7-21-93

Happy

D0435620

# PITTSBURGH PIRATES
## *Still Walking Tall*

Kip Richeal

SAGAMORE PUBLISHING
Champaign, IL

Production Manager: Susan M. McKinney
Cover and photo insert design: Michelle R. Dressen
Editor: Russ Lake
Proofreader: Phyllis L. Bannon

Library of Congress Catalog Card Number: 92-63138
ISBN:0-915611-69-4


Printed in the United States.

This book is dedicated to Milton and Helen Richeal. They are my parents, but they are so much more. They never told any of their children what *they* wanted them to be in their adult lives. That choice was to be their own. Their guidance and assistance, however, was never out of sight and for that, I will be forever grateful. They never pushed or prodded, but the completion of this project is not just the fulfillment of my own dream. It is their dream as well, and the words on the following pages are theirs as much as mine.

———————————————  ஜ  ———————————————

# CONTENTS

# ACKNOWLEDGMENTS

When this book was completed, it became the realization of a dream. Many dreams and goals are difficult to fulfill without the help of others. I would like to thank those who believed in this project and helped see it through to its completion. They include:

—Jim Trdinich, Richard Cerrone, Jim Lachimia, and the rest of the media relations staff of the Pittsburgh Pirates Baseball Club for their untiring efforts in providing me with the utmost courtesy and assistance during this project; manager Jim Leyland, coaches, players, trainers, and front office staff of the Pirates for believing in themselves and putting together three marvelous and memorable summers of baseball.

—Lanny Frattare, the Voice of the Pirates, for his kind words and unforgettable contributions to this book. Since 1976, he has graced the fans of Pittsburgh Pirate baseball with his vast knowledge of the game and a voice that provides a true indication of the professionalism that surrounds him. Thanks also to Kent Derdivanis, Steve Blass, and Jim Rooker for providing interesting and timely anecdotes throughout the season, both on and off the air.

—Joseph Bannon, Sr., Joseph Bannon, Jr., Susan McKinney, Jude Lancaster, Michelle Dressen, and the rest of the fine people at Sagamore Publishing for allowing me an opportunity that I had before only thought of as wishful thinking. Your patience, encouragement, and assistance have been greatly appreciated.

—John Perrotto, of the *Beaver County Times*. It was his goal from the day he became a sportswriter to cover the hometown Pittsburgh Pirates, and he realized that goal in 1987. Since then, he has studied and followed the team religiously. I am grateful for his insight and for making my venture into uncharted territory a much smoother expedition. I am also grateful to Ed Rose, sports editor at the *Times* for believing in my ability several years ago and for being the bridge that every writer must cross to see if this is indeed the profession he or she wants to pursue. Thanks also to Clif Page, graphics editor at the *Beaver County Times*, and *Times* photographers past and present: Greg Lynch, Sally Maxson, Brian Plonka, Pete Sabella, Dan E. Stauffer, and Lourie Ann Zipf.

—Paul Meyer, of the *Pittsburgh Post Gazette*, who offered his thoughts on several topics that have taken place with the Pirates over the last few years, as well as Steve Hubbard, of the former *Pittsburgh Press*; Alan Robinson, of the Associated Press; and Pittsburgh-based free-lance writer, John Mehno.

—Judith Augustine, of the Pittsburgh Chapter of The Make-A-Wish Foundation. This is an organization that spreads hope to youngsters all around the Pittsburgh area and allows them to live dreams that may otherwise have never been possible. Her thoughts and expressions gave me a fuller realization of the common bond that is shared between the organization she works for and the children it represents.

Words of thanks also go to Patti Gerard who somehow made me realize you can be comfortable in front of a camera; Joseph Young and James Riggio, who ably assisted me with research throughout this book; Patrick Eaton, who provided medical knowledge and research when called upon; Scott and Patrick Steckman, for their photographic efforts; and my good friend, Jerry Sandusky, who is one of the most inspirational and patient people I know.

"What goes around, comes around."

This is the truest of all the baseball truisms. For those of us who are in love with the great game of baseball, we are destined to experience the cyclical nature of the sport.

Baseball is based on the principal that to "score" a player must safely touch all the bases, returning to home plate, the point from which he started.

We should never be surprised that in the game, events have a tendency to reoccur. No two baseball games are ever totally alike, but historical periods for a baseball franchise have a way of repeating themselves. Teams go through winning and losing eras. A follower of the game will experience the joys of a moment at one stage of life, and then, years later be forced to witness a particular game that causes much pain.

The Bill Mazeroski home run in game seven of the 1960 World Series is the greatest moment in the history of the Pittsburgh baseball franchise . . . and that win over the New York Yankees has provided the Pirates and their fans a significant milepost by which to judge and compare all that has been a part of the team's history.

Because of the nature of the game, Pirate fans who have savored Mazeroski's game winning home run for over 30 years, should have been expecting what happened to them on October 14, 1992. That's not to say that the loss in Atlanta was payback for enjoying the Pirates' World Series win of 1960. It does speak to the fact that as the Yankees were forced to stand in stunned disbelief at Forbes Field that year, so it was that the Pirates of '92 were faced with the same emotions watching Sid Bream score from second base on Francisco Cabrera's base hit to left field.

Since 1976, I have had the opportunity to witness, as the "voice" of the team, a long list of great moments. I have watched the Pirates go from one of the winningest teams in the seventies to one of the poorest clubs in the eighties, and then rebuild themselves to a position of prominence in the National League in the nineties.

Kip Richeal has captured the essence of the Pirates' struggles through the eighties and rebirth in the nineties. His book takes us back to the days of Danny Murtaugh and Roberto Clemente and places in perspective the 1972 loss to the Cincinnati Reds and its relationship to the 1992 defeat to the Atlanta Braves.

Kip has given us an in-depth, behind-the-scenes look at the feelings and emotions of the individuals who helped in the rebuilding process. His story recounts the ability of the team to overcome professional and personal adversity in winning three straight division titles. By following manager Jim Leyland's leadership, the Pirates proved their championship make-up while suffering that vile loss in Atlanta.

"Still Walking Tall" is about winning and losing in the game and winning and losing in life. It is about ups and downs, highs and lows, success and failure. It is a book about men who faced their challenges like champions, written by a man who has faced life like a champion.

Lanny Frattare

# *Memories of '72*

The evening of October 14, 1992, will forever be etched in the memories of Pittsburgh Pirates baseball fans. Much like a sunny Cincinnati afternoon on October 11, 1972, when World Series fame and fortune eluded the Pirates with one swing of a bat and one wild pitch.

On that day some 20 years before, Pittsburgh took a 3-2 lead into the bottom of the ninth inning of the fifth and deciding game of the National League Championship Series against the always-tough Cincinnati Reds. The Pirates were playing in their third consecutive NLCS and were gunning for their second straight trip to the World Series, having beaten the Baltimore Orioles four games to three the season before.

The Pirates won the National League Eastern division title with little fanfare in 1972 as they took over first place on June 19 and never let go. The team finished 11 games better than the second place Chicago Cubs and gave ample warning that this was a dynasty in the making. With the division title well in hand, rightfielder Roberto Clemente provided the crowning touch to the Pirates' season on September 30. It was on that day that Clemente became the 11th player in major league history to collect 3,000 hits when he doubled to left centerfield off New York Mets pitcher Jon Matlack. Those who remember witnessing Clemente's greatness have the moment stored in their eternal memory, and those who never saw him get goose bumps when they hear of the legend he created.

"I had the pleasure of coming to the Pirates in an era where there were a lot of good players who were people you could learn from," said former Pirate pitcher Steve Blass, who was a teammate of Clemente's and currently serves as a member of the Pirates' radio and television broadcasting crew. "Roberto Clemente was like that. He was an accomplished technician on the field—a very gifted person. It was a great privilege to come to the ball park every day just to watch him play, because you just knew he was going to bring excitement to the game."

"Clemente was one of those individuals that you could actually say—and mean it—that he was one of the best ever," said Bill Virdon, who was a teammate of Clemente's during the 1960 World Series and served as the Pirates' manager in 1972, Clemente's last season. "I don't think anybody ever played the game better. Definitely not at the age of 38, when he was the best player on our 1972 team."

Five Pittsburgh Pirates, including Clemente and Blass, were invited to the 1972 All-Star Game—another example of the power this lineup exuded and the finesse of one of the finest pitching staffs in baseball. All-Star games certainly looked good on any player's resume, but titles were more important to this club. By running away with the 1972 National League Eastern division crown, the Pirates had won their third division championship in a row. They were more than ready to meet the Cincinnati Reds for the second time in three years in post-season play.

Steve Blass was the pitching hero of the 1971 World Series for the Pittsburgh Pirates, as he won two games over the Baltimore Orioles, including a four-hitter that won Game 7. Blass, who led the Pirates' staff with 19 wins during the regular season, stayed true to form in the '72 NLCS opener, as he limited the Reds to a Joe Morgan home run. The Pirates started off right with a 5-1 victory. Cincinnati tied the series in Game 2 as it scored four first inning runs off Pirates' starter Bob Moose and hung on for a 5-3 win. Moose, who died tragically in an off-season automobile accident in 1974, would eventually be remembered for one untimely pitch in this series that would ultimately change the course of Pirate baseball history.

The Pirates used three pitchers to win Game 3, 3-2, at Cincinnati's Riverfront Stadium, thanks to Al Oliver's RBI double that broke a 2-2 tie in the eighth inning. Cincinnati's Ross Grimsley kept the Pirates from celebrating too soon as he silenced the Bucs bats and lifted the Reds to a 7-1 decision in Game 4.

In 1985, Major League Baseball went to a seven-game format—just like the World Series—to decide each league's championship series, much to the delight of the fans because it added the possibility of seeing two extra games. The move was also beneficial to baseball because of the extra television revenue that would undoubtedly be generated from the additional contests. Most of the divisional playoff games are now seen at night for prime-time viewing, but in 1972 the Pittsburgh Pirates and Cincinnati Reds thrilled a national TV audience in an afternoon that featured one of the best fifth-game showdowns ever registered in divisional playoffs.

The Pirates put Blass on the mound once again to try to carry his team to another World Series, while the Reds were relying on their ace, Don Gullett, who was Blass's mound opponent in Game 1. The Pirates struck first by scoring two runs in the second inning on a single by catcher Manny Sanguillen, a double by third baseman Richie Hebner, and a single by second baseman Dave Cash. The Reds cut the lead in half in their third, but the Pirates answered again on Cash's run-scoring single in the fourth.

Cincinnati's Cesar Geronimo cracked a solo home run in the Reds' fifth to make it 3-2, and things looked good for the Pirates when left-handed specialist Ramon Hernandez relieved Blass in the bottom of the eighth and retired Morgan on an infield grounder with the tying run on third. Hernandez then struck out Bobby Tolan. Morgan and Tolan were two of the Reds' premier left-handed batters, but it was the second time in the series that Hernandez had put the two away in succession to lift the Pirates out of a jam.

Pittsburgh was three outs away from its claim to a World Series title defense, but it would face the Reds' right-handed power in the bottom of the ninth, which began with All-Star catcher Johnny Bench. Pirates manager Bill Virdon called on his ace right-handed closer, Dave Giusti, who had posted the best earned run average of all Pirate pitchers that season at 1.93.

Bench immediately showed why he is a Cincinnati hero by sending Giusti's fourth pitch over the right field wall for a home run and a 3-3 tie. Giusti seemed shaken as he allowed back-to back singles to Tony Perez and Denis Menke, and the Pirates were suddenly in a tremendous jam. Virdon wasted little time in calling for Bob Moose out of the bullpen since he was fresh and hadn't pitched since his Game 2 loss a few days earlier.

Moose, who was a native of Western Pennsylvania, had his first test against Geronimo, whose home run pulled the Reds to within 3-2 in the fifth. This time, however, Geronimo flied out to rightfield, while George Foster, who was running for Perez, moved to third on the play. The winning run was 90 feet away for the Reds, but things got a little easier for the Pirates when Cincinnati's Darrel Chaney failed to get Foster home and instead popped out to shortstop.

The Pirates were one out away from escaping to extra innings, but through one of the worst acts of fate ever delivered to Pittsburgh baseball fans, that out never came. Hal McRae stepped to the plate for the Reds with thoughts of ending the Pirates' hopes with one swing of his bat. But those hopes were dashed without even a whiff by McRae as Moose's third pitch skipped the dirt to the right of home plate and bounced past a diving Sanguillen, who did everything he could to block the ball. In just a few brief seconds that seemed more like an eternity, Foster raced home with the winning run as the baseball skittered back to the base of the Riverfront Stadium backstop.

Just like that, the Pirates' monumental season was over. A season filled with strong hopes for a talented team that would not get the chance to be labeled a dynasty. The Pittsburgh players—some slower than others—walked aimlessly off the Cincinnati field that day and carried a somber silence into their dressing room, which had a funereal-like atmosphere for several long minutes. Finally, someone spoke up. It was the voice of leadership that the Pirates so desperately needed at this moment— Roberto Clemente.

"Can you help it?" Clemente asked his teammates. "Can you help it? Don't worry about it. There's nothing you can do about it."

Clemente then tried to console the one Pirate player who seemed to feel the lowest at that moment.

"Giusti!" he said as he knelt by the side of the pitcher who gave up the game-tying homer to Johnny Bench and allowed the eventual game-winning run to reach base. "Damn you, Giusti, look straight ahead! Pick up your head. We don't quit now. We go home and come back in February."

Dignity was a word Clemente used a lot, and there was no way he was going to let his teammates lose theirs on this heartbreaking afternoon. He continued to move around the room and console each and every team member until he convinced them that their heads should remain high for everyone to see.

That evening, back in Pittsburgh, Clemente celebrated a successful season with other members of the Pittsburgh Pirates and vowed that his team would return to compete again in 1973. But that was the last time many of his teammates would ever see the great rightfielder alive.

On New Year's Eve, 1972, Roberto Clemente was on a plane flying to Nicaragua to help those in desperate need following a devastating earthquake that ripped through that country just a few days before. The plane was heavily loaded with relief supplies— blankets, food, clothing— and Clemente wanted to do his part to help the victims. The plane, which carried four other passengers besides Clemente, went down over shark-infested waters off of Puerto Rico. Clemente was 38.

"His death was unbelievable," Bill Virdon recalled. "It was the morning after all the New Year's Eve parties when I first heard the announcement, and I just remember how stunned I was. You had to ask someone else if they were hearing the same thing. It was very sad and unfortunate. People like that shouldn't die young. He was too good a person, too good an athlete, too good an ambassador to life to die like that."

"Roberto Clemente carried himself with so much pride," Steve Blass said. "I only hope I learned to carry the kind of dignity he had during my career."

The dignity of one of Pittsburgh's greatest sports legends was lost in a body that was never found after that New Year's Eve plane crash, but Roberto Clemente's tragic ending would be just one of the many stories that would parallel the Pittsburgh Pirates of the early 1970s to their counterparts of 20 years later. The happiness and the heartache. The anxiety and the anguish. The love and the turmoil.

The memories returned in great waves to those who could remember Bob Moose's fateful errant pitch into the five o'clock shadows of home plate that afternoon in 1972. Now, 20 years and three days later, the Pittsburgh faithful knelt at their television sets again, as Doug Drabek took the mound in the bottom of the ninth inning of Game 7 against the National League West champion Atlanta Braves.

The Pirates had fought so gallantly to reach this Game 7, having fallen behind to the Braves 3 games to 1, but rallying behind complete-game pitching performances from veteran Bob Walk to win Game 5, and rookie knuckle-ball sensation Tim Wakefield to capture Game 6. Drabek was the National League's Cy Young Award winner in 1990, when he finished 22-6 in the Pirates' first of three consecutive N.L. East title drives.

He had finished strong in 1992 by winning five of his last six decisions and was Pirate manager Jim Leyland's choice to start Games 1, 4, and 7 against the Braves should the series go that far. It did, and despite suffering the losses in his first two starts of the series, Drabek headed to the mound at Atlanta-Fulton County Stadium in the last inning of the last game, having thrown 120 pitches to that point, with the Pirates holding a 2-0 lead. There was no action in the Pirate bullpen, so it appeared that the game was Drabek's to win or lose.

The inning took 17 minutes to complete, and just as it happened 20 years before, the Pirates never had a chance to get that one final out. Terry Pendleton, mired in a two-year playoff slump for the Braves—despite having outstanding regular- season statistics—opened the ninth with a double that just stayed within the limits of the rightfield foul line and bounced into the corner.

David Justice followed with a sharp, but definitely playable grounder to the right of Pirate second baseman Jose Lind. Lind had become one of the Pirates' slickest infielders since his call-up from the minor leagues in August 1987, and was consistently in the top five in fielding percentage among National League second basemen. His specialty is his range, and it is common to see Lind rob one batter of a base hit up the middle on one play, and then dive deep into the hole to his left on the very next play to steal another sure hit.

Despite his acrobatics, Lind had been constantly over-looked for his defensive prowess, mainly because he has never established himself as a consistent .275 to .280 hitter. He finished 1992 with a .255 career batting average, and with Chicago's Ryne Sandberg providing power with his always near-.300 batting average, the Gold Glove Award for second basemen usually ended up in Sandberg's hands. Sandberg is also an outstanding fielder, and he once set a major league record for chances without an error. But he has never possessed the range or leaping ability that Lind has, and Pittsburgh baseball fans have long felt that Lind had been grossly overlooked on several occasions to win the award handed out for defensive ability.

Earlier in the afternoon of this series-deciding game, Jose Lind discovered that he was being overlooked no more. The 28-year-old native of Dorado, Puerto Rico, learned that he had won the 1992 Gold Glove Award. Chico, as his teammates called him, was finally being recognized for the great plays that are his trademark on the field.

"Jose Lind is incredible," Pirates manager Jim Leyland said earlier in the season. "I would certainly hope that one day he would get the recognition that's due him. We see him every day, but it's great when you're on the road and you hear the fans who don't see him very often. That's when you know he's appreciated when you hear everyone else oohing and aahing over the plays he makes."

The ground ball hit by Justice was a play that Lind makes nine times out of ten in his sleep, but this time the ball flicked under the tip of his glove as he reached to his right and squirted into short right field. Lind was charged with an error, and the Braves had runners on first and third with no outs.

Sid Bream, who played first base for the Pirates from the end of the 1985 season through 1990, was the next Atlanta batter, and Drabek was way out of the strike zone on four consecutive pitches. Leyland had waited as long as possible, but the waiting was over. As much as he would have liked to left his top pitcher in the game, he knew it was time to take him out.

"Well, you could see when Doug didn't get a strike in on Bream that he was out of gas," Leyland said. "I wanted to leave him out there, but I couldn't. Not when he had nothing left on his pitches. It wasn't hard to tell he had had it."

Drabek reluctantly agreed with his manager's decision.

"I think everyone could feel [that I was tired]," he said. "But in that situation, you just don't notice it. I felt well enough to go out and do the job, but when I walked Bream, I figured I was coming out of the game."

And now, as Drabek took his seat in the Pirate dugout, he realized he was no longer in control of the outcome.

"All you can do in that situation is just sit through it and cheer for the guy that comes in for you," Drabek said.

The Pittsburgh Pirates had been well documented for the past three seasons as running a bullpen-by-committee. They had no solid closer. It was whomever Leyland felt could get the job done in any particular situation. He looked to certain pitchers for ground-ball outs in double-play situations, and he looked to others for fly-ball outs when the moment presented itself.

Atlanta had leftfielder Ron Gant at the plate with the bases loaded and still no outs, and the thought had certainly crossed Leyland's mind that Gant had taken reliever Bob Walk out of the park in Game 2 with a grand slam that helped propel the Braves to an easy 13-5 victory. So Leyland opted for Stan Belinda, whose strong-armed, three-quarter delivery led the Pirates pitching staff with 18 saves in 1992.

Belinda's hard-throwing motion has a tendency to make the ball rise when it reaches the plate, and when a strong hitter catches up to the speed of the pitch, the results can be devastating to the pitcher who threw it. It is a style Belinda developed when he pitched at State College High School in central Pennsylvania, and although he has been moderately successful since joining the Pirates in May 1990, he has been the victim of a few game-winning home runs by the opposition.

What Belinda and his teammates needed most was a ground ball that would hopefully lead to a double play. The Pirates could afford to give up one run with the 2-0 lead, but there wasn't much room for error after that. Curiosity arose when Leyland summoned for Belinda in the first place, because he is the one pitcher on the Pirates staff who is not known for ground-ball outs. Of all the outs Belinda recorded during the regular season, about 66 percent were on fly balls, and he had only forced one double-play ball all season.

"We wanted to get a fly ball from Gant, and that's why I brought in Belinda," Leyland explained afterward. "Even if it was a sacrifice fly, that was OK, as long as we kept him in the park."

Belinda kept Gant in the park, but just barely. His 2-0 pitch to the powerful Braves leftfielder was launched deep into the Atlanta skies, and even Belinda hung his head when he saw the ball leave Gant's bat. But Pirate leftfielder Barry Bonds calmly backed up on the outfield warning track and hauled it in for the first out.

The 50,000 or so Atlanta fans who stayed around to see the finish (yes, there were some who left after Drabek mowed down the Braves in the eighth inning) gave a tremendous ovation as Pendleton crossed the plate with Atlanta's first run, but the situation was actually a blessing for the Pirates. The Braves still had the tying run at second in Justice, but now there was one out and catcher Damon Berryhill, a potential double-play candidate, was at the plate.

The next move figured to be Belinda's removal for either left-hander Bob Patterson or right-hander Bob Walk, who were warming up in the Pirate bullpen. Both pitchers had a propensity for the long ball, but they also had a better chance of serving up a ground ball, which was what the Pirates so desperately needed.

But Leyland remained firm in the Pirates dugout, figuring Belinda was his man to get the Pirates out of this jam. Belinda pitched the Pirates out of a ninth-inning jam to clinch the N.L. East title just a few weeks earlier against the New York Mets, so maybe Leyland figured a little deja vu was in order.

His first pitch to Berryhill was a ball, high and inside. The crowd, which remained standing through the entire ninth inning, was almost deafening now as Belinda rocked from his stretch to deliver to the plate once again. A hush fell momentarily as home plate umpire Randy Marsh rang up a strike against Berryhill.

Marsh became an interesting sidelight to this incredible evening, because he had started the game at first base. John McSherry was in the umpire's box behind home plate to start the game—as he was in Game 1 of the series—but after the Pirates had batted in the second inning, McSherry broke into a cold sweat and made his way to National League President Bill White's box on the first base side. Soon, the other five umpires were huddled around the 320-pound McSherry, as television monitors closed in on his paling face and weary expression.

At first, it was feared McSherry was suffering a heart attack, and he reluctantly pulled himself from the game. He was escorted to the Braves training room, and from there was taken by ambulance to Atlanta's Piedmont Hospital for observation. Midway through the game, an announcement was made to the media that McSherry was suffering from a severe case of dizziness and would remain in the hospital at least overnight.

After an 11-minute delay in the game, Randy Marsh emerged from the Braves dugout like Superman from a phone booth wearing his protective gear for calling balls and strikes. Little did he know how pivotal his decisions would later become.

Damon Berryhill now faced a 1-1 count in the ninth against Belinda, as he settled into his stance and hoped to play the role of hero that so many kids dream about. Belinda challenged with a fastball on his next pitch, and Berryhill watched it cross the plate at his knees. But Marsh's hand never went up to call the strike, and Belinda was behind 2-1. The next pitch tailed outside, and Belinda was one pitch away from putting the tying run at third, and more importantly, the winning run at second.

Needing a strike, Belinda thought he had it with a slider that looked better than the 1-1 pitch he had thrown earlier. Again, however, Marsh felt the pitch was somehow not adequate, and the crowd roared as David Justice moved to third, Sid Bream to second, and Berryhill to first.

Rafael Belliard, an outstanding defensive infielder but an extremely weak hitter, was the next scheduled batter, having replaced Mark Lemke at second base, who was lifted for a pinch-hitter in the seventh. Atlanta manager Bobby Cox's bench was running thin, but he went with Brian Hunter, an excellent right-handed batter with good defensive skills both in the outfield and at first base. With Hunter pinch-hitting for Belliard, Cox could no longer make the move that seemed so necessary in everyone's eyes.

"The move definitely called for a pinch-runner for Bream," Cox said later. "But really, my hands were tied. I didn't have anyone else to bring in."

Sid Bream had endured three operations on both knees over the last three years, which can be a definite hindrance to speed on the base paths. But Cox needed Bream for possible extra innings, because Hunter was going to have to stay in the game and play leftfield, and Ron Gant would have to move to the infield with both Belliard and Lemke out of the game.

So Bream remained at second as Hunter stepped into the batter's box. Each pitch was met with a surge of anticipation from both dugouts with every Braves and Pirates fan watching. Finally, the crowd roared as Hunter lifted a fly ball to short rightfield. It turned out to be too short, however, as Lind raced back and watched the ball nestle into his glove. Justice gave a slight hint of trying to score from third on the play, but there was no way he would challenge *anyone's* arm on such a short fly ball with his team's World Series hopes on the line.

Now there were two outs, and the Pirates still clung tenuously to their one-run lead. Just before Hunter batted, Atlanta hitting coach Clarence Jones told seldom-used catcher Francisco Cabrera to grab a bat, because he would pinch-hit for pitcher Jeff Reardon if Hunter didn't get the winning run home.

Cabrera was an 11th hour call up from the Braves Class AAA Richmond farm club on August 31—the last day to make such moves. He batted 3-for-10 during the last month of the regular season and flew out in his only NLCS appearance against the Pirates. But here he was, the center of attention—the last hope for the Atlanta Braves.

By now, no one was seated in Atlanta- Fulton County Stadium, and everyone who cared about baseball in Pittsburgh was praying, holding hands, crossing fingers—whatever it took to get that last out. As Cabrera stepped to the plate, Belinda remained the man that Leyland would count on, and the one that so many would later second-guess . . .

# *Fall of a Dynasty*

Tragedy to a sports fan is seeing your favorite team come up short year after year, and losing three National League pennants in a row makes a lot of folks think about searching for the nearest bridge to jump off. The hearts of Pirates fans sunk to new lows on the night of October 14, with many saying things such as, "That's it! I'm through with the Pirates," "How could they possibly choke again?"

One man who was interviewed by a local Pittsburgh television station immediately after the game even opined that the entire series was fixed. "How else could it end up the way it did?" the man reasoned.

This was not a series that was fixed or tampered with. And those who called the Pirates chokers didn't follow the team during the 162-game regular season. It was a series that was hard-fought by two extremely talented baseball teams. Both refused to give in until the very last pitch of the series, and both were physically drained because of it. Pride wore strongly under the uniform of every player on that field during the series, and it continued to shine well afterwards.

Before all hope is lost about ever bringing a World Series title back to Pittsburgh, it should be remembered that there was a time when Pirate baseball was almost no more. Baseball has existed in the city of Pittsburgh for over a century, but fan appreciation for the sport, and its team, has too often been non-existent. For various reasons, fans have stayed away in droves from the team that first brought prominence to the National League in the late 1800s and has continued to build a tradition that ranks as one of the finest in terms of championships won and lost.

The Pittsburgh Pirates joined the National League in 1887 and got their nickname after signing infielder Louis Bierbauer away from the less-established American Association following the 1890 season. If losing a pennant seems tragic to fans, imagine losing 113 games and compiling a .169 winning percentage, which is what the team did that season. Bierbauer was one of the American Association's best players, and that league protested the manner in which Pittsburgh signed him. They held firm beliefs in territorial rights to a player, and the move seemed to be an early form of free agency, although that phrase would not become popular for another 90 years or so.

At the time, the team was called the Pittsburgh Alleghenies, but when the American Association's protest forced a decision from an arbitration committee, an Association spokesman said in a statement before the board, "The action of the Pittsburgh club in signing Bierbauer was piratical." After the arbitration committee ruled in favor of Pittsburgh by allowing it to keep Bierbauer, people began calling the team the Pittsburgh Pirates.

The Pirates played in the first World Series in 1903. A mid-June 15 game-winning streak propelled the team into first place in the National League, and it was a position they would hang onto for the rest of that season. The new American League was younger and far less- established, but when it became apparent that its champion would be the then-Boston Pilgrims, newspapers everywhere began calling for a series between these two league champions.

And so it was born. The Fall Classic. The crowning of a champion in baseball that has become the World Series. The Pirates lost that first meeting with the Boston club in a best-of-nine series, five games to three, but they have since appeared in six others, and won five. Over the past 106 seasons, there have been many baseball ups and downs in the city of Pittsburgh. Many players have passed through the gates of three very different baseball parks during that span of time, each with their own creative style, each with their own legend to carve.

ᴤ

In 1985, baseball in Pittsburgh took a back seat for several weeks to ugly stories of drugs and corruption. A once-proud franchise had plummeted to its lowest depths, both on and off the field, and it suddenly appeared that wherever the Pirates took the field to begin the 1986 season, it would not be in Pittsburgh.

Rumors were rampant as speculation already had the Pirates sold and moved to either Denver or New Orleans. Some also believed that South Florida deserved a major-league baseball franchise, while others claimed that the city of Buffalo was in the process of building a new stadium solely for the Pirates to move into.

A couple of last-place finishes by a very bad baseball team could have been the easiest excuse for the poor attendance figures that were on the verge of running the Pirates out of town. But position in the standings didn't seem to be the biggest factor.

In early July 1970, the Pittsburgh Pirates moved from the beloved confines of Forbes Field to the totally enclosed, new age Three Rivers Stadium. Three Rivers was designed for football as well as baseball, but many Pirates fans felt that the Steelers were the city's primary reason for building the facility.

It is a six-level wonder with a perfect circular shape and symmetrical measurements. From home plate to the outfield foul poles, the distance is 330 feet. It is 375 feet to each alley and 400 feet to straightaway centerfield. The surface is artificial turf, and the entire facility resembles a concrete doughnut. Several major league franchises were making moves to these types of stadiums during this era, with Cincinnati, St. Louis, and Philadelphia among the cities to build facilities with a similar architectural design.

Those cities, however, have never had serious attendance problems, either in their old stadiums or the modern ones. Pittsburgh never lacked for fans, either, before the move to Three Rivers. While attendance records weren't exactly falling year after year, the people of Pittsburgh enjoyed the cozy atmosphere of Forbes Field, which had stood at its position on the campus of the University of Pittsburgh in the Oakland section of the city since its opening in 1909.

When Three Rivers Stadium opened, it faced the same challenge as Jay Leno replacing Johnny Carson on television, or Bear Bryant on the football sidelines at Alabama. Not only did people find it more suitable to football than baseball, they turned in a staggering amount of other complaints. Three Rivers was "stale," some complained. It lacked the charm and atmosphere of Forbes Field. Parking and concessions were too expensive. There was not enough parking, and the access routes both in and out of the stadium were inadequate. Mostly, people missed old Forbes Field. It was only the second facility the Pirates had ever played in, having replaced Exposition Park, which normally seated about 10,000 patrons, but could hold nearly 16,000 if they let the fans stand around the outfield perimeters.

In the early 20th century, Pirates owner Barney Dreyfuss felt baseball was a game that was about to take off. He could see the ever-increasing fan interest all around the league, and he decided he was not going to let it pass him by. He was also concerned about the current location of Exposition Park, which was in Allegheny. The park itself was located in a poor neighborhood, and Dreyfuss felt that was what kept many of the city's upper-class citizens away from the ball games. It wasn't a very humanitarian perspective, but Dreyfuss had to consider who would ultimately buy tickets.

"Many people laughed at me when I said I wanted to build a modern facility that would hold about 25,000," Dreyfuss was quoted in a Pirates history collection. "They told me the Giants don't have that large a park with all of New York to draw from. One friend bet me a $150 suit of clothes the park would never be filled."

Dreyfuss easily collected his new suit as his new stadium filled to its capacity five times within the first two weeks of its opening. That day was June 30, 1909, before a standing-room-only crowd of 30,338. The visiting Chicago Cubs beat the Pirates, 3-2, just as the Cincinnati Reds did on July 16, 1970, in the inaugural game at Three Rivers Stadium.

Forbes Field had symbolized the city of Pittsburgh. It was made entirely of steel. The production of steel was the main source of employment and income for the city and its residents for many decades. The timing could not have been better for the park's opening, as Pittsburgh earned its second World Series appearance in 1909 against the Detroit Tigers. The Pirates hosted three of those World Series games with 83,885 fans passing through the turnstiles. That was more than the attendance of the team's two previous World Series combined.

&

When Barney Dreyfuss died, the Pirates built a monument to honor him and placed it in centerfield at Forbes Field. He was best known for his innovation, his sense of awareness, and the courage to take a chance once in a while. His judgment missed sometimes, such as when he passed on a friend's advice to sign a young, unknown pitcher from a semi-pro league in Idaho. That pitcher was Walter Johnson, who later became the major league's second-winningest pitcher of all time as a member of the Washington Senators.

But those miscues were few and far between, and Dreyfuss more than made up for them by bringing some of the best talent and most well-liked players the city of Pittsburgh has ever known. There were names like Connie Mack, Pie Traynor, and Fred Clarke, who all managed at one time or another in the Pirates organization. There was also the brother combination of Paul and Lloyd Waner, who were better known as "Big Poison" and "Little Poison." No player, however, had more impact on a Pittsburgh Pirates team than Hans "Honus" Wagner, the man baseball purists called the "Flying Dutchman."

Wagner grew up in Western Pennsylvania and went to work in the coal mines at the age of 12. He worked in those dark, dusty mines from sunup to sundown and only saw the light of day on Sundays and holidays. He made about 70 cents for every ton of coal he could load, and that amounted to about $3.50 a week.

He fell in love with baseball while watching others play on the local sandlots, and he knew that it was his ticket out of the mines. His older brother arranged a tryout for him with Steubenville in the Tri-State League, and soon he was making $350 a month as a professional baseball player.

Honus Wagner won the National League batting championship in 1900 with the Pirates—his first year in the majors—

with a .381 average, which is still the best ever for a right-handed Pirate hitter. He finished his career with a .328 lifetime average and hit over .300 17 times. He won the league batting title seven more times and although he was never considered a power-hitter, he finished his career with 1,732 runs batted in, drove in 100 or more runs seven times and led the league in RBIs five times.

He was called the Flying Dutchman because of his speed on the base paths, and he backed up that moniker by leading the league five times in stolen bases and finishing with 722 for his career. His fielding efforts at shortstop were nearly flawless, and a sportswriter once wrote, "Wagner's legs are so bowed, you could roll a barrel between them, but not a baseball."

Once in the winter of 1901, Honus Wagner was about to make $3,000 for his second year with the Pirates, but a man named Clark Griffith, owner of the American League's New York Highlanders, sought Wagner out in a driving snowstorm. Griffith offered Wagner $20,000 to leave the Pirates and join the Highlanders, and even though the offer was overwhelming, Wagner refused.

"I told Griff I didn't think there was that much money in the world," Wagner said in a 1950 interview with *The Pittsburgh Press* newspaper. "But he pulled out twenty thousand-dollar bills and laid them down there on my table. I must admit it was tempting, but I told Griff I was perfectly satisfied [in Pittsburgh], and Barney Dreyfuss had treated me fine."

Wagner was never paid more than $10,000 a season during his entire career with the Pittsburgh Pirates. It was a ritual for Dreyfuss to call him in the winter to tell him his contract was ready. Wagner would look at the blank contract and fill in the $10,000 amount—which was still an outstanding figure in those days.

Honus Wagner died December 6, 1955, just eight months after presiding over a ceremony to unveil an 1,800-pound statue of the Flying Dutchman in his best swinging motion, at Pittsburgh's Schenley Park. The statue remains a Pittsburgh icon, and it now stands outside one of the four entrance gates to Three Rivers Stadium.

The statue honors Wagner for his "baseball immortality," and calls him a "champion among champions, whose record on and off the playing field of the National Game will forever stand as a monument to his own greatness and as an  example and inspiration to the youth of our country."

Ed Barrow, the owner of the New York Yankees during Wagner's playing days,  probably put it best when giving his opinion of who the best player ever was. "The Flying Dutchman stands alone," Barrow said. "Babe Ruth was the game's greatest personality and its greatest home-run hitter. Ty Cobb was the greatest of the hitters, and the only man I ever saw who could single-handedly  unnerve an entire ball club. But there is no question that Honus Wagner was  the greatest all-around base-ball player who ever lived."

&

The Pittsburgh Pirates have certainly been blessed more so with talent than  malcontent over the years, but the early 1980s was one of those down periods in every organization's existence. It was a time when fan  disinterest was  at an all- time high, and while many wondered how a team with so much talent through most of the 1970s could draw so few fans, they were about to find out  how many less an awful team could draw.

The Pirates won six division championships in the 1970s —including five of the decade's first six—and two World Series. They drew 1.5 million fans  while winning the World Series in 1971, but saw their attendance decline  every year after except two on their way to another world championship in  1979.

The Pirates won the Eastern division championship in 1974, but only 1.1  million fans passed through the gates of Three Rivers Stadium. Only about 964,000 showed up to witness a second-place finish in 1978, and although the Pirates played host to ten NLCS  championship games in the 1970s, the  average attendance was 42,276, which was about 10,000 short of capacity for  Three Rivers at that time.

In 1982 the Pirates still fielded a better than .500 ballclub, but could barely draw one million fans. After finishing second in 1983, things turned  truly sour for the Pirates. Their record began to slip as then-general  manager Harding Peterson tried desper-ately to keep the ballclub up to date. He signed aging veterans, who had seen their better days, and traded for old  retreads.

There were names such as Steve Kemp, Gene Tenace (whose contract was guaranteed for three years even though his best year was 1972 with the world-champion Oakland A's), Amos Otis (who hit .165 in 40 games and was released in mid-season), Jason Thompson (the first of several Pirate long-term contract disasters), Lee Mazzilli, Al Holland, and Sixto Lezcano, a 31-year-old Puerto Rican outfielder who claimed it was his dream to fill the uniform of the great Roberto Clemente. The fit was never even close, as Lezcano batted just .207 in his first season and was released in spring training the following year. His contract was guaranteed at two years for a total of $825,000.

Probably the most memorable name to join the Pirates during this time of uncontrolled spending and ill-advised decision making was George Hendrick. "Joggin' George," as he became known to local fans and media alike, came to the Pirates from the St. Louis Cardinals on December 12, 1984, for pitcher John Tudor and utility man Brian Harper. It was Peterson's hope that Hendrick and Kemp could instill some life into a quickly fading body, and although both players had enjoyed success earlier in their careers, they could not live up to Peterson's expectations.

Kemp was perfectly willing to follow Pirates manager Chuck Tanner to the end of the earth because that was the size of his heart. When he joined the team, Kemp instantly became the Pirate with the most dedication in the clubhouse. Twice, he had driven in over 100 runs in his career with the New York Yankees, and it was felt that at age 30 he could still give the same kind of production to the Pirates. But while his heart said he could, a partially torn rotator cuff injury said he couldn't. And the move cost the Pirates several more million dollars in salary to a player who could not perform.

George Hendrick was a player who *was* capable of performing— even at the age of 35. He had driven in over 200 runs for the Cardinals in 1982-83 and Peterson again felt run-production like that was what the Pirates needed. What the Pirates didn't need, however, was another headache. But that was exactly what Hendrick amounted to. Almost from the beginning, he made it quite clear that he did not want to play in Pittsburgh, and his efforts often confirmed his sentiments.

Hendrick immediately distanced himself from the media by refusing most interview requests. And he totally alienated himself from the fans, who were ultimately the final contributors to the players' salaries. He dogged almost every play in the field for the Pirates and never hustled on the base paths—whether he had hit a home run (which were few for the Pirates) or bounced into a difficult ground ball.

"I've always tried to have some kind of communication with the different players who have been with the club," said Pirates radio and television play-by-play announcer, Lanny Frattare, who has been with the team since 1976. "I never get too involved with their personal lives, you know, but I always try to give them a friendly hello, or ask them how the family is. I talk about whatever comes up. In all my years here, I think George Hendrick was the only player I never had that kind of rapport with, nor did I care to. He just went out of his way to alienate himself from anyone involved with the Pittsburgh Pirates organization and he never gave the city a chance."

Harding Peterson made one more unusual move in April, 1985, when he shipped relief pitcher Kent Tekulve, one of the most popular Pirates and a clutch performer in the Bucs' 1979 World Series win over the Baltimore Orioles, to Philadelphia for reliever Al Holland. Tekulve, who was known as "The Rubber-Band Man," for his wiry frame and lanky side-arm delivery, was revered by Pirates fans for his work in local charities off the field as well as his heroics on it.

Acquiring Holland, whose salary was less than half of Tekulve's, was not a bad move statistically, but it would soon prove to be one of the many negatives from a public relations standpoint for the Pirates. Upon his arrival in Pittsburgh, Holland was summoned to appear before a federal grand jury investigating ever-increasing speculations of drug usage in baseball. That was only the beginning of the Pirates rapid fall from the top.

That fall started slowly, as the Pittsburgh Pirates remained competitive for a few more years after their storybook World Series championship in 1979 over the Baltimore Orioles, their old nemesis from 1971—which had been a dream season. A chance to endure miracles and witness heroics that brought back memories of Bill Mazeroski's ninth-inning home run that won Game 7 of the 1960 World Series for the Pirates over a heavily favored and deeply talented New York Yankees club.

Much like several Pirates teams from the past, there were many heroes in 1979. First, there was manager Chuck Tanner, who oozed optimism no matter what dark cloud hung over his team, and then there was second baseman Phil Garner, who batted .500 for the series and made several spectacular plays in the field. The Pirates had an aging pitcher in Jim Rooker, who provided one more chance in the series for the Pirates to pull out a championship, and an aging outfielder in Bill Robinson, whose 24 home runs and 75 RBIs in 1979 sparked several Pirates rallies.

Heroes came through trades in the form of shortstop Tim Foli and third baseman Bill Madlock. They were acquired in separate early-season deals during Harding Peterson's better days as the Pirates' general manager, but together they solidified an infield that would dive on nails to stop a ground ball from going through. Speed was a factor, and centerfielder Omar Moreno provided much of the Pirates' lightning on the base paths. Then there was the pomposity of rightfielder Dave Parker, whose arrogance was matched only by his superior arm strength both in the field and at the plate.

But one hero stood above all the others. His teammates, and soon the entire city of Pittsburgh, called him quite simply, "Pops."

Willie Stargell is forever mentioned in the same breath of every Pirates fan who ever dreams up a list of the greatest players in the team's long and storied history. Stargell played for no other team but the Pirates, and in today's age of fast movement and free spending, that is an accomplishment in itself. He was known for his power, and the timing with which he displayed it.

When he was in his prime, Willie Stargell could summon the long ball with just one sledge-hammer style swing of his enormous bat. Babe Ruth was known for being the only player to ever hit a ball completely out of Forbes Field. Stargell is the only man to ever put a ball out of Los Angeles' Dodger Stadium —not once, but twice—in a park where even reaching the bullpen is difficult. Stargell christened the opening of Three Rivers Stadium many times over with his deep, long blasts to all parts of the outfield stands. He is the only man ever to hit a ball into the massive stadium's upper deck four times.

Although he retired as a player in 1982, Stargell may best be remembered for his accomplishments during the 1979 season. He was the Pirates' captain, and his leadership would prove to be of the greatest importance to the team's success that season. He often courted the media in his rocking chair beside his locker, and he rewarded his teammates with gold stars, "Stargell Stars," for their outstanding efforts during critical times throughout the season.

The Pirates finished first in the National League's Eastern division in 1979 with a 98-64 record and eased to their seventh World Series appearance by sweeping their other playoff nemesis, the Cincinnati Reds, in three straight games. Next up were the Orioles, who had also been absent from the series since their '71 loss to the Pirates.

Baltimore had the champagne on ice after four games, as it built a three-games-to-one lead and was set to clinch at Three Rivers Stadium on a gray Sunday afternoon with 23-game winner Mike Flanagan on the mound. Jim Rooker was nearing the end of his playing career for the Pirates. He was 37 years old and had been on the disabled list twice during his 4-7 season, which culminated in a 4.59 earned run average.

He was a part of "The Family," the nickname the Pirates had taken on after several of the players began playing the popular disco tune, "We Are Family," in the clubhouse after games at incredibly high decibel levels. Manager Chuck Tanner came to Rooker after Game 4 and said the ball would be in his hands.

"I still get goose bumps when I think about it," said Rooker, who today is a member of the Pirates radio and television broadcasting crew. "I didn't feel any pressure because it was a culmination of a dream come true. We were down, 3-1, and we weren't supposed to win that game. How could I feel any pressure?"

Right before Game 5, Tanner learned of his mother's death. Life could seemingly get no bluer for the man who casts an eternal smile on his family, his players, and the world. He was torn, but he knew all along there was only one place his mother would have wanted him to be. "She wouldn't have wanted me anywhere else, but at that stadium," Tanner said.

His players took the news hard because they were the kind of team that cared for one another, not only on the field but away from it. They took it upon themselves to play as hard as they possibly could for their manager and Tanner, in his own optimistic way, delivered a message that seemed to highlight that silver lining that somehow overcomes every dark cloud.

"I told them that my mother was the biggest Pirate fan of them all," Tanner remembered. "I told them she thought we weren't playing too well in the first four games and she just went up to get us some extra help. I know she was watching every pitch from wherever she was, and I know it would have made her proud the way the players dedicated the series to her when it was all over."

The Pirates knew it wasn't over yet and with pressure seemingly in the distance, Rooker gave Tanner and the Pirates one of the best efforts of his career, and although he left the game after five innings with his team trailing, 1-0, it was an effort the Pirates would reward. Bert Blyleven relieved Rooker in the sixth, and the Pirates finally solved Flanagan with a pair of runs in the bottom of the inning. The Bucs added two more in the seventh and three in the eighth, and won 7-1. It was Bill Madlock and Tim Foli, the early-season trades that turned out to be blessings, who provided the offense for the Pirates, as Madlock had four hits, and Foli totaled three RBIs.

The Orioles went home undaunted and still felt the series was in their hands. "If someone told me before the series we were going home with a 3-2 lead and had [Jim] Palmer and [Scott] McGregor pitching, I'd have said we were OK," Baltimore manager Earl Weaver said.

Chuck Tanner would also turn to his ace for Game 6. John Candelaria had been one of the Pirates' steadiest pitchers since his call-up from the minors in 1975, and he was the one Tanner often looked to in the most crucial situations.

"Candy was one of the greatest pitchers I've ever managed," Tanner recalled. "He could always reach back for something extra and rise to the occasion. He was *only* facing Jim Palmer, one of the greatest pitchers of all time, but he was so cool out there. It was like he was pitching in the Northern League somewhere. To him there was no pressure."

Palmer and Candelaria lived up to their billing by tossing shutouts at each other through the first six innings, but the Pirates broke through with an RBI single by Parker in the seventh. Stargell added a run on a sacrifice fly, but his heroics were still to come. Then Tanner went to Tekulve, his ace out of the bullpen, and the Pirates added two more in the eighth to win, 4-0, and even the series at three games apiece.

Game 7 would feature McGregor, the outstanding left-hander for the Orioles, against Jim Bibby, a hard-throwing right-hander who finished the regular season 12-4 for the Pirates. Baltimore got the jump early when Rich Dauer homered to left in the second inning to give the Orioles a 1-0 lead. The score stayed that way until the Pirates finally began to peck away at McGregor. Bill Robinson led off the sixth with a single, and that cleared the way for Pops to do his thing.

"I rested Willie a lot during the first part of the 1979 season," Tanner said. "At the same time, I wanted to make sure he stayed in shape and got his at bats. Finally, around the beginning of September, I said, 'OK Willie, you're in the lineup the rest of the way. The money's on the line, and we're looking for someone to carry us.' He said, 'OK Chuck. I feel like the season's just started, and I'm ready to go.'"

Stargell carried his team to the Eastern division championship and launched a home run in the Pirates' convincing, 7-1 win over Cincinnati in Game 3 of the NLCS. But this at bat in Baltimore's Memorial Stadium was about to become, perhaps, his greatest moment of all time. McGregor's specialty pitch was the breaking ball, but when he tried to slip one by Stargell this time, he didn't succeed.

"I was out in front of the pitch," Stargell said. "I didn't want to commit myself too soon, but I got the right bat speed on my swing. I didn't think it was going to carry enough to go out, but I was hoping."

The pitchers in the Pirate bullpen were hoping also as the ball floated toward them in the right centerfield area of Memorial Stadium. The ball flew high and deep into the cold Baltimore night, but there was a definite feeling of anxiety in the hearts of every Pirate fan, coach, and player during those long, agonizing seconds of its flight. Pitcher Don Robinson frantically coaxed the ball to clear the outfield wall, as though his huge, waving arms would somehow carry it those few extra feet. The rest of the pitchers in the bullpen either stood silently or held their arms in the air with crossed index fingers on each hand. Every person on the Pirate bench jumped to his feet at the crack of the bat and instinctively moved to the top step of the dugout.

Willie Stargell, who hit 32 home runs during the regular season and is the Pittsburgh Pirates' all-time leader with 475 career home runs, had his most significant moment ever on this 1979 October evening, when his correctly-timed swing sent Scott McGregor's breaking-ball pitch into the Pirates' bullpen. Pitchers jumped up and down in the bullpen. Players and coaches hugged each other in the dugout. Bill Robinson trotted down the third base line ahead of his teammate, waving his arms in the air, and then turned to hug the leader of the "Family."

"Willie Stargell proved to be an outstanding leader," Chuck Tanner said. "He carried us through the tough times and was instrumental during the great times. His home run in the seventh game only typified his MVP season in 1979."

"I didn't know if it was going to go out or not," said Stargell, who shared regular-season MVP honors with St. Louis's Keith Hernandez in 1979. "But I was sure thrilled when it did."

The Pirates seemed lifted by Stargell's heroics, while the Orioles were obviously deflated. Reliever Grant Jackson held the Pirates' slim 2-1 lead for 2-2/3 innings, but soon gave way to Tekulve after walking two batters with only one out in the eighth.

Baltimore elected to pinch-hit Terry Crowley, a left-handed hitter who had doubled off Tekulve in Game 4 of the series. Again, it was "Pops" who provided the words of wisdom in a time of dire need.

"Teke," Stargell said, as he lumbered to the mound from his first base position. "Show the people why you're the best in the league. If you don't think you can do that, then you play first base and I'll pitch."

Tekulve smiled. Stargell smiled. And Tekulve got Crowley to ground out to second. The base runners advanced on the play, and after Tekulve intentionally walked Ken Singleton, the Orioles' last hopes, perhaps, were down to Eddie Murray, a very dangerous hitter, who was not having such a dangerous series. Murray drilled a sharp liner to rightfield that first appeared as if it would drop in for a hit. But Dave Parker got under the ball, slipped and almost fell, then adjusted himself for the catch.

The Pirates gave Tekulve a cushion in the ninth by scoring a pair of runs, and after getting the first two Orioles out in the bottom of the ninth, Tekulve induced Pat Kelly to fly out to center to wrap up the fifth World Series championship in Pirates' history in seven tries.

"World Champions!" Tekulve would say over and over long after the game had ended. "It's ours and nobody can ever take it away from us."

The 1979 Pittsburgh Pirates weren't exactly the same as the team that was branded for destiny in the earlier part of the decade, but they carried the quality that most often befits a championship team—togetherness. They were a family. They were more similar to the championship team of 1960 that no one figured to win, but somehow did it anyway. They could play from behind, they could hold a lead. They played with determination, they played with emotion. They were the first team to ever win a World Series without having a pitcher win at least 15 games during the regular season (Candelaria had 14; Bruce Kison, 13; Blyleven and Bibby, 12 each), and they became the only team to rally twice from 3-1 deficits to win two World Series. If Willie Stargell was Pops to the Pirates, then Chuck Tanner may possibly have been their grandfather. He was the one who sparked optimism when the normal slumps would occur, and he knew when to offer a kind word and the right time to say it. He was the one who told the players to have fun, and winning would take care of itself. They did— and it did.

"There might be teams that were, or will be, just as good as our team in '79," said Tanner, who remained in baseball through the 1992 season as an advance scout for the Milwaukee Brewers. "There also might be better players. But there will never be a group of men who were as dedicated to the game as that group of Pittsburgh Pirates."

It was soon after the heroics of 1979 that the walls began to close in on the Pittsburgh Pirates. The club followed its World Series accomplishment with a decent attendance figure of 1,646,757 in 1980, which is not uncommon for any team defending a world championship, but it struggled to stay above .500 on the field and finished third in the division at 83-79.

Bill Madlock won the National League batting title with a .341 average during the strike-shortened 1981 season, but the Pirates finished fourth in the first half of the season and last in the restructured second half. Over one million fans turned out in each of the 1982 and 1983 seasons as the Pirates posted identical 84-78 records and finished fourth and second, respectively. But it was during this time that the unrest began to take shape.

Harding Peterson had lost his flair for making the right moves in the front office, and that's when he too often tried to counter the Pirates' fall by signing high-priced, over-the-hill free agents who would prove only to gobble up the majority of the Pirates' payroll. In 1984, the Pirates turned in a last-place effort with a 75-87 record, and did it in a way that totally destroyed the fans' sense of loyalty.

For a very long time, Pittsburgh fans had been blue-collar, no-nonsense type fans. For years, there has been a waiting list for Steeler season tickets, because the football team's nickname has long epitomized what the city is all about. The 1970s brought four Super Bowl championships and two World Series titles to the city, and the fans reveled in every minute of that glory. They appreciated the hard work, the dedication, and the discipline the players displayed, as well as the friendly attitudes they would offer if confronted for a handshake or an autograph.

What the fans didn't appreciate was the abrupt turn-around that their beloved Pirates were exhibiting. It was one thing to have a down year once in a while. Those things happen, and they can be tolerated if effort is shown on the field. That is something any true fan will always appreciate. While it is true that most fans expect a winner, they will also applaud a strong showing and a true measure of effort, such as running out a ground ball, or diving once in a while for a close play in the field. The 1984 Pirates gave them none of that.

Up until this time, the Pittsburgh Pirates had been linked to only two sets of ownership. One was Barney Dreyfuss and his heirs, who eventually sold the majority interest of the ballclub to a group headed by Columbus, Ohio realtor John Galbreath in July 1946. It was on May 23, 1985, that Dan Galbreath, John's son and president of the Pirates since 1970, decided he had seen enough.

The Pirates hit record lows in 1984, as total attendance reached only 773,500. The last-place finish did nothing to ignite the fans' interest, nor did the ever-increasing whining of several marquee players who had suddenly decided Pittsburgh wasn't the place for them anymore. Among the disenchanted were such notables as Madlock, Candelaria, and Parker, three of the Pirates' World Series heroes only five years earlier.

"Things were in a pretty sad state of affairs at that time," said pitcher Bob Walk, who signed with the Pirates as a free agent in 1984. "Some of the guys made it a big deal every day in the papers about how they wanted to get out of Pittsburgh."

Fed up with Peterson's ill-advised expenditures and nonsensical acquisitions, Dan Galbreath called for a press conference that early May morning and announced the firing of his general manager. Peterson was extended the offer to resign, he refused, so Galbreath did it his way. The Pirates were 12-25 at that early point in the season, and already 11-1/2 games out of first place.

"We have a payroll that is in the middle to the top-middle of all the baseball clubs in the league, and we are in last place," Galbreath said of his decision to fire Peterson. "I find that position hard to support."

"The losing was hard to accept," the Pirates' manager at the time, Chuck Tanner, said. "We lost Stargell to retirement [in 1982] and we lost Parker, Foli, Madlock, and Candelaria to either trades or free agency. We had to rebuild, and we had the guys to do it with. There were guys like Barry Bonds, Jose Lind, and Bobby Bonilla in our farm system, but they were just babies, and they were going to need time. It was a cycle that every team goes through, and we tried to hang on by signing older players. That just didn't seem to be the answer."

In Harding Peterson's defense, Galbreath kept a tight purse string on his payroll, which somewhat limited the number of top free agents that Peterson could actually approach. One can only carry a team so far with a patchwork lineup, and that was what the Pirates had become. Peterson, however, never argued that case in his defense and just sort of quietly slipped out the door with the knowledge that poor decision making became his eventual downfall in the Pittsburgh Pirates organization.

The Pirates were a team in desperate need of help. Like when Gotham City needed help in the movies or comic strips, and it shined the Bat sign in the sky to summon Batman, Dan Galbreath sent out a signal for help, and his old friend, Joe L. Brown, couldn't refuse.

"The Pirates were a team in need of rebuilding," Walk said. "It's OK to plug a hole now and then with an experienced veteran, but we needed a whole new outlook. Guys at that time, however, didn't want to stay around and help rebuild the team. They looked at the Pirates as a sinking ship, and they wanted to get off."

Brown was the perfect man in Galbreath's eyes to right that sinking ship. If Galbreath needed experience, he had only to look at past Pirate history records, which showed Joe L. Brown to be the man who put together the 1960 World Series championship team after taking over baseball's laughingstock Pirates from Branch Rickey in 1955. When things started going bad during the mid-1960s, Brown again tore the team apart and reconstructed it to form the nucleus of the 1971 championship team. He retired from baseball in the mid-70s, but his fingerprints remained on the team that would eventually go on to capture the 1979 World Series.

Brown was living in Southern California in May 1985, enjoying retirement with his wife, Din. But when Galbreath called him the night before the announcement of Harding Peterson's dismissal, Brown looked at his wife and knew in his heart he couldn't turn down the offer.

"The Pirates and the Galbreaths had been too good to me," Brown said at the time. "Retirement was enjoyable in California. We had settled into a more leisurely life and were together without any pressure. But when Dan called me, I knew I was a cooked goose. I loved that family too much and when a friend says he needs you, you go."

Brown accepted his friend's offer and soon walked into a situation that he had never seen — or dreamed imaginable—before.

"One of the immediate things that stood out was how the team had turned into a loser," Brown recalled. "The attitude was awful. And there was no effort, no cohesion."

Brown felt the disintegrating attitude was coming from the older players, whom he considered in reality to be the heart and soul of every ballclub.

"We had guys like Hendrick going through the motions," Brown said. "And Madlock was going around the clubhouse telling everyone how bad the ballclub was, and how there were no prospects to look forward to in the minors. Then we had Candelaria telling everyone over and over how he wanted out of Pittsburgh. This was a team in disarray, and I felt we had to clear the air. There were a lot of people I was disappointed with, and a lot more we had to move."

When ownership changed hands for just the second time in the Pirates' existence during the following off-season, many—

including players, coaches, fans, and front office personnel—
wondered if baseball in Pittsburgh would become extinct. Much
of the talk had new owners buying the team and moving it to
another city. But before that could even come about, death almost
hit the Pirates in an even larger fashion.

ॐ

The news broke quickly in the midst of the 1985 baseball
season. Suddenly cocaine had become the hot topic of America's
pastime. There were stories of drug usage among major-league
players in unbelievable proportions. Stories that went back to
the early 80s with names that would fill any All- Star lineup.

Once upon a time, there was the story of Dock Ellis, who
pitched a no hitter for the Pirates in 1971 while under the influence of LSD, but even that incredible anecdote was topped by the
names and places that were dropped during the summer of 1985
in Pittsburgh Federal Court.

It came to be known as the biggest baseball scandal since
the Chicago White Sox threw the 1919 World Series by accepting
payments from high-priced gamblers. Eight players—including
the legendary "Shoeless" Joe Jackson—were acquitted by a federal grand jury in that scandal, but they did not escape the wrath
of the hard-nosed commissioner of baseball at the time, Judge
Kenesaw-Mountain Landis, who despite the jury's verdict, banned
all eight players from professional baseball for life.

The Pittsburgh drug trials, as they came to be known,
involved the guilty pleas and convictions of seven drug dealers
from around the country. They were tried, in part, for selling
cocaine, the drug of the 1980s, to the many notable baseball
players they came in contact with. And with the trials taking
place in Pittsburgh, curious Pirates fans began to wonder which,
if any, of their heroes would be implicated in the proceedings.

Stories broke about drugs being sold in the Pirates' clubhouse and on team charters by people who were passed off as
players' friends. Confessions unfolded during the trials, and it
was discovered that even the team's mascot at the time, the Pirate
Parrot, had bought cocaine and introduced players to a drug
dealer.

Then came the bigger names. Players who at one time or another wore a Pirate uniform supposedly with pride, but now with shame. Former or current Pirates like Parker (who had since moved on to Cincinnati through free agency), Dale Berra, Lee Lacy, Al Holland, John Milner, and Rod Scurry all had been implicated during the trials for anything from cocaine abuse to participation in distribution to recreational use, as they testified against the dealers that supplied them. Seven of the players were granted immunity from criminal prosecution in exchange for their testimony.

"It was a black eye," said Pirates marketing director Steve Greenberg, whose job it was to fill the seats that had spent most of the 1984 and 1985 seasons feeling so very lonely. "The aura of baseball was just abused."

There were six current players at the time and one former player who fell into the category of "major offenders," according to then-commissioner Peter Ueberroth. They were Parker, Berra, Enos Cabell, Joaquin Andujar, Jeff Leonard, Lonnie Smith, and perhaps most notably along with Parker at the time, Keith Hernandez. Even though those players were granted immunity from prosecution, Ueberroth, much like Judge Landis some 65 years earlier, exercised his own power and penalized 21 players for their involvement after dividing them into three categories.

In the most notable category were the major offenders. They would each receive a one-year suspension from baseball or pay ten percent of their 1986 base salaries to drug-prevention centers. They would also have to provide 100 hours of community service each year in 1986 and 1987 and submit to random drug testing the rest of their careers. None chose to sit out the season.

Then came the medium offenders. They were charged with engaging in direct use rather than distribution of cocaine, and their punishments were either a 60-day suspension or forfeiture of five percent of their salaries to drug prevention centers, 50 hours of community service, and random testing for the remainder of their careers. Again, none chose the suspension. Among the offenders in this category were Lacy, Holland, Claudell Washington, and Lary Sorensen.

The last group of players were considered minor offenders. Their charge was indication, but little or no evidence of cocaine use, and the only punishment they faced was random testing for the rest of their careers. Scurry fell into this category, as did Dusty Baker, Vida Blue, Gary Matthews, Dickie Noles, Tim Raines, Manny Sarmiento, Alan Wiggins, Daryl Sconiers, and Derrel Thomas.

According to Keith Hernandez, one of the early signs of drug usage in major league baseball was in 1980, when he estimated that 40 percent of the players used or tried cocaine. He termed it, "the romance year, the love-affair year."

The seven drug dealers that were convicted were handed the stiffest penalties, including Curtis Strong, Shelby Greer, and Dale Shiffman, who each received 12-year prison sentences. But they were not the focus of practically every major media outlet in the country. It was the list of witnesses that drew the attention of the hordes of cameras and microphones that rained down on the city. The seven players who had been granted immunity from criminal prosecution so J. Alan Johnson, then Western Pennsylvania's chief federal prosecutor, could build his case against the drug dealers were the focus.

"Baseball wasn't on trial in that courtroom," Johnson said in a 1991 interview with Steve Hubbard of *The Pittsburgh Press.* "But baseball was certainly on trial in the public's mind after the revelations started coming out."

The fans felt scorned and betrayed by the news, and as the proceedings continued to unfold, their anger was replaced only by their shock. Most of the players were ruined by the drug that started out as "recreational." Cocaine shortened Dale Berra's career and ultimately ended Rod Scurry's life. Its aftermath with the trials left reputations tarnished and earnings diminished. None of the players will speak openly about it, preferring instead to leave the dirt swept under the rug.

"I'd rather keep it in the past," Enos Cabell, a former infielder with several major league teams, told Hubbard in the 1991 *Press* interview. "It was a totally negative experience. It hurt my family more than anything else, and that's the thing I'll never forget."

The resentment of some of the players stems from the fact that they had endured their problems long before the trials and voluntarily submitted themselves to rehabilitation. Lonnie Smith, the only current member of the so-called major offenders still on a major-league roster, said he volunteered for rehabilitation in 1983 and never had another problem, but three years later, he had to pay a harsher penalty than many of the other users who were classified as medium or minor offenders.

Of the seven major offenders, Dave Parker was the most outspoken about his feelings of "being pulled into the mess long after the fact." He still remains bitter toward several parties including the federal prosecutors, whom he thought brought the famous baseball players into the minor drug trials as an attention-getting device.

"I'm out of Pittsburgh three years, I'm in Cincinnati, what do I have to do with it?" Parker told Steve Hubbard in a separate interview with *The Pittsburgh Press*. "The way I and some of the other big-name athletes were pulled into it, I thought it was grandstanding. The normal procedure, from what I know, is you send someone to buy drugs, and then you bust the dealer when it's over."

"I hope he's better at baseball than law enforcement techniques," Johnson retorted. "The best situation is if you can make buys, but that's not the way it's always done. It wasn't at all unusual to do it this way."

Parker also blamed former baseball commissioner Bowie Kuhn, whom he said had a "long list" of drug-using players for "years and years" and did nothing about it, nor did Peter Ueberroth, until the trials forced his hand. Parker claimed the list was common knowledge to baseball's upper management, but was shredded when his attorneys tried to obtain it. That theory was heavily rejected by the commissioner's office, who said that such a list, if it existed, would not have been shredded, because Ueberroth had already fined clubs for trying to hide drug problems.

When Parker admitted during testimony that he first used cocaine "with consistency" in 1979, he said he quit three years later because "I felt my game was slipping and that played a part in it."

The Pirates were angry with that statement and the fact that one of their players knowingly took a drug that was hampering his abilities in the field. The team filed a suit seeking to nullify $5.3 million in deferred payments to Parker and eventually settled out of court, costing Parker an undisclosed amount.

Parker is still bitter toward the team for those actions, and told Hubbard  he earned his salary. Parker claimed that even if the Pirates had a case, it should have gone to an arbitrator, according to baseball rules, and not to a Pittsburgh jury, where he doesn't think he would have gotten a fair trial.

"That's just like trying to get Hitler for his war crimes and having the  trial in the U.S.— by a whole jury of Jews," Parker said.

Parker is bitter because he claimed the trials cost him his reputation, money, and maybe even the National League Most Valuable Player Award in a year in which he hit .312 with 42 doubles, 34 home runs, and 125 RBIs.  Willie McGee won the award with a .353 batting average, 18 triples, 114 runs  scored, and 56 stolen bases.

"I had the best year of anybody in that league," Parker told Hubbard. "Possibly in baseball. It was an extra $425,000 in incentives for MVP and  just for the sheer fact I would have won it for a second time would have  meant a heckuva lot personally."

"I was persecuted more than anybody," he said. "Nobody suffered as much  as I did from the drug trials."

Tom Reich, a Pittsburgh-based agent, said many of the players' constitutional rights were violated because they were being punished for  testifying under immunity for "things that would have been otherwise  impossible to prove." He said if the players had not been granted immunity, they would have in- voked their Fifth Amendment rights not to incriminate  them- selves, and neither the prosecutor nor the commissioner could have proved  they did anything wrong.

"I was extremely distressed," Reich told *The Pittsburgh Press.* "To testify  under immunity and then have what was said used against them in other forums, to have penalties imposed on them after the fact was an obvious case of  double jeopardy."

Johnson disagreed with Reich's assessment at the time.

"It wasn't double jeopardy in a legal sense," he said. "Because the players  were never in jeopardy with the law in the first place, and their punishment  was handed down by base- ball."

"It all depends on whether you believe baseball has the right to enforce it's own game, which I do," said Carl Barger, who was a managing general  partner in a Pittsburgh law firm at the time and would soon become a major factor to the Pirates staying in Pittsburgh. Barger also spoke of his fear that the public backlash and drug problems would have only escalated if baseball had done nothing. The backlash wasn't as bad as Barger may have thought, but the public still voiced its opinion at the turnstiles in 1985 and 1986. Attendance dropped to 1.6 million in Pittsburgh in those two years, before it rose again to more than two million in each of the past six years. The players whose names were dragged through the trial's bloody ruins heard the boos everywhere they went, and they also felt the blow of the proceedings in their deflated egos and shrunken wallets.

People in Pittsburgh, as expected, did not look kindly upon the Pirates, following the revelations. Their reasons were numerous and often well founded. They were tired of the sloppy efforts the malcontents on the Pirates were displaying and when drugs were announced in news shorts around the country, it only served for further ammunition from the fans. The best way to get even with a last-place team fielding no-hustle players was to stay away from the stadium. And that they did. Attendance never reached 800,000 in 1984 and 1985, and it looked as though baseball was on its way out of Pittsburgh.

"Because it was in Pittsburgh and it was called the Pittsburgh drug trials, the association was more with the club than it should have been," Steve Greenberg said. "If it had been in Houston or St. Louis, it wouldn't have had the same impact. Because it was in Pittsburgh, we lived with it twenty-four hours a day."

"People often associated the drug problems with Pittsburgh because the trials were centered in the city," said Pirate pitcher Bob Walk, who was a member of the team during the trials. "At the time, usage was going on all around the league. I never saw any of it in the clubhouse or on the planes, but the things in question supposedly happened a few years before the actual trials.

"Those trials really built an awareness to players and fans alike because at that time, the public's perception of cocaine wasn't as great as it is today. Players snorted cocaine back then much like they would go out and have a drink once in a while. It was more like a casual thing to do."

Walk's former manager, Chuck Tanner, agreed.

"People had the perception that Pittsburgh and the Pirates were the main focus," Tanner said. "That would happen to almost any city where trials of such importance would be held. But I didn't care what people thought or said  because what counts is what you know. I know the players implicated were a good group of guys and I did not make it a habit of watching every move they made.

"Baseball was in the spotlight at that time, but for the wrong reason. There were lots of professions that encountered drug problems in the mid-80s. Doctors; lawyers; entertainers. All sorts of professional people were brought out in the open. Baseball just happened to take most of the emphasis because it is a sport that's held in such high regard. Cocaine was spreading fast all over and it was a shame because no way did I ever want to see that happen to our country."

There was a moment during the Pirates' season-opening road trip to San Diego  in 1984 when Rod Scurry, a one-time Pirates' left-handed specialist out of the bullpen, called his parents' home in Reno, Nevada, and seemed despondent. When he blacked out during the conversation, Scurry's father, Preston, called Pirate pitcher Don Robinson and asked him to go to Rod's hotel room.

When Robinson and teammate Dale Berra arrived, they found Scurry  hallucinating about invisible snakes crawling on the walls and on him, and he  said they were trying to bite him. Robinson knew of Scurry's fear of snakes,  but he also knew his words were spoken from the effects of cocaine. The two  players comforted their friend through this bizarre time of terror and eventually identified the problem to manager Chuck Tanner. The Pirates sent Scurry home to a rehabilitation center, where he hoped to defeat the  problem before the problem defeated him.

Drugs weren't a part of Scurry's early life. He was a quiet, laid-back student in high school, and one of the toughest decisions he ever faced was  leaving his family and his home in Sparks, Nevada, after the Pirates made him their No. 1- draft pick out of high school in 1974. When he made the move to Florida to join the Pirates' Bradenton rookie league, he called his home two or three times a day because he was lonely and homesick.

He developed his strength pitch— the curve ball,— but his self-confidence suffered miserably. He remained quiet and reserved and seldom went out with his teammates after a game. Scurry's best season in the majors was 1982 when he posted a 4-5 record, with 14 saves and a 1.74 earned run average. When his numbers started to slip, however, so did his new-found confidence. His record fell to 4-9, his ERA ballooned to 5.56, and Scurry began to look for other ways to compensate for his problems on the field.

Berra was one of the few players on the Pirates roster that Scurry called a good friend, and together with a couple of other players they had known through the minor leagues, they began to mingle with Dale Shiffman, one of the three drug dealers who was given a 12-year prison sentence, and Kevin Koch, the man who donned the costume of the Pirate Parrot and entertained the crowd during every Pirates home game. At first Scurry snorted maybe a gram or two of cocaine a week, but his dosages became heavier with the added pressures of being a major-league baseball player.

After the incident in San Diego, Scurry completed his 30-day rehabilitation assignment, but even then his family felt the problem was only swept under the rug.

"My husband and I went to visit him and I was very disappointed in the rehab center because they treated him more like a major-league star and not as a drug addict," his mother, Betty, said in a November, 1992, Associated Press interview. "They even had a pitching mound for him to continue practicing on."

Scurry was one of the first players to come forward with his drug problem, but one year later, he was still doing cocaine. Shiffman had cut him off, but he found it in other places.

At the news conference to announce his return in 1985, it was evident that drugs had made Scurry weak and pale—a stark contrast to his short, stocky build of before. He spoke of wanting a second chance and of starting anew. But this was only a temporary stall from the eventual destruction of his life. Scurry was given another chance the following season, but was suspended for leaving the club on a trip to Philadelphia. Eventually, the Pirates traded him to the Yankees, but Scurry found that no matter where he played baseball, drugs would ultimately rule his life.

Scurry made short appearances with the Giants and the Mariners after the Yankees released him, but eventually he disappeared from baseball. Once, his name popped up on a drug- related police message in Nevada, but for the most part, he kept his name out of the news. With another baseball season just a couple of weeks removed from the 1992 season, Rod Scurry's name surfaced once more. This time would be the last.

He called his mother from his home in Reno at about 12:30 a.m., on October 29. Scurry was trying to put his life back in order with his wife, Laurie, (who was not at home at the time), and two children, ages 6 and 2, and he wanted to talk with his mother about his marital problems. Betty described her son as "upset, but coherent and lucid," but a little while later, her phone rang again, and her six-year-old grandson asked her to come over quickly.

Police were called to Scurry's home and found him wandering on his front lawn, wearing only sweat shorts and vehemently insisting that snakes were attacking him, trying to bite him. When the police tried to calm him, Scurry began to breathe in short, irregular gasps. Soon, he was unconscious and moments later, at the hospital, he fell into a coma.

It was that quick, but it wasn't painless.

Police called it cardiac arrest from a "combination of substances" that took the life of Rod Scurry. He died a week after the incident outside his home when he was taken off a life- support system. Doctors said he lapsed into cardiopulmonary arrest from a reaction to the cocaine, cutting off his brain's oxygen supply.

He was only 36 years old, which is young in a profession where being left-handed and having the ability to throw a decent curve ball can help a person make a good living for many years to come. The temptation was too strong in Scurry's case, however, and he ultimately paid the heaviest price.

ॐ

If the drug trials in major league baseball did anything positive, they opened the public's eyes to the dangers of this deadly drug.

"I quit because I felt my game was slipping," Dave Parker testified from the witness stand. "I knew that cocaine was playing a part in that."

Lonnie Smith said he sought help after snorting cocaine all night and feeling "too jittery and uncontrollable to play."

"I woke up one night and my nose was bleeding," Keith Hernandez said. "I was experiencing the shakes, and I threw a gram [of cocaine] away, right down the toilet."

Jeff Leonard got himself so hooked that he, too, had to enter a rehabilitation center, and Dale Berra told of buying cocaine twice one day before 1 p.m. Enos Cabell quit to save his family, and because he was "getting older" and "had too much to lose."

Smith told J. Alan Johnson that confessions were difficult, "but if it saves one kid, it may have been worth it." Another person said the trials were probably a better advertising campaign against cocaine than anything up to that day.

"That was because of the media coverage," Johnson said. "Because of the witnesses testifying about the effects of cocaine on them. People had to sit up and take notice. Baseball had to do something about it. Other sports had to address it. I was never under the impression it would do away with drug usage in professional sports, but it shined a light where it had never been shined before."

"The incident put a neon sign on a significant problem that plagued baseball," Barger said in an interview with *The Pittsburgh Press*. "Since then, baseball has cleaned up. It's not one-hundred percent clean, but the improvements are unbelievable."

Barger cautioned though, that cocaine couldn't be eliminated from baseball because it's a part of society, and because the player's union won't allow random drug testing, which, he said, would deter some from using cocaine and identify those who needed help.

The players were upset with the fines they incurred, but they all agreed that the community service was beneficial, as did the people who received those services.

Parker provided some of his speaking services to the Human Involvement Project of Cincinnati, which deals with youths in trouble with the law. The executive director of the program, Althea Day, said Parker's stay-in-school-and-out-of-trouble speech turned around a lot of kids who were immature and put them on the right track. "Sometimes it helps youngsters to hear it  through someone who has stumbled and made a change," Day concluded.

Parker also talked to troubled youngsters at Abraxas III, a drug re-entry  house in Pittsburgh, to which he also donated money, and helped establish a college scholarship fund for underprivileged children.

Dale Berra, the only other former Pirate implicated with the seven major offenders, finished his career with the Houston Astros in 1987. He testified  he first used cocaine at a New Year's Eve party in 1979, and Parker and John  Milner were the first Pirates to use it with him. He said he also used it with Scurry and Lee Lacy, and that his use peaked in 1984. Berra donated money to underprivileged families so children could seek help from The Bridge, a  Caldwell, New Jersey counseling program dealing mainly with drug abuse. He lectured to  students about drugs cutting his career short at age 32, and how people think they can whip drugs, but they cannot, and he told them everyone is vulnerable to drugs.

"I want that period in my life to be forgotten," Keith Hernandez said in a 1989 interview with *Playboy* magazine. "I hate the fact that I'm  part of 'The Pittsburgh Seven' and that'll be a part of baseball history, just like the Black Sox scandal. Using cocaine was the biggest mistake I ever made, because my reputation had been outstanding—and I blew it."

Hernandez finished his career on the Cleveland Indians' disabled list and  most of the others implicated in the Pittsburgh drug trials are also out of baseball. Injuries or age may have been a factor in causing their absence,  but snorting cocaine for recreational, or any other purposes, did not enhance their efforts on the field in any way. On the contrary, it limited their  production and left them with the same feelings that any other common drug  user feels. At the time, they felt bigger than anyone and bigger than the  drug they ingested. But in the long run, cocaine ruled again and took away  the livelihood that so many athletes dared hang out in front of them.

৵

At a time when baseball could easily have been run out of town, Joe L. Brown took the Pirates in his calming hands and began the long and arduous task of reformation. While the negatives heavily outweighed the positives, Brown reassured the Galbreaths that the storm would pass, and soon—but not soon enough— it did.

Eventually, the national media filtered away from this town that was delivering front-page news from a last-place organization. As drugs carried the Pirates into a spiraling dark tunnel, Brown kept his finger on the button and an eye on the end of that tunnel. When the smoke had cleared, Brown finally felt it was time for the Pirates to regain their position of high respect— a position that would hopefully put them back at the top of their division.

"We had to start thinking about a new approach," Brown said. "We decided to go and get some young players and consequently get rid of some fat contracts. A lot of people felt that was what I was trying to do, but it was really the result rather than the goal."

And so the housecleaning began. On August 2, Brown shipped Hendrick, Candelaria, and Al Holland to the California Angels for pitchers Pat Clements and Bob Kipper and outfielder Mike Brown. The Pirates began to take the approach that if you didn't want to be in Pittsburgh, it was OK by them. Candelaria and Hendrick were two of the biggest complainers during the team's darkest times, and by now the fans who were still around couldn't wait to get rid of their attitudes. At the time, Brown was a good prospect for the Pirates to take a gamble on, although he didn't quite measure up to what the club had hoped for from him. Clements pitched in a few games, but not enough to be given serious consideration by the Pirates, and Kipper proved to be a solid set-up man out of the bullpen for several years to come.

Approximately one month later, the Pirates' future was further solidified when Brown traded Bill Madlock, another of the several malcontents, to the Los Angeles Dodgers for first baseman Sid Bream and outfielders R.J. Reynolds and Cecil Espy. Bream displayed a flare for power from the left side and an even greater flare defensively, while Reynolds proved to fit the Pirates best as the consummate fourth outfielder. He could play any of the three positions at any time, and he consistently batted in the .280-.290 range. Bream and Reynolds were valuable assets to the Pirates future and contributed greatly through the 1990 season. Espy was lost to free agency, but later regained by the Pirates and equally proved his wares as a utility outfielder through the 1992 season.

"I just wanted the chance to play," Reynolds said. "I was excited to get the chance to come here."

The commitment had been made by Pirate management to shift to a youth movement— albeit probably a year too late— and it turned out to be a move that brought some of the deserting fans back.

But still, the fears of losing the team to another city loomed quietly over the steel city's vast skyline. If championship years are seasons to remember, then 1985 would be the year to forget for the Pittsburgh Pirates. The club finished last for the second straight year and lost 100 games (57-104) for the first time since 1954. At the gates, the team lost even more. Attendance dropped to 735,900, and the Pirates were figured to have lost $25 million over a three-year period.

"I was used to starting in Triple-A games with crowds of 1,500 or 2,000 watching," Bob Kipper said. "I got here, and it was the same thing. There were still crowds of 1,500 or 2,000 watching me pitch. The only thing that made it seem like the major leagues was that we were playing against major-league teams. Other than that, it was like I was still in the minors. Sorry to say, but you had to go on the road back then to get the feeling of a major-league atmosphere."

"Everyone thought we were the joke of baseball," Reynolds said. "It was embarrassing to walk through an airport carrying a Pittsburgh Pirates bag. People would look at your bag and have that look on their faces that said they didn't even think you were a major leaguer."

Joe L. Brown, as acting general manager, was trying to give the Pirates a fresh start on the field, but for Dan Galbreath, it became quite clear the team needed a fresh start in all areas— including ownership.

"Obviously, a breath of fresh air was needed here," Reynolds continued. "Maybe leaving town would have been the perfect antidote. This was a franchise that needed a change and maybe that meant changing locations, too. It seemed like we had to just start all over again."

When the dismal season was played to its conclusion, the Pirates made their first leadership move by firing manager Chuck Tanner. He was a local product, from nearby New Castle, Pennsylvania, and he had the chance to live every young man's dream. He took over his hometown team and helped shape it into a contender, which culminated everyone's efforts into a World Series championship.

"When I was hired, it was hard to believe I'd be coming home," said Tanner, who had previously managed the Oakland A's and Chicago White Sox. "It was a big thrill to know the Pittsburgh Pirates wanted me, but when I knew the team was going to be sold, I figured there were going to be wholesale changes. I had always been close to the Galbreaths and I felt moving on was the right thing for us all. I don't regret anyone's decision."

When the announcement came that the Pirates were up for sale, Galbreath made it clear he would do everything possible to keep the team in Pittsburgh. The offers came rolling in— believe it or not—but they were all from other cities. And even though they were very lucrative offers, Galbreath turned them away. For now, he was sticking to his word.

While rumors flew rampant that the Pirates were on their way to Denver or New Orleans or any Florida city, attorney C. Kent May, from the Pittsburgh law firm of Eckert, Seamans, Cherin, and Mellott, told his partners, "We can't just stand by and let the Pirates go."

So the law firm and the accounting firm of Price Waterhouse and Ketchum Communications, a public relations concern, offered free services to any group interested in buying the Pirates. That brought in the law firm's managing general partner, and a future major interest in the Pittsburgh Pirates, Carl Barger.

The Pirates' books were opened for the law firm to see, and the results weren't pretty. "It was godawful," Barger said after examining Galbreath's books. "They were losing ten million a year. The team was populated by a bunch of malcontents. There was a war between the city and the team because of a long-term lease agreement and a war between the Steelers and the team because of rights to Three Rivers Stadium. The fans were turned off. It wasn't a great situation, probably the worst. But the fact remained something had to be done."

Barger figured the best way to keep the Pirates in Pittsburgh was to rally corporate leadership from the city's main businesses around them. He first approached Douglas Danforth, who was CEO at Westinghouse Corporation, and Dave Roderick, CEO at US Steel, which is now USX. Both men made it clear they would be interested in joining the effort to save the Pirates, but they didn't want to buy any control of the team. They doubted whether their efforts would be successful, and they didn't want the responsibility of pulling out if it didn't work.

"There were many cold, blank stares when we laid this on the rest of the CEOs we talked to," Barger said. "I guess you couldn't blame them because they were sitting there listening to someone tell them why they should invest in a team that was losing ten million dollars a year and was saddled with a long-term lease."

These early discussions brought forth the term "public-private coalition," which brought about the method that would ultimately keep the Pirates in Pittsburgh for several years to come. First, Pittsburgh Mayor Richard Caliguiri was asked to head the coalition. With him leading the way, the matter of the lease —which had the Pirates in an agreement to keep the team tied to Three Rivers Stadium until 2011—would become one of the lesser stumbling blocks to any sale of the team because he was a man who could provide leadership and experience into any such discussions.

Barger felt a provision had to be provided so the people who were willing to put up the money would have an out if it became necessary. He called it a stop-the-bleeding provision, which meant that if, in spite of everyone's best efforts the plan still couldn't work, meaning if Pittsburgh simply wouldn't back the team, the coalition would have the right to terminate the lease and sell the team.

The provision was granted after a short review, but obstacles began to pop up everywhere.

The Galbreaths were by now very anxious to sell and had slipped from their earlier stance of only selling the team to local investors who would keep the team in Pittsburgh. By now Dan Galbreath was willing to open the sale of the Pirates to all bidders and if that didn't work, he was threatening to put the team into bankruptcy. He even dropped his original asking price from $45 million to almost $30 million. That was still too much for the local group.

"There seemed to be one stumbling block after another," Barger lamented. "I always believed that it would work, but there was a lot of political opposition and newspaper negativism. I knew we weren't going to have a bonanza on our hands, but I felt the franchise would give us financial integrity."

Malcolm "Mac" Prine, who would soon emerge as president and chairman of the board of the Pirates after retiring from Westinghouse in 1987, almost reached the point of giving up.

"It was a slow, agonizing process," Prine said. "There was a time when I was very discouraged, and I felt it maybe just wasn't worth it. But then you begin to think rationally again and tell yourself that it all was worth it. We didn't want to run the risk of permanently damaging our community by letting this chance pass by. But things were at a pretty low level at one time."

Through Mayor Caliguiri's efforts, the coalition was able to raise $24 million thanks to $2 million investments from 12 different individuals or corporations in the private sector. The group, known as Pittsburgh Associates, included Aluminum Corporation of America (ALCOA), Carnegie Mellon University, Eugene and Raymond Litman, John McConnell, Mellon Bank, N.A., PNC Financial Corporation, PPG Industries, Inc., USX Corporation, Harvey M. Walken, and Westinghouse Corporation.

"I didn't know exactly how close we were to losing the ballclub until Carl Barger sat down with me in an informal session and showed me," Pirate broadcaster Lanny Frattare said. "I think Mayor Caliguiri deserved a lot of the credit because he did all this during an election year. His position wasn't safe, and backing the Pirates at a time when there were a lot of other important issues in the city could have been disastrous to his campaign. He put himself out on a limb to save baseball in Pittsburgh because it was something he so deeply believed in."

The city was also expected to contribute $25 million by a bond issue through the Urban Redevelopment Authority. In essence, the team was sold to the city of Pittsburgh for $22 million, but the coalition also accepted debts of almost $9 million from Galbreath. Many individual players make that kind of money in five years today, but at that time, the city was simply finding a way to keep the Pirates in Pittsburgh.

"I've been in law for a long time and that was probably the craziest transaction I have ever been involved in," said Barger, who mostly practiced corporate law.

The sale of the team took place on October 2, 1985, and the coalition took control one month later with no sure certainty that the city would be able to come up with its share of the sale. The deal was officially closed in March, 1986.

≈

The sale of the Pittsburgh Pirates was complete, and three men stood tall for their intelligence and ability to keep the team in the city it had started in some 100 years before. Carl Barger, Richard Caliguiri, and Malcolm Prine took on this task, not only because they were businessmen, but because they were people who cared about losing an organization that meant so much to the city. They realized that for a lot of people, life wouldn't be the same without the Pittsburgh Pirates around. Money and business played a heavy role, but pride and tradition were what ultimately saved the organization.

About a week before Chuck Tanner was fired, Joe L. Brown resigned his position as general manager of the Pirates — this time for good. He did what he said he would do. He helped a friend. But when Dan Galbreath put the team up for sale, Brown figured new blood was in order all around.

The new Pirates regime had its work cut out, and one of its first orders of business was to hire a new general manager and field manager. This was to be a delicate task because now that the commitment had been made to keep the team in Pittsburgh, there had to be the right match to bring the Pirates back to prominence in the National League East. If the heads of the coalition picked the wrong people, it could still have meant the death of baseball in Pittsburgh because of the stop-the-bleeding provision in the original sale agreement. That was the last thing anyone affiliated with Pittsburgh Pirate baseball wanted at this crucial time in the club's history.

There were undoubtedly several big names to choose from on the Pirates' list of prospective general managers. Some with loads of experience and some who were merely big names ready to take on new challenges. In many people's eyes, the Pirates' ultimate choice seemed to be the new regime's first mistake.

The Pirates chose Sydnor W. Thrift, Jr., to lead the team out of its rapid downfall and almost immediately, the wisecracks came pouring in. He was called a kook and a hayseed who had no business making major decisions involving a major league baseball team. While Mac Prine stuck by the coalition's decision by calling Thrift a "marvelous choice," the media became instantly critical. Fans simply went around asking, "Syd who?"

Thrift had at one time been involved in baseball. He had once been a scout in the Pirates organization before moving on to Kansas City and Oakland. Until his hiring as the Pirates general manager, he had been out of baseball a little over nine years and had been living in Fairfax, Virginia, where he had established a successful real estate business with his wife.

The calls of insanity in the new Pirates organization left Thrift undaunted as he took on his new role with eager anticipation. He had no problem with the rude reception he received in Pittsburgh from fans and media alike.

"I can understand it," he said after his inaugural press conference. "I'm sensible enough to know I wasn't famous. I don't think very many people in that room knew anything about me. They didn't understand the number of years I'd spent preparing in-depth knowledge for procurement, scouting, recruiting, and appraising players, not to mention their training and development."

The people involved in that first meeting may not have known him at the time, but they would soon find out about Sydnor W. Thrift, Jr. He was big on scouting and development, seeing that as the proper path to building a championship team. The city would wish him well, but with a wary eye, knowing that baseball was still on the brink of extinction in Pittsburgh.

So Thrift began the long interviewing process to find the Pirates a new field manager. This, too, would have to be the right call because the last thing any team in transition needs is instability from its position of leadership. There were many names being thrown about the town, including the late Billy Martin, the always-controversial figure who, if nothing else at the time, would surely have put fans in the seats with his mere presence.

But the Pirates didn't need a circus act and that would more than likely have been the case if the aging but fiery Martin would have taken the helm.

Thrift was the one who ultimately made the final choice. It was Jim Leyland, a man who was considered a master at the game even though he had never been a big league manager. Through all the changes, everyone in the Pirate organization stressed that "a fresh start" was in order. If that was the case, then Leyland was the perfect choice. He had spent 11 years as a minor league manager in the Detroit Tigers organization and four as third base coach for the Chicago White Sox under Tony LaRussa, who is also considered to have one of the best managerial minds in the game.

"I kept saying from the first day the only name I knew of on our list [of ten or twelve] that was a curiosity to me was Jim Leyland," Thrift said. "I followed his career. I watched him manage at different levels and coach in the major leagues. I said he certainly should be a candidate, but no one—including myself —really knew him."

And so it was. The new beginning for the Pittsburgh Pirates. No one outside of professional baseball (and even some within baseball) had ever heard of the team's new general manager, nor did they have a clue about the new manager in the dugout. Syd Thrift and Jim Leyland were unknowns at the time, but they would soon become a part of one of the greatest turnarounds in major-league baseball history.

# A New Beginning:
# Jim Leyland

It was a sunny February morning—as all winter mornings seem to be in south-central Florida —and the Pittsburgh Pirates were about to begin their 1986 baseball season. They would try to forget the washed-out, last-place finishes of the past two seasons and leave behind the drug scandals that very nearly caused the team's demise less than a year before. It was time to start anew and look toward better days.

There was new leadership in the Pirates organization from corporate ownership, to the front office, to the dugout. It was their job to restore the dignity to a once-proud organization that had somehow lost 191 games over the previous two seasons. Malcolm Prine and Carl Barger were the primary figures in overseeing the Pirates' restoration to prosperity, while Syd Thrift would handle the signings and dealings that come from the general manager's position. As Thrift weeded out the Pirate roster, adding and subtracting names here and there, Jim Leyland would undertake the task of turning those players into believers.

That first day of spring training was one of the most memorable of Leyland's career simply because it was his first as a big league manager. When he sidled into his office at Pirate City in Bradenton, Leyland was immediately approached by long-time Pirates equipment manager, John Hallahan.

"Hully asked me what size uniform I wore, and I told him I didn't care, as long as it said Pirates on it," Leyland remembered about that first day. "It was a dream come true, managing a big league club, and I just couldn't believe I was finally putting on a uniform as a major league manager."

For most first time managers, that's exactly what they feel — a dream has finally come true. But this dream could just have easily turned into a nightmare if Leyland's players would have decided to become the moaners and mutineers they had become the season before.

But Leyland was willing to take that chance, just because he had finally made it to the level that every baseball person dreams of.

"My brother used to kid me about always being the runner-up and never getting the job," Leyland said. "I had gone through interviews with Texas, Oakland, Houston, and Seattle at different times, but I never got the jobs."

He was, more than likely, a slim candidate for the Pirates job as well, until something about his name kept coming up in Syd Thrift's conversations with other general managers.

"One day," Thrift recalled. "I was talking with Dick Wagner [president of the Houston Astros] about something not related to the manager's job. I told him I was having a problem in the selection process and he told me I should talk to Leyland. He said when it had gotten down to the final analysis for the Houston job, it was between Leyland and Hal Lanier. And Wagner really liked Leyland.

The next day, I got a call from Joe Klein [general manager of the Cleveland Indians]. He hadn't talked to Dick Wagner, and no one had talked to each other. But he asked me how we were doing in the selection process and I told him I wasn't a hundred percent pleased with any of our prospects. He told me when he was in Texas, he was in the same dilemma and he narrowed it down to two people. The second name he mentioned was Jim Leyland's and Joe even admitted he probably should have made Leyland his first choice."

The intrigue started to build inside Thrift's mind, and he went back to his bosses with the name of Jim Leyland falling off his lips.

"I found Joe Klein's story very interesting, and I went back to Mac Prine and told him I had a strong feeling about the necessity to talk to Leyland, simply because each day that went by, someone different was recommending him."

Thrift immediately called the Chicago White Sox, where Leyland was stationed at the time, and offered the third base coach a trip to Pittsburgh and an interview for the vacant manager's position.

Leyland was somewhat hesitant because he had just signed a new contract to stay on with the White Sox, and he had grown just a little bit tired of the "token" interviews that he thought were cast to him in the other cities.

"When I got the call for the interview, I didn't think it was really Syd Thrift," Leyland said. "I just thought it was somebody pulling my leg. When I realized it was him, I told him I'd be glad to interview, but I didn't want to be another newspaper article. Sometimes in baseball they like to carry these things out just to keep the interest in the papers. I was happy in Chicago, and I just didn't want to be another name added to his list. I told him if I was, then I wasn't even coming."

Thrift assured Leyland that this interview was very legitimate, and the Pirates had a sincere interest in listening to his baseball expertise.

"I called Ken Harrelson [White Sox general manager] before I called Jim, and he gave me a good report on him also." Thrift said. "Within thirty minutes I knew he was the right man for the job. He had exactly what we were looking for."

Leyland received an added endorsement when White Sox manager Tony LaRussa called Thrift and said he had never made a call recommending anyone for a job, but if there was one guy in baseball who was ready to manage in the major leagues, it was Jim Leyland. "I think he's a better manager than me," LaRussa said.

Thrift was astonished. "I said, 'What are you talking about? He's never managed.' But LaRussa stuck to those words."

It was about a week after that first interview that Thrift called Leyland and offered him the job. "Syd told me if we could agree to terms I had the job," Leyland said. "I came back and worked out the contract and they announced it the following Monday."

And what the media saw was a man who had immediately taken on the persona that typified the citizens of Pittsburgh. His words spoke of confidence and reality at the same time, and he gave the fans a reason to believe in the future of the Pittsburgh Pirates.

"All the fans expect is a good day's work," Leyland said in his first official introduction to the city on November 20, 1985. "As a manager, I don't think you can ever guarantee how many wins you're going to get. I can guarantee that our players will give a hundred-percent effort day in and day out over a 162 game schedule. You can create a lot of fan enthusiasm with a steal of home, and sometimes that enthusiasm will carry over for six or seven days, not only with the fans but with the entire ballclub. Stealing bases and running aggressively is very important. I don't know if we have the people to do it, but I'm going to find out, and I'm going to do it with the people I feel comfortable with."

Many of the same fans that said, "Syd who?" when the Pirates named their new general manager felt the same way about Leyland. He wasn't well known to the novice baseball fan, but those who followed the game religiously knew of his achievements. Leyland spent seven years as a player in the Detroit Tigers farm system beginning in 1963, but never made it past Class AA. He was a light-hitting catcher in his playing days, his best season coming in 1966 when he hit .243 with Rocky Mount (North Carolina).

In 1970, Leyland was appointed to the coaching staff of the Tigers Southern League Class AA affiliate in Montgomery. One year later, at age 26, he received his first managerial assignment when he took over Detroit's Bristol club in the Appalachian Rookie League. He also managed Clinton (Class A) in the Midwest League and Montgomery and Lakeland (Class A) in the Florida State League, before moving on to the Tigers' Evansville (AAA) club in the American Association, where he spent three years as a manager. Leyland's teams advanced to the playoffs in five of his last six seasons as a minor league manager, winning three league championships. All together, his teams made six post-season appearances in his 11 years as a minor league manager.

Leyland was named Manager of the Year in the Florida State League in 1977 and 1978 and then won Manager of the Year honors in the American Association after leading Evansville to the league championship in 1979.

From there it was on to Chicago in 1982, where then White Sox manager Tony LaRussa had Leyland penciled in as his third base coach and right-hand man. That was where he spent the next four years, learning the major league system and honing his wisdom for what would soon become the best career move Leyland ever made.

"I was comfortable in Chicago, and I can't tell you how much I learned from Tony LaRussa," Leyland said in the middle of the 1992 season, his seventh with the Pirates. "I've often said he didn't make me a manager. He made me a *major league* manager. He took me from the minors and made me a third base coach. He gave me a lot of insight along the way and gave me the opportunity to show what I can do. He's a brilliant man, and he's the one that got me over the hump. If it hadn't been for him, I might still be coaching third base for the White Sox."

"I remember meeting Jim Leyland for the first time in 1981," said Paul Meyer, the Pirates beat writer for the *Pittsburgh Post Gazette*. "I was having lunch in an Indianapolis hotel with Sparky Anderson and I was doing a story on [pitcher] Mark Fidrych's attempted comeback. Jim was the manager at Evansville at the time, and he came in and had coffee with us. As soon as he left the table, Sparky said to me, 'That guy's going to be a major league manager within five years.' Sparky, of course, was right on target and when I told Jim this story a few years later, he remembered every minute of our meeting."

On that first spring training day some five years after Sparky Anderson's bold prediction, Leyland showed a spring in his step that would last right through the 1992 season. He had proven his ability to manage in the minors, and he realized he might be stepping into a cauldron in Pittsburgh. But it didn't matter. Jim Leyland was a major league manager—finally.

&

The turnaround would not happen overnight. Leyland knew that. He knew that he could take a liking to Pittsburgh. The question was, would Pittsburgh take a liking to him?

"My father was born in [nearby] Butler, Pennsylvania, but I had never been in Pittsburgh in my life," said Leyland, who was born in Toledo, Ohio. "I had heard a lot about the area, but that was basically it. I knew we had an act to clean up, and that it would take time, but I didn't know if the people would have the patience with me."

The "act" Leyland referred to was, in large part, the drug trials that had rocked baseball and the city of Pittsburgh less than one year before his first season as a big league manager. The circumstances surrounding that period in baseball history were of little concern to Leyland, because he played no part in it and had no effect on its outcome. What did concern him was the team he was inheriting. He wondered how they would handle the new situation with a new manager and a new coaching staff. What could he do if they decided to lay down for him the way they did for Chuck Tanner the season before?

"I wasn't going to let that happen," Leyland said. "When I look back on it, I knew my team wasn't going to be a very good one that first year. But I also knew Pittsburgh carried a lot of tradition with names like Stargell, Clemente, Mazeroski, and so many more. Chuck Tanner had done a great job as manager here. He was a part of that tradition when they won the '79 World Series.

"My idea was, I'm a baseball manager. I can't come in and turn it around overnight, but I felt like I *could* manage. And, if given enough time, I felt like I could do the job and do it well."

Leyland may not have known much about the city the first time he visited, but Pirate management wanted to make sure he would find out.

"I moved to the city, as the Pirates asked me to do, and I've found I'm very happy here," Leyland said. "I plan on living here for the rest of my life. I don't know how much longer I'll manage here, but I plan on staying."

One thing the Pirates definitely had in mind going into that 1986 campaign was to give Leyland his time. Carl Barger and company were not oblivious to the fact that this was a team that needed a tremendous overhaul, and they were not going to throw this man out the door after just one year— even if the Pirates didn't win a game all season. So with management behind him, Leyland now had to wonder how the players would accept him.

ᔰ

"Everyone pretty much knew there was going to be a changing of the guard," Bob Walk said of Leyland's first year. "Our spring training literally looked like a tryout camp with all the new faces around. But we knew the Pirates were going to try to rebuild the farm system and especially the Triple-A team. Some guys knew it would be a matter of time before they were traded, and it just seemed like they were more curious about where they would be going instead of trying to help us win.

"The situation was good for guys like Barry Bonds and Sid Bream because Jim could put them out there and tell them, 'We're going with you guys, sink or swim.' I think that helped them because they didn't have any added pressures on them, like worrying about making mistakes and losing their positions. It would have been foolish to think we could have competed right away. You're only going to get one shot at this rebuilding thing, so the Pirates had to make sure they were going to do things right."

That Walk has been around long enough to reap the benefits of the Pirates' reconstruction is a credit in itself. He was a rookie when he pitched in the 1980 World Series with the Philadelphia Phillies. He went 11-7 after being called up on May 26 of that year and struck out 94 batters in 152 innings. He started out 6-0 before suffering his first major league loss, 3-2, to the Atlanta Braves on July 20. He started Game 1 of the 1980 World Series and defeated Kansas City, 7-6.

Despite his impressive rookie year, the Phillies traded Walk to Atlanta during the following off-season for outfielder Gary Matthews. Walk started slowly for the Braves and subsequently went on the disabled list at the end of May with a rib injury. He stayed there until August 9, but his initial season with the Braves never blossomed as he finished 1-4 and posted a 4.60 earned run average.

Walk bounced back to finish 11-9 for the Braves in 1982, but spent most of the following season on Atlanta's Class AAA Richmond club. He lost his first six decisions there and posted a 10.59 ERA during that stretch. He came back strong to finish 11-6 the rest of the way and dropped his ERA to 3.60. He led the league in complete games (11) and innings pitched (185) and tied for the lead in starts (28), but despite those numbers, the Braves pitched him in only one game. The outing was not impressive as he gave up three runs and seven hits in 3-2/3 innings pitched.

The Braves released Walk in spring training of 1984, and the Pirates signed him to a minor league contract with their Class AAA Hawaii team on April 7. Walk wasn't sure at the time if he'd ever see the majors again, but his signing with the Pirates would soon prove to be a perfect match.

"The Pirates were the only team to offer me a job," Walk said. "Chuck Tanner guaranteed me at the time that if I was doing the job by mid-season in Hawaii, he would make sure I had a job in the big leagues, whether it was with the Pirates or some other team."

Walk did more than help himself at Hawaii. He was 9-5 midway through the season, with 85 strikeouts in 127.1 innings, and was leading the league with a 2.26 ERA. The call from the Pirates came on July 16 of that year, and Walk delivered that very night by striking out a career-high eight batters in the Bucs' 4-1 victory over the Los Angeles Dodgers. A week later, however, he went on the disabled list with a sore right shoulder and spent much of the rest of the season there.

The disabled list would soon become a common place for Bob Walk. He has never been a player who whimpers at every hangnail, preferring instead to pitch through whatever ails him and worry about the pain afterward. But sometimes the pain gets to be too much. Whether it's a rib injury or the more familiar groin and hamstring pulls Walk has become so accustomed to, the injuries take their toll. For most players, nine trips to the disabled list in a four-year span would tell that player it was time to think about another profession. But Walk, who spent a total of 66 days on the D.L. for various ailments in 1991, keeps right on going.

"It gets frustrating to see a player come up lame that many times in his career," Jim Leyland said. "But Walkie is the kind of guy that just keeps pulling himself back up. I love having him on the team because he'll do just about anything you ask him to. All he wants to do is win."

Walk has done that quite well since coming to Pittsburgh. The Van Nuys, California native has a 69-47 record with the

Pirates since 1984 and through 1992, he was the only major league pitcher to have a winning record in each of the six previous seasons, while having at least 10 decisions. He is often seen as the kind of pitcher that can put his defense to sleep. He stands in the stretch for a long time; often slow and very meticulous, always looking for that one edge that might get him out of a jam. Despite his propensity to injury, Walk has formed himself into one of the most resilient and versatile pitchers on the Pirates' staff. If Leyland needs a last-minute starter, he can always turn to Walk. If long relief is what it takes, Walk can be seen throwing in the bullpen during the middle innings of a game. Sometimes even a save isn't out of the question.

"It really depends on what Jim wants me to do," Walk said. "I don't really care, because pitching is what I get paid to do. Whether it's in spring training or in the National League play-offs, I'll go out and give the team the best I can."

Walk has the current distinction of being the Pirate with the longest tenure, but when the Pirates were going through their rough transition period, he thought he might be on the way out with some of the other veterans.

"I think the difference was that I wasn't worried about all that negative stuff when I came to the Pirates," Walk said. "The guys on that 1984 team were all established and weren't fighting for their careers like I was. I felt I had to care for myself and no one else. Whether Candelaria wanted to get out of Pittsburgh or not had no bearing on my situation."

When the managerial change was announced after the 1985 season, Walk immediately thought his career was suddenly in danger again.

"I had always pitched well for Chuck Tanner, and when they made the changes, I felt like I was going to have to prove myself again. I figured Jim Leyland didn't know me from anyone else, and I was going to have to start worrying about my situation all over again."

But Leyland had other thoughts in mind when it came to sifting through his new pitching staff. Walk's steadiness and tough demeanor were two qualities that really stood out in the manager's eyes.

"I could see he was a no-nonsense type of guy," Leyland said. "He'll do just about anything you ask him to. Whether it's as a starter, long relief or short relief. Walkie is always there for the ballclub."

It's been that way ever since in the relationship between Bob Walk and the Pittsburgh Pirates. Walk posted a 12-10 record in 1988 and followed that with a 13-10 mark in 1989, and his first appearance in the All-Star game. He was 7-5 in 1990 with a save and was the winning pitcher in the Pirates' Game 1 victory over the Cincinnati Reds in the National League championship series.

Despite spending so much time on the disabled list in 1991, Walk finished 9-2 and the ballclub rewarded him with a two-year contract that would avoid free-agency and keep him in a Pirates uniform through the 1993 season. Walk lived up to that gesture by finishing 10-6 in 1992, with a 3.20 ERA and two saves in 135 innings pitched.

"Walkie is a player every manager dreams about," Leyland said. "He'll go out there and give you the innings and never bat an eye while doing it. Every year the so-called experts keep saying his time is gone. But every year Bob Walk keeps putting on that Pirates uniform and pitching his ass off. You can't ask for much more than that from any ballplayer."

And to Walk, the uniform is what it's all about. Putting it on. Taking it off. Day after day during the summer months. It is every kid's dream, and Walk has felt fortunate to live in such a world.

"I've always tried to take things one day at a time," Walk said. "When I got released by the Braves in 1984, I had [put in] three years in the majors. I figured if I could get a couple more years in, I'd get a decent pension.

"I was happy as hell to be back in the big leagues when the Pirates called me up. They gave me this chance, and things have been great ever since. I love the city of Pittsburgh, and I feel like I've been wearing this same uniform all my life. I don't even think about my years with the Braves or Phillies anymore. I like to think of myself as a Pirate my whole career."

❧

The pomp and circumstance emanated from Three Rivers Stadium on April 8, 1986. Despite the gloomy skies and lingering

sprinkles that threatened the start of the new baseball season—
the new beginning in Pittsburgh, as the fans would hope— Jim
Leyland eagerly made out his first lineup card as manager of the
Pittsburgh Pirates.

Rick Reuschel would be his opening-day starter against
the New York Mets and a rifle-armed young hurler named
Dwight Gooden. The Pirates had always enjoyed good crowds
for opening day because it is a tradition in every major league
city. This one, however, was built on anticipation. The Mets were
loaded with talented players such as Gooden, Darryl Strawberry,
Keith Hernandez, Gary Carter, Ray Knight, Lenny Dykstra, and
Mookie Wilson. The list went on and on for manager Davey
Johnson, as his team would walk away with the N.L. Eastern
division crown and eventually rally for an exciting four games to
three win over the Boston Red Sox in the World Series.

The Pirates were the team in transition, ready to look at
young players with even younger looking faces, while adding
just a slight mix of veteran leadership. R.J. Reynolds would
provide a little bit of both in center field, while a young Sid Bream
was placed firmly at first base to provide the defense that Pirate
fans would soon grow to appreciate from him. The veteran
leadership would have to come from players such as Reuschel,
Johnny Ray, Rick Rhoden, and probably the fans' favorite Pirate
player at the time, catcher Tony Pena. Youth would come in the
form Reynolds, Bream, Joe Orsulak, Bob Kipper, and the up-
and-coming Barry Bonds.

Jim Leyland bounced out of the dugout at around 7 p.m.
as his name was introduced over the stadium's public address
system, and a chorus of cheers rang heavily from the 48,953 fans
in attendance. Leyland took the customary position beside home
plate for a manager who has just been introduced, and then
rotated slowly, waving and tipping his cap to acknowledge the
crowd's warm reception. The rest of the "new look" Pirates took
their place down the first base line beside him, and another
chapter of Pirate baseball was about to unfold.

The Mets opened an early lead on Reuschel in that game
by scoring twice in the first inning, but Reynolds brought the
crowd to its feet in the Pirates' half of the first by sending a
Gooden fastball deep to center field for a lead-off home run. The
blast ignited hope for a successful beginning for the Pirates, but

while Gooden calmed himself after his mistake pitch, Reuschel just didn't seem to have his best stuff. The Mets showed why they were destined to be the class of the division by holding off any further Pirate rallies and winning the opener, 4-2.

While he knew his team had a long way to go before it could contend, Leyland was optimistic that a bright future would lie ahead if the Pirates' players and fans believed it could be done. And that was just a little bit  more than he believed going into spring training.

"There were a lot of things to look at," he said. "It was a touchy  situation, because you have to deal with the media and they want you to answer  questions about your team. You want to be honest with them, but at the same  time you have to be careful.

"I knew I had an awful team, but I couldn't be critical of my players to  the press. I couldn't afford to lose my players right from the start. I knew we had to make a lot of changes, but I had to be diplomatic about it, too. I just always tried to talk about the positive side. A lot of our guys had  major league experience and pretty good careers as well."

Most of those careers were nearing their end, noticed Leyland. He and Syd Thrift realized that they had to weed out the worn and tired veterans and infiltrate even more youth into this already baby-faced ballclub.

The Pirates traded Jason Thompson and released Sixto Lezcano and Johnnie LeMaster in the last week of spring train-ing, and about 40 games into the  season, Steve Kemp was also given his walking papers.

Releasing players is never an easy assignment for a man-ager on any level.  In the high-priced world of major league baseball, it is even tougher. You're basically telling a man that his productivity is no longer beneficial to your  organization, and it is time that he moves on to another field or endeavor.

"It really is a tough job telling a player he has to move on," Leyland  said. "We had guys who were productive major league players in their day,  but the time had come that they had to move on in the scheme of what we were  trying to do. We didn't want to get rid of everyone, but there were  definitely some changes that had to be made.

"It sounds like a fish market when you say, 'This one's a keeper; throw  this one back.' But that was almost how we had to put our club together. Over the years it's been [general managers] Syd Thrift, then Larry Doughty, and now Ted Simmons who made those tough decisions, and they've done a tremendous job."

But the job of telling the player he is no longer a part of the team usually falls on the manager's shoulders.

"It's never easy to tell a player that he's gone," Leyland continued. "Whether you love a player or don't particularly like him, it'll never be easy. I've always believed there is one basic standard. Be up front, honest and tell the truth. If you do that, you may have a player who is temporarily upset with you, but if you lie to him, he's going to be long-term upset. Players don't want to be lied to. At Christmas, I still hear from players I released in the minor leagues. That means a lot to me.

"Even when the team wins, a manager might never have a perfect day, because he may have to tell one of those players who contributed to the win that he's going down to the minors; or he's been released or traded. I've been managing for eighteen years and if I manage another eighteen years, that job will never be easy."

That is one big reason why Leyland immediately developed a unique rapport with his players. Just about every player on every team Leyland has managed will say he is a player's manager. The kind that doesn't give you a lot of pep talks and clubhouse sermons.

He usually arrives at the stadium about six hours before a home game to let thoughts and strategies run through his mind. There are discussions with his coaching staff, and once a health report is given by trainers Kent Biggerstaff and Dave Tumbas, Leyland will make out the night's lineup card. He is a firm believer in the lefty-righty theory when it comes to making his lineup. If the opposition has a right-handed pitcher on the mound, Leyland will go with his left-handed lineup. And it is the opposite when the Pirates face a left-handed pitcher.

Just about all major league managers keep records of their players against pitchers around the league and Leyland is certainly no different. If he has a utility player who happens to have an outstanding career average against someone like David Cone or Tom Glavine, he won't think twice about inserting that player into the starting lineup against that pitcher.

"People talk about role players," said former utility out-fielder Gary Varsho, who was traded to the Pirates before the 1991 season, but released in November 1992. "But with the Pirates, a role is something you have for breakfast with your coffee. On this team you are a player. You are one of 25 players on the team, and with Jim Leyland as your manager, you *will* play. You may not play as much as other people, but Jim knows you can contribute, and he's not going to tell you anything different. He always tells guys who don't get to play a whole lot that the team has its regulars, but he'll try to match you up against a guy you might do well against. He's very up front and he lets you know you're with the team to contribute to a winner."

It is that kind of rapport that is most noticeable when visitors enter the Pirates clubhouse for the first time. There is comfortable living room furniture spread around the room and a huge television console perched high on the wall. There is a more compact and portable TV-VCR tucked away in another area so players can look at tapes of certain pitchers they will be facing or get a look at why their own swing might have taken a nose-dive.

There are card games that sometimes get boisterous, and quiet discussions in a corner where friends can console each other or help with problems that come up in everyday life. And then there is the basketball court.

Perhaps the best way to get your mind off the troubles in your own sport or profession is to take a stab at something else. Major league baseball players can't always walk away from the field to practice law or medicine, but they can build a miniature basketball court in the middle of their clubhouse and pretend for a few precious moments they are Michael Jordan soaring in for a spectacular dunk, or that Larry Bird has come to town to sink a few three-pointers before heading out to pitch a complete game against the Mets.

This is something most of the Pirates look forward to every day, and they hold various singles and doubles tourna-ments with brackets and seedings posted on the wall that would make the NCAA tournament committee feel envious.

"I've always felt it's not always the front office or the fans that give you the encouragement to believe in yourself, but the locker room," Barry Bonds said. "It's the people that you have in there who make the atmosphere. The locker room is where everything starts before a game, and the locker room is where it always ends."

Jim Leyland makes himself a part of all the action in the clubhouse in one way or another, but he never makes himself a nuisance. He will not intrude on a player's personal life, but he makes it a habit every day to walk around the Pirates clubhouse and greet each player in some fashion. Whether it's a, "Hey, whaddya' say, Andy?" or "How's the family, Dougie?" he lets his players know they have someone they can talk to and turn to if things aren't going so well.

"When you're young and starting out on a new team, hearing something like that makes you feel more at ease," pitcher Doug Drabek said. "Jimmy involves you in his thoughts and makes you feel like a person and not just a ballplayer. I think that carries over to the players and lets them know that he really does care."

Leyland doesn't carry a lot of expectations for his players, the only one being that they show up on time and come ready to play. Much like what the shop foreman would expect at any kind of factory, or what your own boss would expect from your efforts at work. All the while, Leyland has done things with a kind heart and a tremendous amount of patience.

"Patience was the word everyone stressed that first year," pitcher Bob Kipper said. "I know I heard it a thousand times. They stressed it to the players, and they stressed it to the fans. We knew we were going to take some lumps, but we also knew we were headed in the right direction."

The Pirates did take their lumps in 1986. After falling to 0-2 in the young season, the Bucs won five in a row and seemed like they would provide a challenge—no matter how slight—to the other teams in the division. That five-game winning streak, however, would be the longest string of consecutive victories the Pirates would put together all season. They followed by losing eight of their next nine, including five in a row, and another pair of six-game losing streaks had them completely out of the picture by the end of May, when they fell 14-1/2 games behind the front-running Mets.

The Pirates were destined for their third consecutive last-place finish during this initial phase of the rebuilding process, but October 1 of that season would be a date that Jim Leyland will always remember.

"I never set any kind of timetable for the team or anything," he said. "I preferred to take things day by day, and I lived to accomplish my responsibilities for each day. But there was one thing that every single member of that ballclub worked their asses off to do and that was to *not* lose 100 games. When I got the job before the season, I told my brother in the winter that if I lost 100 games as manager of that club, I'd resign. There was just no way we were going to do that."

The Pirates were 62-95 on October 1. They were playing a somewhat meaningless game against the St. Louis Cardinals at Busch Stadium, but each member of that Pirates team knew just how special the game really was. The club had already improved over the previous year's 57-104 record, but losing 100 games would stick out like a sore thumb in the eyes of the fans who expected bigger and better things.

It was an ordinary day in major league baseball, but it was an exhilarating day for Jim Leyland as his club defeated the Cardinals 4-3, and avoided the noose that would undoubtedly have been fitted for their necks by the all-too-common second-guessers. The Pirates won again the following day over the Cardinals before dropping their final three games of the season at New York. Their 64-98 record was only a seven-game turn-around from the season before, but to the 1986 Pittsburgh Pirates, it was a huge and positive sign that said, "Yes, we have turned the corner."

"I was happy as hell when we won that sixty-third game," Leyland joked. "But you could see the people believed in us. They showed their appreciation the whole year by saying, 'Well yeah, they're not very good, but they're busting their tails and they're hustling. They got a plan.' They were going to give us the benefit of the doubt and I think that was the biggest step the fans of Pittsburgh ever took."

The Pirates just made it over the one million mark in attendance— the first time in three years they had done so—and despite the club's third straight last-place finish, those numbers said that the fans were interested again, and that the Pirates truly had taken bigger steps forward.

Thrift also took some big steps during and after the season to build the nucleus of the ballclub. Bream had steadied himself at first base, as the Pirates had hoped he would, and a new star named Barry Bonds would come up in mid-May to build the foundation for his Pirates legacy.

Thrift watched his club carefully during the entire season and made little roster moves at first. Near the end of the season, however, he reacquired former Pirate farmhand Bobby Bonilla from the Chicago White Sox in exchange for right-hander Jose DeLeon, who had seen his better days earlier in his Pirate career.

He then called up a young, hard-throwing pitcher named John Smiley all the way from Class A, who was projected to go a long way in the Pirates' scheme of things.

Then came one of Thrift's first significant moves. It happened on Thanksgiving Day 1986, a trade that sent pitchers Rick Rhoden, Cecilio Guante, and Pat Clements to the New York Yankees for Doug Drabek, who would become a Cy Young Award and 22-game winner for the Pirates in 1990, Brian Fisher, and Logan Easley.

"Syd always had a vision for what it would take to bring a winner here," Sid Bream said. "He started putting his plan into action that winter."

There was no clear-cut time for Thrift's plan to unfold, however, Pirate management knew the fans wouldn't allow an exorbitant amount of time to build a winner. But they had to stick with the plan nonetheless.

While the plan called for Thrift to make the moves where he saw fit, none would start out as unpopular as the one he pulled off right before the beginning of the 1987 season. It was April 1, but Thrift looked at the Pittsburgh media gathering in the Pirates' spring training complex in Bradenton, Florida, and said, "This isn't any April Fool's joke."

Thrift had taken the most popular Pirate —catcher Tony Pena—and held him out on the trading block. The St. Louis Cardinals were in desperate need of a catcher, and Pena seemingly fit the bill, because not only did he have the defensive skills for the position, he was also a pretty fair hitter, with a .286 batting average in six full seasons with the Pirates and 63 home runs.

Despite Pena's popularity, and despite the fact the Pirates were going to lose maybe the best defensive catcher in their history, Thrift made the deal with the Cardinals. In return, the Pirates received pitcher Mike Dunne, catcher Mike LaValliere, and outfielder Andy Van Slyke. None of the players were household names at the time, but Van Slyke probably carried the most attention. His acquisition definitely carried the most weight in the trade, because the Pirates were in need of a true centerfielder and Van Slyke, who was never a regular starter with the Cardinals, was the man to fill that need.

Fan reaction came pouring in to the major Pittsburgh media outlets— television, radio, print—all with the same reactions. "Who does Thrift think he is?" one person asked. "I thought the Pirates were trying to improve," others would say with very noticeable hints of sarcasm. But Thrift and the Pirates stuck by their decision and welcomed the trio with open arms.

"I think everyone was still a little skeptical about how we were going to turn it around," Walk said. "We knew they wanted to rebuild, but when Syd went out and traded Tony for those three guys, it sent a message to everyone that they were serious about making this a better club. I think everyone started believing then."

It may have taken a monster trade to make the players believe that the Pirates were actually committed to winning again, but the fans sensed it much earlier. They sensed it in the youthful enthusiasm of a new manager who wasn't afraid to juggle his roster the way he saw fit from time to time, and dared to challenge his players to get the most out of themselves each and every night. The fans liked his style and wanted to see more of the plan that called for a challenge at every turn.

They also took a liking to the general manager, who only a year before was being run out of town before he even had a chance to wield his sword of authority. Syd Thrift was pushing all the right buttons with his daring trades and thoughtful roster moves. He was on his way to genius status in a position where even geniuses get bounced around once in a while.

The fans also liked the Pirates' new attitude. The hardcore Pirate fans noticed the desire to win from each player almost as soon as he or she entered the stadium and nestled into a seat. There was the hustle of R.J. Reynolds in 1986 and the defensive wizardry of first baseman Sid Bream. Together, the two provided punch, power, and a growing sense of maturity that both veterans and rookies could build on.

Perhaps one thing stood out above all others, however, in that nightmarish, but educational 1986 season for the Pittsburgh

Pirates. It was the beginning of a new era for the Pirates and the dawn of one man's soon-to-be-spectacular career. While Pittsburgh hoped to rebuild through time and patience, it also needed to find a catalyst. The Pirates could no longer afford to wait for the moon to come to them. They had to reach for the moon. On May 30, 1986, that is exactly what they did by bringing Barry Bonds up from Class AAA Hawaii and throwing him to the wolves in leftfield.

This was a time to decide just how serious the Pirates were when it came to rebuilding a contender in Pittsburgh.

# *Taking Stock in Bonds*

He was the son of a major leaguer. Sometimes that can be good, sometimes not. After all, there are pressures that are automatically incurred when the other little kids can say, "His daddy is so-and-so." Even adults who don't know you, but certainly know your father's name, will anticipate the day you grow into your old dad's spikes and do your best to keep the family light glowing.

Barry Bonds grew up watching, studying, and learning from some of the best baseball players ever. He studied the pitching mechanics of Juan Marichal and shagged fly balls with Hall-of-Famer Willie Mays, who was in his hey-day with the San Francisco Giants. Above everything, though, Barry Bonds learned love and the importance of being a man in all his decisions from his father, Bobby.

"You only have one daddy," Barry Bonds says time and time again. "Sometimes managers and coaches try to be like your daddy, but they're your managers and coaches. They *ain't* your daddy."

Bonds watched his father through his prolific major league career, which was spent mostly with the Giants, and followed him to the ballpark every day. What a thrill it must have been to have stood in the outfield at Candlestick Park at age 11 or 12, that famed bay wind swirling in behind you, while a baseball races at your glove with the speed and force of a jet engine. This is no ordinary childhood, unless, of course, your name happens to be Barry Bonds. For this is what young Barry did through much of his early life.

He followed the routines that major leaguers go through: the pre-game stretching, the ritual of batting practice, and the fun and games that went along with all of that. He was not the only player's son to put on a smaller Giants uniform and roam the outfield grass, but he was probably the most diligent.

Barry Bonds not only followed. He studied. And he learned. Many times he also participated. Giants' coaches never minded throwing him a little batting practice once in a while, and even they were taken aback by the sleek form in his left-handed stance and the sharp eye that introduced every pitch to a near-textbook swing.

He was growing into a baseball person, and many people within the San Francisco Giants organization knew the son of one of their best players was going to be someone special. But Barry still liked being Barry, a kid growing up and having fun. Live for the present. Be a kid. Have fun. That was how he liked to look at life.

Sometimes Barry was the Giants' bat boy. And on other occasions, he didn't even know a baseball game was going on. "A bunch of the kids and I used to play our own games in the hallways by the clubhouse," he recalled. "We just said, 'Aw man, we don't wanna watch the game. We're having fun playing our own baseball.'"

It was a makeshift game, to be sure, but for Barry Bonds it was a chance to excel at the game where his name would ultimately define the word excellence.

ชา

Barry Bonds was born July 24, 1964, in Riverside, California. His father, Bobby, played baseball quite well. He enjoyed a 14-year playing career as an All-Star outfielder and spent four more years as a coach in the major leagues. Most kids would be proud to be the son of a professional athlete, and Barry was certainly no different. But Bobby also wanted his son to learn the humility and respect that he learned from baseball and carry that with him through whatever career he would choose to pursue.

So Barry learned from his father and from others within the confines of Candlestick Park in San Francisco, where his father spent much of his major league career. He listened to advice and stored in his memory whatever tips that were offered to him.

Athletics appeared to be his ticket as a teenager because of his sleek build and the skillful ease with which he played any game. As his body matured, so did his ability, and by the time he graduated from Serra High School in San Mateo, California, Bonds was a three-sport star in football, basketball, and baseball.

He decided to pursue his education at Arizona State University, where he majored in criminal justice and insists he thought more of becoming a lawyer than a professional baseball player. But those aspirations soon diminished when Bonds lit up the Pac-10 conference with a .347 career batting average, 45 home runs, 175 RBIs, and 57 stolen bases. Bonds was named to the All-Pac-10 team for three straight years and was named to the College All-World Series team as a freshman and sophomore (ASU didn't make the World Series in Bonds' junior year).

Bonds was named MVP of the NCAA West II regional tournament as a freshman, and he tied an NCAA record as a sophomore with seven consecutive hits in College World Series play. He hit .368 in 62 games during his junior year at Arizona State in 1985 and led the Sun Devils in home runs (23) and RBIs (66). His selection to *The Sporting News* College Baseball All-America Team was a foregone conclusion.

With every college game he played, it was becoming apparent that Barry Bonds would have to store thoughts of practicing law in the back of his mind for a while. Baseball was becoming a hit to him, and soon the major leagues would be calling.

❧

If finishing last did anything for the Pittsburgh Pirates in 1984, it gave them the No. 1-draft choice in the 1985 free agent draft. It was a choice they couldn't afford to go wrong with because of the team's commitment to rebuilding. If this pick was a bust, there was no telling how far the team could be set back.

At the same time, the Pirates realized they would have to bring their selection along slowly. Rushing a young prospect— especially a No. 1-pick—can sometimes lead to disaster. There is the constant feeling of pressure that is almost sure to hit the young man at some point. If the hope for the team's future is put under the spotlight too fast, it could cost the player a career that he had worked for years and years to sharpen.

In the big leagues, fans can often be merciless. And in major media outlets such as New York, Chicago, or Los Angeles, the media can be downright torturous. The Pittsburgh media has always been fair with the hometown players—giving credit where credit is due— while at the same time not pampering an athlete beyond the realm of believability. But even so, Pirate brass figured whomever they chose in this all-important draft, they would have to be careful with him. They couldn't afford to lose him to the fans and the media before they had a chance to put him on the field in a Pirate uniform.

Speculation rose heavily that the Pirates would make the young phenom from Arizona State University their first selection. He was, after all, the son of a former major leaguer— a great major leaguer at that— and he had all the tools to someday lead the Pirates out of their major hole and back to the peaks of respectability.

When the day finally came, the Pittsburgh Pirates pulled no surprises and made Barry Bonds their No. 1 selection. Bonds, at the time, was delighted to have been the Pirates' first choice and he felt no qualms about joining a team that was starting again from the ground up.

"I was actually quite fortunate to have been a young ballplayer at that time," Bonds said as he thought about being the first player drafted by the Pirates and the sixth player overall. "The Pittsburgh Pirates were a rebuilding team, and it was interesting to think they would be counting on me to help them turn things around. I think if you're a young ballplayer, you should always want to do your best to live up to the role the team has for you, but at the same time, it's a feeling you should relish and be proud of."

Bonds was 20 years old when he was chosen to lead a major-league franchise back to the top. It would not happen overnight, as everyone in the Pirates organization was well aware of. But Bonds was confident that day would come.

Confidence oozes from his 6-foot-1, 185-pound body. He stands at the plate with an attitude that he will hit you, no matter what your name is on that pitcher's mound, or what your specialty pitch happens to be. "You may get the best of me once in a while," his eyes seem to say, "But more often than not, I am going to get you."

Bonds began the 1985 season at Prince William, the Pirates' Class A affiliate, but it soon became apparent that he wouldn't stay at the minor league's first level very long.

"You could tell from the beginning he was gonna be a great one," the Pirates' manager at the time, Chuck Tanner, said. "He had everything we could have wanted in a ballplayer. He could hit. He could play the outfield. He could throw the ball like a cannon. He was young, but you could just tell it wasn't going to take him long to get to the big leagues."

Bonds stayed in "A" ball for exactly one season. He hit .299 in 71 games at Prince William and totaled 76 hits including 16 doubles and 13 home runs. He also delivered 37 runs batted in and stole 15 bases. He had three multiple-home run games in that first season and blasted three homers in a single game at Durham on July 19. The following week Bonds homered in three consecutive at bats over a two-game span against Durham and was named Carolina League Player of the Month for July.

While Bonds' career was taking shape in the minor leagues, the Pirates were busy reshaping their future in the majors. Joe L. Brown had left as acting general manager and Chuck Tanner was fired just a week later. The Galbreaths were out after nearly 40 years of ownership, and the new public-private coalition was set to take over, with Malcolm Prine, Doug Danforth, and Carl Barger spearheading much of their efforts.

Syd Thrift was named the new general manager, much to the shock of fans and media alike, and soon after, the Jim Leyland era would begin. This conglomeration had one common goal—to make the Pirates contenders again in a league where most of the other teams thought they were only pretending.

The Pirates started the 1986 season with a fresh array of new faces, but Barry Bonds' was not one of them. The Pirates felt he was almost ready, but there was still some seasoning to take care of, and Class AAA Hawaii seemed just the place to take care of it. While Bonds was batting .311 through 44 games with the

Islanders, the Pirates were losing 24 of their first 40 games and falling quickly to their familiar position at the bottom of the National League Eastern division standings.

It was May 30, and the Pirates were in fifth place, 13 games behind the front-running New York Mets. With a little prodding from manager Jim Leyland, Syd Thrift decided it was time to call for the Pirates' future. The ballclub bought Bonds' contract that very day, and he made his debut against the Los Angeles Dodgers that night.

His soon-to-be magic bat had no hits in that inauspicious premiere, but from the looks of his hustle and his swing, the Pirates knew they had a player in Bonds. His first major league hit—a double off the Dodgers' Rick Honeycutt—came the very next night, and soon the hits came in greater quantities.

Leyland placed Bonds in the lead-off position in the Pirates' order from the very beginning in hopes of utilizing his ability to hit to all parts of the field and take advantage of his dangerous speed. Leyland admitted a couple of years later that it wasn't really the greatest spot in the order for Bonds to hit from, but he had no one else on his roster that could do the many things that Bonds was capable of doing.

Bonds grew fond of his new manager, and probably for that reason never made great waves about hitting from the lead-off position. It was a spot he admittedly didn't think he was being best utilized in, but he was a rookie, and his father had always taught him to respect the manager and know that he is the boss.

"I was very lucky to have a manager who stuck with his young players," Bonds said. "I mean, he's the kind of guy that'll stick with you through at least 200 at bats, if not more. He figures if you're going to learn, you might as well get your spankings in the major leagues instead of going back and forth to the minors."

During that first season, it was Bonds who did most of the spanking as he pounded 16 home runs— the most ever by a Pirate rookie since Al Oliver hit 17 in 1969—and drove in 48 runs. His flare for the average didn't come around that first year as he batted only .223, but he worked opposing pitchers for 65 walks and led the Pirates in stolen bases with 36, which was the most by a Pirate rookie since Omar Moreno stole 53 during a full season in 1977.

"I think I struggled a little bit my first year," Bonds said. "There was probably some pressure because when you're a No.

1 draft choice, people have these high expectations and perceptions of you. But I was around a lot of good baseball people and they helped me develop the confidence. Overall, I was pretty satisfied."

One thing that wasn't satisfying to Bonds or any other member of the 1986 Pittsburgh Pirates was the team's 64-98 record and third straight last-place finish.

"It was frustrating, but you could see the team coming," he said. "Syd Thrift believed in developing young talent, and I was fortunate to work a lot with Bill Virdon, who is considered one of the best outfield coaches in the game today.

"We just didn't have the dominating pitching staff like other ballclubs. The talent was there, and the development. You just didn't know when it was going to arrive."

In Bonds' eyes, the Pirates would arrive when the young players learned to gel with one another and gain the trust and confidence that was needed to carry them to the top of this ominous hill known as the National League Eastern division. Thrift had suddenly pushed many of the right buttons by bringing in fresh, young talent while at the same time, decreasing the team's payroll. Although Tony Pena was making $1.15 million at the time he was traded, the move could not be seen as a total cost-cutter, because the Pirates truly needed the players they received from the Cardinals, and Pena was their top commodity.

"Guys like Andy Van Slyke and Mike LaValliere needed to be everyday players," Bonds said. "And I don't think they ever got that chance in St. Louis. When they got that opportunity with us, you could really see the confidence start to build."

Before things could get better for the Pirates, however, it would take a commitment from all the team's members—players new and old; rookies and veterans; manager and coaches. Everyone had to come into the 1987 season with a positive attitude if there would be any hope of a turnaround. But it appeared the Pirates' new spring training additions weren't exactly chomping at the bit.

ϿϮ

It was with tears that Tony Pena said good-bye to his teammates that April 1 afternoon. He had experienced ups and downs with the only ballclub he had ever played for, and he always carried himself with a smile. But one opportunity he never had with the Pirates was to be part of a championship team. He would get that chance in his first season with the Cardinals, who lost the 1987 World Series, four games to three, to the Minnesota Twins. He would remember his friends in Pittsburgh and also the good times he shared, but soon he faced up to it, as most players do, with the attitude that he had a chance to help a contending team.

While it was a sad day for Pena to leave the Pirates, Mike LaValliere and Andy Van Slyke felt even worse, because they were being brought *in* to Pittsburgh.

"It was kind of a weird feeling," LaValliere recalled. "I was going to be one of the Cardinals' two catchers, along with Steve Lake, and I remember how Steve caught nine innings in a 'B' game that morning in spring training, and I was just running sprints, getting ready for the 'A' game that afternoon."

But when LaValliere saw his name scratched from the afternoon lineup, he figured immediately that something was up. As it turned out, it wasn't the news he wanted to hear.

"The first thing that came to my mind was trade," LaValliere said of seeing Lake's name penciled into the afternoon lineup. "I knew there was always that possibility and it was something I felt I could deal with. I just always thought to myself, 'There are only two places I don't want to be traded to. One is Montreal, the other, Pittsburgh.'"

So, LaValliere and Van Slyke watched the "A" game from the Cardinals' bench and learned soon afterwards of their fate.

"I was pretty well disgusted after they told us," LaValliere said. "I felt I was going from a first-class organization in St. Louis, where the team was well-appreciated, to a place where not too many nice things were being said about the baseball team. It was also tough because I was going from a contender to a last-place team for the three years before."

"You could say it was somewhat of a shock," Van Slyke said as he thought of the voices of Cardinal management who announced his fate. "I mean, you know there is always the possibility of a trade, but when you get yourself settled in a nice area and then find out they're shipping you to a place that had become the most undesirable baseball town in the league, it really kind of hits you."

Pittsburgh had developed a reputation in the eyes of young ballplayers who had never really learned of the city's baseball history and tradition that dated back to the late 19th century. Young players such as Van Slyke and LaValliere only knew a few details about the Pittsburgh Pirates—and they weren't the kind of details that remained in your memory forever. They knew of three consecutive last-place finishes and drug trials that nearly chased the team out of the city almost two years before. They remembered lack of hustle and enthusiasm when the Cardinals played the Pirates, and most of all, they remembered Three Rivers Stadium.

"I'll never forget visiting there my first time with the Cardinals," LaValliere said. "I thought it was a beautiful city, but when the game started I couldn't believe it when I looked around and saw all the empty seats. There were probably only 7,000 or 8,000 people in the stands."

Van Slyke took the news even harder because he had grown up in the Cardinals' organization. The Utica, New York native was the Cardinals' first-round selection in the June 1979 free agent draft, and like Bonds, did not spend much of his career in the minors. He was called up to the majors in 1983 and has remained there ever since.

Van Slyke and his wife, Lauri, built a home in Chesterfield, Missouri, a suburb of St. Louis, and their ties grew stronger to the Cardinals with each passing year.

"I don't care what organization you come up with," Van Slyke said. "You just naturally develop a special feeling toward that organization. There is something about them that gets embedded in you. When I heard I was traded, it was hard to believe I was no longer a St. Louis Cardinal."

Like LaValliere, what made Van Slyke's situation even harder to deal with was being traded to the Pittsburgh Pirates. He, too, felt the sudden fall from championship grace to what was perceived just two years before as baseball's slum.

"When I was playing with the Cardinals, I got the impression that Pittsburgh was a place where I would not want to play," Van Slyke said. "They were drawing 3,000 or 4,000 people to their games and that didn't particularly excite me, especially since I was used to playing in front of 30,000 or 40,000 every day in St. Louis."

Every day. Those were words that Van Slyke and LaValliere were not familiar with in St. Louis. They were both high on the Cardinals' list of young talent, but both were seemingly looked over time and time again when positions opened up in the field.

Van Slyke was especially shuffled around the diamond of St. Louis' Busch Memorial Stadium as he had been tried at one time or another at first base, third base, and all three outfield positions from 1983 to 1986. He was rarely in the lineup against left-handed pitchers because of manager Whitey Herzog's platoon system, and it was Herzog himself who once said, "With Andy Van Slyke, what you see is what you get."

"It got frustrating at times," Van Slyke said, pondering the words from his former manager. "As much as I liked playing there, I think some people in the organization never had the faith that I could be an everyday player."

The Pirates had enough faith in Van Slyke to make him the key player in the trade, and one team executive would soon call him the "cornerstone" of the franchise. His best season with the Cardinals was in 1986 when he hit .270 and had 13 home runs and 61 RBIs in 137 games. The Pirates figured to position him in rightfield next to Bonds, who was being tabbed the centerfielder of the future. Bonds would be the Pirates' key to the future all right, but Van Slyke would eventually have some say about whether that future would be in centerfield.

For Mike LaValliere, the trade was also a chance to solidify a starting position in the major leagues. The thought of joining a last-place club did little to lighten his attitude, but that soon changed when LaValliere met his new boss.

"I had only talked with Jim Leyland once before when the Cardinals were in Pittsburgh and we were passing the time during a rain delay," LaValliere said. "I didn't get time to build an impression of him, but he appeared to be a likeable guy and one who knew his baseball.

"My first real impression, though, came when Andy and I drove down to Bradenton the day after the trade. We weren't the least bit thrilled with the thought of going to the Pirates camp there and when we were stuck in traffic on the Skyway Bridge that leads from St. Petersburg to Bradenton, Andy even mentioned something about how he kind of wished the bridge would collapse and swallow us into the Gulf of Mexico."

That just wasn't their day, because the bridge did not collapse, and the two were able to survive the traffic and make their way to Pirate City.

"When we first got there, I remembered how an equipment guy asked me what size shoe I wore," LaValliere recalled. "I have real small feet and they didn't have my size at first. All I had were my red spikes from the Cardinals and the guy took those and painted them black. Right then I thought, 'Oh boy, this is gonna be a lot of fun.' I had worn uniform No. 10 in St. Louis, but the Pirates gave me No. 4, because Jim Leyland wore No. 10. When we had our first meeting with Jimmy, one of the first things he said to me was, 'Do you want No. 10?' I looked at him real surprised and said, 'Well, no. That's your number.' He said, 'If you want No. 10, you can have it. I can wear any number.'

"Right then I felt, 'Well gee, if the guy's willing to give up his uniform number for you, you have to give him a chance.' Right then I got the feeling I was going to be an important part of the Pittsburgh Pirates' plans and the negatives started to go away."

Leyland assured LaValliere that day that he was not just a throw-in to the trade, and he would be an integral part of the club's future. He told him he would be the Pirates' catcher against all right-handed pitchers, and that he was looking forward to LaValliere's defensive prowess behind the plate.

"He said he was counting on me," LaValliere said. "And that really meant a lot to me."

The Pirates had good reason to count on LaValliere as he had become St. Louis' regular catcher by the 1986 All-Star break and had earned a spot on Baseball America's National League Rookie All-Star team. He threw out 26-of-65 (40 percent) base runners attempting to steal against him and allowed just one passed ball in 827.1 innings, which was the lowest rate in the majors.

Leyland also spoke highly of Van Slyke in that first meeting and gave him the confidence that he, too, was definitely being counted on in the revitalization of an up-and-coming ballclub.

"Andy Van Slyke is tremendous," Leyland told reporters. "He's a guy who can steal 30 or 40 bases, hit 20 home runs, knock in 90, hit close to .300, and he plays great defense. What else do you have to do?"

Something a manager needs his players to be is happy. Not that players should wear false smiles on their faces every time they are in the clubhouse or on the field. But happy in a satisfied sort of way. The player should be comfortable with his surroundings and not alienated by others, just as he shouldn't alienate his teammates. This was never a problem with Van Slyke, who has always been popular with teammates for his sense of humor and sharp wit. But in the early stages of the trade and the beginning of the 1987 season, Van Slyke still appeared to be uncomfortable with his new location.

Playing right field, Van Slyke started the season miserably as he hit just .238 through the first two months of the season. Leyland was uncertain whether the slow start was due to Van Slyke's unhappiness in Pittsburgh or a possible distaste for his position in the outfield.

On May 30, with the Pirates three games under .500, in a tie for fifth place and eight games out of first, Leyland decided to do a little bit of gambling. He moved Barry Bonds from centerfield to left and moved Van Slyke to center. The move was a match made in heaven for the Pirates as Van Slyke endeared himself to the position, as well as to the fans by making difficult plays seem routine and impossible plays seem miraculous. He finished out the season there and would become a Gold Glove winner five years in a row from 1988 to 1992.

In many people's eyes, the position change was purely coincidental in the resurgence of Van Slyke's 1987 season. Although he broke out of his slump soon after and finished the season with a .293 average, 21 home runs, 84 RBIs and 34 stolen bases, he attributed the turnaround more to finally coming to grips with the trade — and himself— and acclimating to his new home.

Van Slyke and his family spent the first six weeks of the season living in a Pittsburgh hotel, brooding about the ill fortune they were seemingly beset with on that fateful April 1.

"I had to adjust to a lot of things early that season," Van Slyke admitted. "I had to get my family settled into a new city with new surroundings. I was with a new team and I had new teammates. I was also playing every day for the first time.

"It was a tough experience because the trade came right at the end of spring training and we were all set to go back home to St. Louis. Then all of a sudden, you're not going home."

Instead, Van Slyke, Lauri, and their three sons Andrew James, Jr. (age 5 at the time), Scott (3), and Jared (who was barely four months old), were holed up in a hotel room in a city that had been cast as baseball's first step to hell only a couple of years before.

It wasn't until mid-May that Van Slyke and his family settled into a house in the Franklin Park section of Pittsburgh, and soon he started providing the statistics the Pirates were hoping to see from him.

"When I committed to buying the house in May, that's when I told myself I was starting to feel like I belonged here," Van Slyke said.

"I began to realize what the atmosphere was, and I liked it. There weren't the negative things that other baseball people were making Pittsburgh out to be. This was a rebuilding club that was putting together a lot of talent. I began to see that this franchise was ready to start turning things around."

And with the turnaround, the Pirates were giving these young players the proper chances they might never have received in St. Louis.

"In my heart, I always knew I could be an everyday player," Van Slyke said. "What I needed was a chance to prove myself, and I've gotten that chance here."

"Pittsburgh took on a reputation around the league as being a ratty place to play," said LaValliere, who led major-league catchers by throwing out 49-of-115 base runners in his first season with the Pirates, earning him a Gold Glove Award. "I think that's why it hit us so hard about being traded here. But it's a great place and nothing like what we had thought it would be."

❧

While the Pirates were sticking with their theory of rejuvenation, the results didn't show immediately on the field. They had planted themselves in their now-familiar spot in the N.L. East cellar by late May, moved out briefly in June, and dropped back again by the end of that month.

There were a couple of faces still around from the last-place clubs of seasons before, and even though they were never considered malcontents, Thrift continued to build for the Pirates' future. Veteran pitcher Don Robinson, the team's top reliever at the time, was traded to San Francisco on July 31, and Rick Reuschel, the best starting pitcher on the roster followed Robinson to the Giants three weeks later. Second baseman Johnny Ray also didn't fit into the club's future plans, and he was shipped to the California Angels on August 29.

The reasons for these moves by Thrift were two-fold for the Pirates, because all three of these players were high-priced veterans who were nearing the end of their careers. Of the three, Ray would stay in the majors the longest, but with annual salaries at the time of $650,000 for Robinson, $657,000 for Ray, and $750,000 for Reuschel, the Pirates were able to take some cost-cutting measures, while at the same time stock the ballclub with eager, young talent waiting for a chance.

In return for Robinson, the Pirates got relief pitcher Jim Gott, who would become the bullpen stopper for a team that was ready to contend in 1988. Every good stopper needs a setup man, and that's what the Pirates received for Reuschel when Jeff Robinson came over from the Giants. While the Pirates received little in return for Ray, the move opened the door for a slick-fielding infielder at the team's Triple-A level named Jose Lind.

On August 23, the Pirates had just lost their fourth game in a row to the Atlanta Braves and had fallen to 53-71. At that rate, they were on a pace to lose 93 games, which would have been a nominal improvement from the season before, but nothing for the fans or players to get excited about.

The club was getting set to start a nine-game homestand against Western division foes Cincinnati, Houston, and Atlanta, which was usually just a formality to finish out the last month-and-a-half of the season. But that homestand will be remembered as the beginning of the Pirates' new era, and the exorcism of the wretched spirits of 1984, '85 and '86.

&

It started simply enough. Doug Drabek, the young starting pitcher the Pirates had acquired the preceding November from the New York Yankees, beat Tom Browning and the Reds, 5-4, in front of 11,020 fans at Three Rivers Stadium. This meager crowd still consisted pretty much of the die-hards who cheered the Pirates through thick and thin, but as the days wore on, attendance would be noticeably improved.

The Pirates swept the Reds and the Astros, and picked up their seventh win in a row in the first of a three-game series against the Braves. Over 26,000 fans showed up for two of the games against Houston, and although the Pirates lost to the Braves in their bid for an eighth consecutive victory, the game was significant because the attendance figure went over the one-million mark, and it was only September 1.

"I think we were starting to come together at that point," Barry Bonds said. "We developed quicker defensively more than offensively during the season, and that was a big key. We didn't have a strong bullpen yet, but we were defensively sound and that kept us in a lot of games."

With the trades completed and new bodies in new places, the Pirates built on their 8-1 homestand by running off a 7-2 road trip through Houston, Chicago, and Philadelphia. On September 20, the Pirates were 71-77 and facing the much-hated New York Mets at Three Rivers Stadium. The hatred was not from the players, but more so from the Pirate fans. It wasn't easy to forget the Mets' pounding of the Pirates in 17 out of 18 games in 1986. What was even worse was the way the Mets, who were considered cocky and egotistical by Pirate fans, seemed to revel in their mastery over the Bucs on their way to a world championship.

"They did beat us up pretty good that year," Bonds said. "They were a deep and talented ballclub, but you just had to wonder when that stuff was gonna end."

The Pirates weren't faring much better against the Mets in 1987 as they had won just four of the first 14 meetings between the two teams. On this night the Pirates and Mets went into extra innings and although the Mets were battling for a division title with St. Louis, the Pirates suddenly had some reason of their own to play. Only a month ago the team seemed headed for a fourth consecutive last-place finish, but the 18-6 tear the Pirates were on suddenly brought hope of climbing out of the division cellar.

A year or two earlier, this was a game the Pirates would have probably closed shop on long before extra innings came around. But now there was something to play for. The pride that Jim Leyland had preached so diligently was starting to come forth, and the dignity that Pirate legend Roberto Clemente had spoken of some 15 years before was starting to resurface.

John Smiley, another young Pirate pitcher brought up through the farm system, held the Mets in relief through the 14th inning, and the Pirates won it 9-8, in the bottom of the 14th. There were only 19,122 fans, but the cheering sounded more like 40,000, as everyone in attendance realized that the Pirates had climbed out of last place thanks to a loss by the Chicago Cubs. The fans were happy not only because the Pirates' good fortune came against the Mets, but also because it was late September and their team was not in last place.

"We got on a good run at a good time," pitcher Bob Walk said. "The streak we had at the end of that season shined a spotlight on the fact that we had reached a point where we had a decent bunch of guys on this team."

The Pirates closed the 1987 season by winning five of their last six games and managed to grab a fourth-place tie with Philadelphia at 80-82. The 27-11 run since August 24 was remarkable for the Pirates because there was no telling what another last-place finish would have done to the team's psyche as well as their fan support. At season's end, the Pirates' attendance figure stood at 1,161,193, and it appeared the club had won back the hearts of the fans.

"We were playing hard and hungry the last part of the season," Leyland said. "We were bound and determined to get better and as we got better, we started to win more games. It was a different atmosphere taking shape in our clubhouse. It was a great feeling to come in here with a win under our belts night after night. And the one thing I'll never forget about 1987 is the fans giving us a standing ovation at the end of the season. It made each and every one of us feel good about ourselves."

"At the end, all we felt we had to do was fill a couple of holes to be there," Walk said. "If we hadn't had that streak, I think it would have been another winter of indecision and uncertainty. But being right at the end of the year, it gave us a jump-start to 1988."

There was no telling what kind of effect the late-season surge would have on the Pirates' future, but it was definite that the Pirates were a new team that was capitalizing on its mixture of youth and veteran leadership.

"The team had just about finished all of its house-cleaning," *Pittsburgh Post Gazette* sportswriter Paul Meyer said. "I think the trade for LaValliere and Van Slyke became the beginning of the team's turnaround, and Jim Gott was a positive catalyst to the season-ending streak the Pirates went on. There were a few things yet to be done, but you could see the future was there."

Syd Thrift had taken the role of miracle worker by cutting the Pirates' payroll considerably and still infusing the talent that would one day become a contender. Van Slyke finished the 1987 season with a .293 average, 21 home runs, and 82 RBIs; LaValliere hit .300 and won a Gold Glove; Mike Dunne, the pitcher in the deal for Tony Pena, went 13-6 for the Pirates that season, but eventually fizzled in the club's future plans.

After a 1-8 start, Doug Drabek staked his reputation as a second-half pitcher by finishing 11-12 and was named National League Pitcher of the Month for August with a 5-0 record and a 2.79 earned run average. Brian Fisher, who came from the Yankees in the Drabek deal, finished 11-9, but his career would wind down soon after due to shoulder injuries. Although Jim Gott was 0-2 for the Pirates over the last month-and-a-half of the season, he saved 13 games during the late-season surge and had a 1.45 ERA. And Jose Lind made Pirate fans forget all about Johnny Ray by hitting .322 over the final 35 games and displaying a range that even some of his teammates couldn't believe at second base.

On the field it was Jim Leyland who kept the team afloat during the troublesome times and kept it on an even keel when the wave of success came through during the last part of the season. That would be his trademark— always think positively, but never let yourself get lost in what your job entails.

The 1987 Pittsburgh Pirates knew there was a long way to go before they reached the top of their mountain, but thanks to an incredible season-ending surge, the top of that mountain suddenly didn't seem so far away.

# Two Steps Forward, One Step Back

There were two ways to look at the stretch run that ended the 1987 season for the Pittsburgh Pirates. One, it may have been a fluke. The team may not have been as good as it showed in those last few weeks and could possibly have returned in 1988 as the also-ran that many experts had predicted.

The better way to look at the club's finish, however, was the way Jim Leyland preferred to look at everything in life—with a positive attitude. "I believed we had a good team going into 1988," Leyland said. "We were young and I wasn't sure we were ready to contend just yet, but I knew we had the enthusiasm from the fans and the players and that came about because of the way we finished the season before. Everyone came to spring training excited and ready to start the season."

The fans again were an important factor in the Pirates' plans for 1988. The Pirates turned to innovative ideas such as promotional giveaways on a more regular basis and began to make Three Rivers Stadium a more enjoyable place to watch a baseball game. Eventually, there would be family seating sections and sections that did not allow alcohol.

And while the Pirates' marketing department did everything it could to put people back in the seats, Pirate players did their share by becoming more involved in the community. Their main responsibility was to win baseball games, but they showed a human side uncharacteristic of clubs of just three or four years before.

The fans liked what they saw in the new Pirates. They admired the youth and hustle they exhibited, and they adored the way that players would suddenly offer a smile or a handshake and take the time to sign an autograph. They also noticed the realization in the players' eyes that there was still a tremendous job to be done, not only on the field, but off as well.

The picture wasn't as rosy in the Pirates' front office, as general manager Syd Thrift seemed to suddenly be wallowing in his successful moves and practically breaking his arm trying to pat himself on the back. He was becoming a somewhat difficult person to deal with because of his tremendously large ego and his will to seek more power than anyone was willing to give.

Club president Mac Prine, for one, was not amused by the ever-increasing thirst for power that Thrift was displaying, and he in no uncertain terms told the Pirates' board of directors that it was either the way he saw it, or no way at all.

"Mac is a very strong-willed and sometimes inflexible guy," Carl Barger said in newspaper interviews at the time. "Syd was equally the same, and at that time we didn't want to have those disturbances because we felt we were right at the borderline of making this thing work. We tried to get a meeting of the minds, but no one wanted to budge. At that time, it would have been insane to fire Syd because of everything he had brought to the Pirates. When no one would make any concessions, there wasn't a whole lot we could do."

The board elected not to support Prine in his stand against Thrift's power crunch, so he made the decision to resign. Barger was named the club's new president, and Douglas C. Danforth was named Chairman of the Board. Thrift had won this power struggle, but as Barger, Danforth, and the rest of the board were to find out, it wouldn't be the last.

≈

The players saw 1988 as a season of hope for the Pittsburgh Pirates. Barry Bonds remembered his first season when the team took its lumps against the Mets in 1986, and although that Pirate team was nowhere near competitive, there was a sense of urgency in winning 63 games to avoid a second straight 100-loss season.

"We played as hard as we could in '86," Bonds said. "We were building a team and finding out about each other and you could see the guys coming together to play for one common goal. I know the Mets beat us up pretty good that year, and if it wasn't for them beating up on us in '88, who knows what could have happened."

It became a rivalry in 1988. Finally, the Pirates had something to play for, and the Mets were inevitably the team that would stand in their way. In a decade with few highlights and a host of disappointments, the Pittsburgh Pirates were finally going to be heard from.

The season started with a six-game road trip through Philadelphia and St. Louis, with three games in each city. Mike Dunne, who had pitched so well the season before after coming over in the Van Slyke and LaValliere trade, won the opener, 5-3, in front of over 46,000 fans at Philadelphia's Veteran's Stadium. The Pirates lost the second game in 14 innings and were rained out in the third. The Bucs then took two out of three in St. Louis to start the season at 3-2.

Doug Drabek's turn came up in the rotation for the Pirates' home opener against the Phillies. The home opener is a tradition in every major league city. No matter how good or bad your team may be, opening day is certain to be a sell out because of the hype that is generated by the media and the curiosity that abounds from fans wanting to get that first glimpse of their hometown heroes.

Tradition followed the Pirates on this day as a record crowd of 54,089 filled Three Rivers Stadium to see the Pirates and Drabek ease by the Phillies, 5-1. The Pirates proceeded to win 13 of their next 17 games and had played in first place through much of April and early May.

"They'll go away," the rest of the National League must have been thinking. Experts figured it was only a matter of time. But the Pirates stayed in the chase. Pittsburgh was either tied or alone in first place for 19 days in April and May, which was about 19 more than they had been during the four years previously. On May 3, the Pirates fell to second after dropping the second game of a three-game series in Los Angeles. The sweep by the Dodgers helped keep the Pirates off the New York Mets' backs for a while, but the Mets were soon to realize their eventual division championship would not come as easily as it did in 1986.

The Pirates played .500 baseball in May, but their 16-6 April record had them at 30-20 and in second place, 4-1/2 games behind the Mets. Thoughts of a June swoon were ignored as Pittsburgh dropped only one game to the Mets in the standings and were nine games over .500 (43-34) heading into the dog days of summer. Clearly, July and August are usually the times when the also-rans take a back seat to the legitimate contenders in major league baseball. If a team means business, it had better be prepared for the crunch that follows over the next 60 to 90 days.

"It was funny because we didn't go into the season thinking we were going to win it all," Bob Walk said. "But we also knew we weren't the doormats of the league any more, and that can give a lift to any team that *was* the doormat for as long as we were."

No one knew for sure if the Pirates were headed for a serious showdown with the Mets in 1988, but it was quite clear that indeed, they were not the Eastern division doormats the other teams had wiped their feet on over the last four years.

The Pirates were for real, and they were displaying it with solid pitching, timely hitting combined with the right mixture of power and run production, and a defense that management always felt would be important if the team were to ever reach the pinnacle of success again. Maybe they would fade in the setting sun of the season, or maybe they would rise to a level that many felt impossible to reach only three years before.

Either way, the fans were appreciative of the team's efforts once again, and would show it by breaking the Pirates' all-time season attendance record. By season's end, 1,866,713 patrons passed through the turnstiles at Three Rivers Stadium and gave further credence to the fact that the Pittsburgh Pirates had righted their ship and were on a collective journey to a destination they had not seen in nearly a decade.

July 1 started a west coast road trip for the Pirates. It was a trip that would surely have a lot of bearing on the team's fate as they were still in second place, only 5-1/2 games behind the Mets. Jeff Robinson won the opener in relief over the San Francisco Giants, but the Pirates lost the next two games of the series and dropped the first of a three-game set in San Diego. They dropped two games in the standings and were beginning to make the non-believers' words come true—that the Pirates would eventually fold.

"I've always said I didn't want the Pirates to be a token stop on anyone's schedule," Jim Leyland said. "I mean, we're here to win ballgames and even though I felt deep down that this pennant race we suddenly had found ourselves in was somewhat cosmetic, I didn't want the players to lose sight of the excitement they had generated for themselves and especially for the city of Pittsburgh."

The excitement was restored in the middle game of the San Diego series as Walk held the Padres in check, and the Pirates escaped with a 3-2 win. John Smiley shut out the Padres, 2-0 in the final game of the series, and the Pirates followed with a three-game sweep of the Dodgers in Los Angeles. The team took a five-game winning streak into an 11-game home stand against the west coast teams and immediately made it nine in a row with a four-game sweep of the Giants. The Pirates won three of their next four and had cut a 7-1/2-game deficit to just a half-game during that sixteen-day period.

"It was kind of nice because we were suddenly being noticed by people all around the country," Walk said. "It was kind of easy to stay with the Mets mentally through the first two-thirds of the season because we were having fun. But all of a sudden, around early to mid-August, we all looked at each other and said, 'Wait a minute. We're still here.' We were used to fighting for fifth place and now we were fighting for first."

With that realization and a crucial seven-game trip to St. Louis and New York on the horizon, the Pirates were about to find out just how far they had come—and how much farther they still had to go.

It was late July, still a lot of time left in the season, but perhaps too much time for these young Pirates to think about their situation. They were floating on uncharted waters, and the next eight weeks would probably be the most critical in the team's storied history.

The Pirates took two-of-three in St. Louis and with their deficit at a mere two games, the four-game weekend set in New York was considered by many to be a make-or-break series for the ballclub.

"We were following the Mets all year," Barry Bonds said. "So in that sense, it was an important series. We felt if we were ever going to take a hold on the division, we were gonna have to beat them to do it."

It didn't happen.

The opener figured to be a pitchers' duel as the Pirates were sending their young, hard-throwing left-hander, John Smiley, against Mets' lefty Bob Ojeda, whose specialty was a strong curve and excellent control.

The Mets took in over 198,000 fans for the four-game series, and even a Pittsburgh radio station got into the Pirate pennant fever by sending its morning disc jockey team to New York to basically create havoc and show that the city was backing the Pirates. Scott Paulsen and Jim Krenn, of rock and roll station WDVE FM in Pittsburgh, did their broadcast live outside the gates of Shea Stadium and proudly displayed a banner with the station's— and Pittsburgh fans'—new slogan which read, "MUCK THE FETS!" (Figure it out).

It was the 101st game of the season for the Pirates, and to that point they sported an impressive 58-42 record. The Mets were only two games better at the time, and they could feel the heat of the Pirates' resurgence with every glance at the box scores and every reminder of the division standings.

Smiley and Ojeda lived up to the pre-game billing as they each took their turns mowing down the other team's lineup. The Pirates' collective power of Van Slyke, Bonds, and Bonilla could do little against Ojeda's best, but Smiley was equal in stopping the Mets' strength, which featured Darryl Strawberry, Howard Johnson, and Gary Carter.

The game was scoreless into the eighth inning as neither team mounted much of a scoring threat. It seemed that one big hit would do it, or one costly pitch could be the biggest mistake of the season. As each team searched for a hero, the Mets found theirs not in Johnson, or Carter, or even Strawberry. It was shortstop Kevin Elster who provided the drama as he sent Smiley's only mistake of the game into the left field seats in the bottom of the eighth inning, much to the delight of the 49,000-plus New York fans, to give Ojeda a 1-0 victory.

For perhaps the first time all season the Pirates appeared shaken. They had handled their new-found success with great poise through the first four months, but to lose a game in this fashion— a game of such importance, such magnitude— left a sick feeling in the pits of their stomachs.

Losing this game—the first of this critical four-game series—was a crushing experience, even though most of the players and coaches wouldn't admit it at the time. "It's one game," they would all say, "We've been able to stay with them all season."

The Pirates, as it turned out, were never able to recover from that gut-wrenching loss. They were noble with their words, but their bats remained silent as Sid Fernandez pitched another shutout the following day and the Mets were able to increase their lead to four games. The Pirates fell even further behind on Sunday as Ron Darling pitched the Mets to a 2-1 decision. Doug Drabek helped the Pirates avoid a sweep by beating Mets' ace Dwight Gooden, 7-2, in the final game of the series, but the damage had been done. The Pirates doubled their deficit during their weekend in New York, and that slight margin was enough to turn the lights out on a successful season.

"I think everyone became just a little more nervous when we went into that series," Walk said. "It was probably expected because we were such a young team, but we never wanted to admit it. We felt we belonged where we were, and we refused to be taken lightly. It's unusual for a young team to turn things around so quickly, and I think we just got caught up in all the sudden pennant fever."

The Pirates dropped five of their next six games and fell seven games behind the Mets, who were looking more and more like the team that had taken the division and a world championship in 1986. With the race still close in late July and early August, Thrift did his part to try to bolster the team over the top by trading for a couple of veteran players with admirable statistics, but also high price tags.

Thrift picked up veteran left-handed pitcher Dave LaPoint from the New York Yankees, who was making $425,000, and infielder-outfielder Gary Redus, who was making $460,000 with the Chicago White Sox.

"The trade came at a time when I was about to become a free agent," said Redus, who played with the Pirates through the 1992 season. "You figure that teams going nowhere like the White Sox were, will look to trade that kind of player and a team in contention may want to pick you up."

The Pirates weren't quite finished at the trade table as they swapped outfielders with Seattle, giving up Darnell Coles for a more powerful Glenn Wilson, who carried an $850,000 price tag with him. The Pirates hoped the final piece of the puzzle would come with infielder Ken Oberkfell, whom the Pirates received in a trade with Atlanta. Oberkfell was making $725,000 at the time, but the Braves agreed to pay half his salary for the remainder of the season.

Despite the new additions, the Pirates continued to slip further behind the Mets in the standings. They were able to cut the Mets' lead to 3-1/2 games on August 23, but a 3-9 slump over a 16-day stretch dropped them 8-1/2 games behind and just about out of contention. The Pirates went 14-11 over the rest of the season, but the Mets left no doubt by winning 20 of their last 24 to finish 15 games ahead of the Pirates.

"The Mets were just too good," Barry Bonds said. "They were a very talented ballclub, and we weren't at their level yet. We gave them everything we had, and probably more than they bargained for, but they had it when it counted."

"If you think back at all the rebuilding the Pirates had to do, it seems surprising that they were in a pennant race so quickly," *Post Gazette* sportswriter Paul Meyer said. "It's probably cliché to say they weren't ready to win, but I just don't think they were good enough. They were becoming a solid club, but the Mets were a helluva team, and the Pirates just weren't as good as the Mets yet."

As clichéd as it may sound, Leyland also figured that deep down his team wasn't quite ready to challenge the big boys yet.

"I was very proud of our team," Jim Leyland said. "We battled all year, but in my heart I knew we weren't ready for a title yet. Being in a pennant race in August is really cosmetic to me. It's nice for the fans and for the club, but a real pennant race— a real test of your team's character and ability—comes in September.

"Still, nothing took away from the fact that we had made progress and as that season went on, I felt like I knew a little bit more each day about where we were going."

Leyland was also beginning to find out where his players were going. Some went to the All-Star game, while others went to the moon with their statistics backing every bit of the Pirates' pleasant transformation. The record-setting attendance figure gave proof that Pittsburgh wanted its baseball team, and made Pirates management feel much more secure that the coalition's efforts of just three years before were not going to waste. Richard Caliguiri, the mayor of Pittsburgh who helped form this coalition, died from a blood disorder known as Amyloidosis in April of that season, but his name lived on as the Pirates wore his initials on their sleeves through the remainder of the season.

Andy Van Slyke hit .288 with 25 home runs and 100 RBIs for the Pirates, and when people began to see his acrobatics in the field, he was suddenly thrown into the spotlight as one of the best players in the game. Bobby Bonilla put up similar numbers with a .274 average, 24 homers, and 100 RBIs. His numbers were good enough early in the season to be voted the National League's starting third baseman in the All-Star Game over Philadelphia Phillies legend, Mike Schmidt.

Barry Bonds continued to excel from the lead-off position in the batting order, as he hit .283 and smashed 24 home runs. Jose Lind hit .262 and developed as a major leaguer even more in the field, while Doug Drabek won 15 games, Smiley won 13, and Walk won 12. Jim Gott solidified his position in the bullpen by saving 34 games, and Jeff Robinson played the perfect set-up man for Gott.

There was a lot to be said for the Pirates' second-place finish in 1988. A year before they had climbed out of the cellar for the first time in three years, and even though the baseball experts figured them to finish no higher than fifth, the Pirates proved them wrong with a youthful exuberance that had not been witnessed in Pittsburgh for nearly a decade.

But while optimism grew heavy for the coming seasons and new hopes were being bolstered, front-office management was not exactly painting a rosy picture. Ownership would probably not have minded Syd Thrift's intentions when he made the July and August trades to hopefully boost the club's chances to overtake the Mets, but they had a problem with Thrift's lack of communication in making the deals.

Thrift made the decisions to trade on his own, and did not consult those who also played a role in the structure and design of the ballclub. While the Pirates gave hope to the fans for the 1989 season on the field, Doug Danforth and Carl Barger were agonizing over another apparent power struggle with their determined general manager.

Ego was again becoming a factor in the Pirates' front office. The problems  surfaced as early as August, but club management—including Thrift—did its best to play them down. Finally with four days left in the regular  season, Barger decided to face the situation openly.

"We have some problems that I would characterize as significant," he said  at the time. "They must, and will, be resolved."

"No decision has been made yet," Danforth said of the state of the Pirates general manager's position. "But it is no secret there have been problems within the organization. We are trying to sort it out, but we will not be  hasty."

Thrift, always the straight-shooter, had an answer for his bosses' comments. "There are two ways to get fired," he retorted. "Either be good or  bad. I don't believe I was bad."

Still, he wasn't good enough for Pirates ownership as the club fired him two days after the season ended. Barger and Danforth once again cited  Thrift's huge ego and his inability to be a team player within the  organization's framework.

"Syd was simply not content to do his job," Barger said in interviews following the dismissal. "All this business about interference, that's a crock. Syd wanted to have everybody's job. He didn't want to be a part of a  team. He wanted to *be* the team. We were facing some severe problems in the organization unless something was done and the decision was not mine alone.

"We labored over the problem for months and we knew we were probably going to take it on the chin. We knew if we did well, it was because of Syd, but if we didn't do well, it was because Syd wasn't there. We understood that, but we honestly felt we did what we had to do."

Thrift again had an answer to his former bosses' claims.

"I felt I was doing things the way I was supposed to operate," he said.  "Maybe they felt like I left them out of trade talks and decisions and I was operating in here by myself. But we set up a budget with salaries and I wasn't required to check with them unless I did something that had a dramatic  impact on the budget."

Thrift claimed his budget was set at $6.2 million, and when all the wheeling and dealing was completed, the actual figure stood at $6.4 million.

"I didn't think that was a dramatic impact," he said.

"When I think of all the successful Pirate teams in the 60s and 70s," Pirates broadcaster Lanny Frattare said. "It was Joe Brown and Danny Murtaugh working together. Then it was Harding Peterson and Chuck Tanner. In the mid-80s, during the turnaround period, it was Syd, Mac Prine, Carl Barger, and Jim Leyland. They were all working together, but then Syd started pulling himself away from what had been a real solid nucleus. As the success for the team started coming in, he started taking a fair amount of credit for it.

"What makes a team successful is when everybody knows their role and does their job. I think Syd is an extremely talented baseball man who deserves an awful lot of credit for helping us to reconstruct this Pirate franchise. But what finally hurt him and the ballclub was his taking a bit too much credit for the success. That wasn't totally wrong, but he started distancing himself from other talented people who had a hand in making the club successful."

Many would look at the move curiously, because ego or no ego, Thrift had done a tremendous job in building the Pirates back to a legitimate contender. To destroy that chemistry at such a crucial point could be disastrous if the team was not able to come back strong the following season.

"Changes at a time like that can be traumatic," Leyland said. "A situation like that is never easy. I'm the manager and it's none of my business when front office decisions like that are made, so I made sure not to get involved. But it still affects my job and made it a tough, tough time. We went through a lot, but I guess that can happen in any business. You just have to move on and do the best you can."

So, the Pittsburgh Pirates looked to 1989 with thoughts of hiring a new general manager. Whether they would seek help from the outside or stay within the organization, they were not yet sure. It was the first major change since the overhaul began in 1986, and it would definitely be another crucial decision.

The Pirates were a team looking to continue their trek forward. They had spent the entire middle of the decade at the lowest point any team could reach, and their thirst for victory came to almost a full reality in only three short years. Forward was the natural direction everyone in the organization wanted

to take, but sometimes, as the Pirates would learn, we are forced
to live by the adage, "For every two steps forward, we must take
one step back." That was to be the case for the 1989 Pittsburgh
Pirates. Two steps forward. One step back.

                                    ॐ

        Optimism was at an all-time high as spring training opened
in   February 1989. The players, as usual, were upbeat about
starting another new  season, but the real excitement came from
the fans. Season ticket sales were up from the season before
because of the Pirates' gallant effort against the New York Mets.
And while the fans were delighted with the team's second-place
finish in 1988, many expected a run this time around that would
put their  team over the top.
        When Syd Thrift was fired as general manager only two
days after the 1988  season ended, the Pirates looked delicately,
but not diligently, for a  successor. This was to be the first order
of business before anyone could  think of where the club was
headed in 1989. After a very brief  search around the league, the
Pirates named Thrift's assistant, Larry  Doughty, to the position.
        Doughty was Thrift's assistant for just one year, but had
spent the  previous 18 seasons in the Cincinnati Reds scouting
department. He was considered an adept baseball man, who like
Thrift, could spot talent and had  the tools to get a player signed
on the dotted line. He was also well-liked  in the organization,
which led the public to believe that he was  simply a yes man for
Barger and Danforth in the Pirates' front office, but it   soon
became apparent that decisions regarding the makeup of the
team would  be his, and his alone.
        Doughty was a rather silent GM in the off-season, having
done little to  change the face of the club. His biggest deals were
signing Glenn Wilson to a two-year contract on November 7 and
agreeing with Gary Redus on a similar  contract about a week
later. He then kept Bob Walk in the fold for at least  three more
years by signing him to a three-year contract at the end of
November.
        On January 12, with the Pirates less than a month from
spring training, Doughty made a quiet move that would turn out

to be a somewhat pleasant surprise for the ballclub over the next couple of years. Bill Landrum was a journeyman relief pitcher whose last stop was with the Cubs, but when he signed with the Pirates, no one could have predicted the impact he would have on the Pirates' future.

The Pirates were thinking of winning now, and Doughty was thinking along the same lines. But he also had to think in terms of the future when it came to which players to sign and which ones to trade. Concentrating on one aspect more than the other, can tip the scales, and that is usually the first step toward a short life expectancy in a general managerial position.

The ballclub was solid at just about every position. There was Sid Bream at first base and Jose Lind at second. Bobby Bonilla spent most of his time at third in those days, and the outfield was more than adequate with Barry Bonds and Andy Van Slyke covering most of the ground. Mike LaValliere and Junior Ortiz were a capable lefty-righty combination behind the plate, and the Pirates were building one of the strongest young pitching staffs in the major leagues.

The biggest concern was at shortstop where, for years, the Pirates had decent players who could field, but their offensive production would more than play down any defensive contributions they could make. Over the years the Pirates fielded such light-hitting shortstops as Frank Taveras, Al Pedrique (who was released after the 1988 season), Rafael Belliard, and Felix Fermin.

Doughty looked at this position with genuine concern because some of the better teams in the major leagues were bolstered by the shortstop position. St. Louis had been successful for years with Ozzie Smith, and Detroit won a World Series in 1984 with MVP shortstop Alan Trammell leading the way. Though the Baltimore Orioles had been an up-and-down team of late, Cal Ripken, Jr., led them to a World Series title in 1983 and remains the cornerstone of that franchise.

Although Smith has never hit as well as Trammell or Ripken, these players all carried the same ingredient that went with the success of their teams. They were—and still are—leaders. Doughty needed a player like that. One who could field and who could hit consistently around .275, while providing a little bit of home-run power and run production. Fermin was a career .265 hitter for the Pirates, but he had zero home runs to back his offensive statistics and only six runs batted in. The last time the Pirates had a shortstop who resembled anything close to a decent hitter was probably in the days of Honus Wagner. Since he was long gone, however, it appeared the club would have to look elsewhere.

₰

Doughty had stayed silent through much of the off-season regarding personnel moves, but seeing the plight of the team's weakest position and the possible opportunity to do something about it, he did. With a little more than a week to go before the club broke camp and headed north for the beginning of the season, Doughty traded Fermin to the Cleveland Indians for Jay Bell, whose claim to fame before that was becoming the 11th player in major league history to hit a home run off the first pitch ever thrown to him when he faced Cleveland's Bert Blyleven.

Doughty was high on Bell because he possessed the defensive skills and range that many of the past Pirate shortstops had, but he could also hit for power once in a while and would hopefully become the club's man in the middle for a long time to come.

Bell started out in the Minnesota Twins organization, but ironically was part of a five-player deal in August 1985, that sent him and three other Twins prospects to the Indians for Blyleven, the pitcher that served up his first major league home run.

"I liked the Twins organization and when I first signed, I thought I'd be with that team forever," Bell said. "Unfortunately, you learn that it doesn't always work out that way, and the realization [of trade] sets in. The three full years I spent with Cleveland were very beneficial, however. I learned a lot and met some people who were very instrumental to my career."

But the change to Pittsburgh was not a sign of dread for Bell, who felt like he was seeing the writing on the wall in the Indians' organization. He spent most of the 1986 season at the Indians' Waterbury farm club and appeared in just five major league games at the end of the season.

Bell started the 1987 season in Class AAA Buffalo, where he hit .260, but he managed only a .216 average in two separate stints with the Indians that covered 38 games. He began the 1988 season in Cleveland, where he appeared in 73 games and hit just .218 with two home runs and 21 RBIs. He started 46 of 59 games through early June and batted .193 during that span. On July 10, Bell was optioned to the Indians' Class AAA Colorado Springs affiliate and stayed there until September 6. He hit .276 in 49 games for the Sky Sox, with seven home runs and 24 RBIs, and then batted .341 over Cleveland's final 16 games with one homer and four RBIs.

"I almost felt like Cleveland was giving up on me," he said of his slow 1988 start. "In spring training [of 1989] I never got to work out with Jerry Browne, who was their regular second baseman at the time, and things just weren't going the way I thought they would. I was actually happy about the trade because I knew the Pirates had a good, young team with a lot of confidence. They were learning how to win, and I just felt things were going to be better for me."

The Pirates were counting on Bell to make things better for them as well, and Jim Leyland felt ready for the season when he inserted Bell into his opening-day starting lineup.

The Pirates opened the 1989 season in Montreal and lost in the bottom of the ninth when Jeff Robinson couldn't protect a three-run lead. Robinson was on the mound in the late innings because ace reliever Jim Gott, who had saved 34 games the season before, had felt some kind of twinge in his elbow after throwing just a few pitches the inning before. No one knew the severity of Gott's injury, but the events of the game were just a preview of the kind of season the Pirates were about to have.

The Pirates dropped two out of three in Montreal and were swept in a three-game series at Chicago. Pittsburgh was 1-5 when it opened at home against the New York Mets, and the rivalry was rekindled when the Pirates won the first game, 4-3, in 11 innings and came back to win an afternoon special two days later, 4-2.

The Pirates had started 3-5, and Jay Bell seemed to be pressing both in the field and at the plate. His usually sure arm started out wild, while his potentially dangerous bat only appeared mild. Larry Doughty watched with a biting lip as Bell started the season with only one hit in his first 20 at bats (.050). The silent Doughty had done an adequate job up to now, but in a rather questionable—and seemingly desperate—move, he made his first major trade as the Pirates' general manager.

Doughty sent right-handed pitcher Mike Dunne and two top minor league prospects (pitcher Mike Walker and outfielder Mark Merchant) to the Seattle Mariners for left-handed pitcher Bill Wilkinson and shortstop Rey Quinones. He was another shortstop who had displayed power in his career, but his talent was only topped by his eccentricity. He was a throwback to the Pirates of just a few years ago, the kind of player who became easily discontented and would exhibit his feelings with lackadaisical play in the field.

The Pirates knew of Quinones' shortcomings, but felt comfortable with the idea of putting him in the same clubhouse with Jim Leyland, whom it was believed could transform any athlete into a dedicated professional.

Meanwhile, Bell was sent down to Class AAA Buffalo for some "seasoning" after watching a few games from the dugout, and the Pirates' hopes were going to ride on the often-errant arm of Quinones.

"Originally," Bell said. "I didn't think I was the right shortstop. Larry made the deal for me, and when I didn't start out well, he felt like he had to make another move to help the team. Unfortunately for him, but fortunately for me, that move didn't work out right. The whole situation was a learning experience for me and it became the turning point in my career."

Bell caught fire in Buffalo as he hit .285 in 86 games and had 10 home runs and 54 RBIs. But while Bell was adjusting his game in the minors, the Pirates were having trouble finding theirs. It was soon discovered that Gott's injury was more serious than first thought. He had torn a muscle in his elbow and would be lost for the entire season.

Suddenly, the Pirates had lost 34 saves from their bullpen and things were about to get worse. Sid Bream felt a snap in his knee when he turned back to first base during an early-season game. The diagnosis was torn cartilage, and he too would be lost for much of the season. In the eighth game of the season, a 4-2 win over the Mets, Andy Van Slyke suffered a severe rib injury when he made a diving catch of a sinking line drive. Two days later, Mike LaValliere suffered torn knee ligaments in a home-plate collision with Montreal's Rex Hudler. He was placed on the 60-day disabled list and missed the next three months. That left the Pirates with back-up catcher Junior Ortiz as the starter, and light-hitting Tom Prince was recalled from Buffalo as his back-up.

Of the four major injuries, Van Slyke was out of the lineup the least amount of time, only one month. But he would not be the same Andy Van Slyke of 1988 as he finished the season with nine home runs, 53 RBIs, and a paltry .237 batting average. The Pirates could only hope that Van Slyke would return to his old form in 1990.

"It seemed like the season was lost after the first two weeks," *Post Gazette* sportswriter Paul Meyer said. "The role players became starters at a lot of positions, and the club had to call up guys from the minors to become the role players. Everything seemed to be thrown out of synch from that point on."

The Pirates were also left with a make-shift bullpen. It seemed everyone got a chance to take the role of closer, but no one took the bull by the horns. Robinson was given the clearest chance early on, but he failed miserably with just four saves in 22 relief appearances and a 4.58 earned run average. Of anyone who was called on in relief during the first half of the season, Bob Kipper probably gave the best showing. The young left-hander appeared in 52 games and had a 3-4 record with four saves and a 2.93 ERA.

It wasn't until the halfway point of the season that the quiet signing that took place during the off-season would begin to pay dividends for Larry Doughty and the Pittsburgh Pirates. Bill Landrum had appeared in a few games over the first half of the season for the Pirates, and Jim Leyland began to like what he saw.

He was fiery, and he had a fastball that could find the strike zone and still keep the opposing hitters guessing. Leyland began throwing Landrum into the fire on a regular basis, and the 31-year-old veteran responded well. Landrum appeared in 56 games for the Pirates in 1989 and had a near 2-to-1 strike out-to-walk ratio. He pitched a total of 81 innings in his new closer role and finished 2-3 with a 1.67 ERA. Even more impressive for Landrum were his 26 saves, which, by far, led any other pitcher on the team.

"Billy was a bright spot in a season where we didn't have too many," Leyland said. "He was a pleasant surprise because it could have been worse if he didn't step up for us like he did."

Landrum saved 13 games in 1990 and 17 in 1991 to help the Pirates win a pair of division championships, but when his arm developed problems near the end of the '91 season, the Pirates decided that his services might no longer be needed. Landrum had gained a hefty salary for his efforts with the Pirates, but management felt going into 1992 that arm troubles and high-priced pitchers just would not be conducive to what the club was trying to accomplish. Cost-cutting measures were being taken by new Pirate management in many areas, and even though there was no real closer besides Landrum, the Pirates released him near the end of spring training.

Landrum had done his part in 1989, but he could not do it alone, and the Pirates fell to a fifth-place finish, 19 games behind the division champion Chicago Cubs.

It was a somber experience for a young club that had come into the season with so much hope and enthusiasm. Youth was displayed during the last two months of 1988, when the club realized it was in a pennant race and succumbed to the Mets, who had been through the experience before. But 1989 gave the Pirates a lesson in humility. They realized that you still had to play the game, and that even though great things were expected, nothing would be handed to you on a silver platter.

Quinones soon became one of several questionable moves made by Larry Doughty in his first year as general manager of the Pirates. He carried a .209 average through 71 games with the Pirates and added three home runs and 29 runs batted in. But his 19 errors and true-to-form lackadaisical style led to his unconditional release in late July. The release of Quinones also led to the second chance that Jay Bell had hoped for.

"I've always said if you can't play for Jim Leyland, you just can't play," Meyer said. "Rey Quinones is a perfect example. If anybody could have gotten through to him, it would have been Leyland. But even he couldn't do it and three months later, Quinones was gone."

With the Quinones fiasco behind him, Doughty traded rightfielder Glenn Wilson to the Houston Astros for catcher Alan Ashby in mid-August. The Pirates needed a right-handed hitting catcher, but Wilson was leading the club in home runs at the time and Ashby was nearing his mid-30s. Luckily, Ashby vetoed the trade by using his 10-and-5 leverage, which meant that any player with 10 years of major league experience, including five with the same team, had a right to veto any trade. One week later, Ashby was released outright by the Astros.

"Larry had a tough first year," Leyland said. "But you've got to remember he was learning on the job. He was just trying to do what he thought was best."

Bobby Bonilla was the only Pirate to appear in the 1989 All-Star Game, and rightfully so. Bonilla led the Pirates offensively, as he played in every game and compiled a .281 batting average. He led the team in hits (173), doubles (37), triples (10), home runs (24), and RBIs (86), and was second only to Bonds in walks (93- 76).

Jay Bell was recalled from Buffalo after Quinones' release on July 22 and hit .285 (69-for-251) the rest of the season. When Leyland inserted him into the second spot in the Pirates' order for the last 48 games of the season, Bell responded with a .309 average and scored 29 runs. This was to be a decision that would solidify the Pirates middle-infield for the next three years and prompt Leyland to say, "The Pirates will have a new manager before they have a new shortstop."

"Jimmy told me when I came back that I was his regular shortstop, and I'd be playing every day," Bell said. "When he said that, things started falling into place and I began to feel a lot more comfortable. His words really set my mind at ease."

Besides Landrum, Doug Drabek and John Smiley were the only bright spots on the mound. Drabek led the Pirates with a 14- 12 record and a 2.80 ERA, while Smiley finished 12-8 with a 2.81 ERA. Bob Walk was also impressive as he posted a 13-10 record in 31 starts, but his ERA was a whopping 4.41 and he had to leave his last three starts of the season due to a recurring groin injury. No other starter had an ERA below 3.05, as the Pirates finished out the season at 74-88.

"I think 1989 toughened us up a little bit," Leyland said. "In my heart I felt we had a team that was good enough to challenge, but the injuries really wiped us out early. We lost four key guys right off the bat, and that made our season a tough one.

"But it was a year where we learned a lot of values. We played hard and even though we didn't win as many games as we wanted to, we fought through adversity and learned to appreciate the value of being healthy. We also learned to appreciate one another, and I think it made a lot of the other guys better ball players. I thought it was a year where we really grew up."

In a sense, Bob Walk agreed that it was a season in which the young Pirates grew up just a little bit and realized the kind of commitment it takes to be a winner.

"We started the season a little cocky," he said. "I don't think we prepared ourselves properly for a lot of the early games. We took an attitude that we didn't have to work hard because we were good, and it caught up to us.

"As far as the injuries, they hurt us a lot, but a good team will find someone to step up when its stars go down. We were a young team on its way up, and when the injuries happened, everyone looked at each other like, 'Oh no, what do we do now?' Now we tend to look at injuries and just say we have to pick up the slack and not sit around and cry in our beer."

"It was definitely a growth experience for our club," Van Slyke said. "We knew we couldn't take anything for granted. I also think it made us stronger. It was a definite learning experience."

The Pirates remembered their lessons from an unusual 1989 season and hoped to carry them into a brand new decade. The steps they took in 1987 and 1988 were giant, to be sure. They climbed out of the basement in '87 and challenged for a division title in '88. But they faced reality in 1989 and found that sometimes you may stumble when you're reaching for the top, but if you get up and keep reaching, you will one day realize your goal. The long wait for these young Pirates would come just one year later.

# 1990: The Bucs Have Arrived

Many called it a five-year plan. Others, like those who were involved in the public-private coalition that kept the Pirates in Pittsburgh, simply meant that five years was what they were asking for to see if the Pirates could transform from the jokes of major league baseball to one of the most respected organizations in the business.

Jim Leyland preferred not to go by any timetable. He instead chose the day-to-day theory, and with good reason. The Pirates, after all, had shown promise near the end of the 1987 season and had raised fan interest to a new level by battling through a 1988 pennant race until mid-August. There was a downside to all this in 1989 due to the injuries of four key Pirate starters, and that showed Leyland that his team's season could be wiped out at any given moment.

To further cloud the results of 1989, the Pirates dropped three spots in the standings to fifth place, and season attendance had slipped by almost 500,000, just a year after the Pirates had broken the club's all-time attendance record. These were just some of the reasons why Leyland didn't want to crow about any five-year plan. If such a timetable were adhered to, this would have been the year that the Pirates would either have to put up or shut up, and Leyland didn't want to have that kind of pressure hanging over his still young, but slightly-seasoned ballclub.

"I just wanted to take things day by day from the very beginning," Leyland said. "I just looked at my responsibilities and tried to live by them."

But even though Leyland traveled the cautious road, there were perceptions and stories in the newspapers at the time that had him predicting a division championship upon the completion of spring training. Leyland— and several other team members— quickly snuffed such thoughts, and Leyland would only say he liked his team going into the season.

"I think I told our players coming out of spring training that I felt we had a good team," he said. "I'm not one to talk much about winning, but I believed we had a real good shot at it and that was the message I was trying to get across to my players. We had players back healthy, and I felt we were going to be a strong club."

Strong would be the operative word for the 1990 Pittsburgh Pirates. They were bolstered at the plate with the power of Bobby Bonilla and Barry Bonds, and they were set defensively with Bonds, Andy Van Slyke, and Bonilla making up probably the best outfield in the major leagues.

Sid Bream turned many difficult plays into routine outs at first base, and Jose Lind was a magician at second. Jeff King, another youngster who was the Pirates' No. 1-draft choice in the June, 1986 free-agent draft, would platoon with newly-signed veteran Wally Backman at third, and the Pirates' infield became complete when Jay Bell took his firm place as the starting shortstop.

"I think the last piece of the puzzle was put into place when Bell became the regular shortstop," *Pittsburgh Post Gazette* sportswriter Paul Meyer said. "I don't really know if Jimmy [Leyland] predicted a division title, but I think he finally felt he had a team that *could* win a title."

Pitching would also be a key to the Pirates' success in 1990, but Leyland was pretty well stocked with Doug Drabek, John Smiley, and Bob Walk set to anchor a starting rotation that would hopefully put the club over the top once and for all. Bill Landrum was back to handle the closer's role in the bullpen, which was good news for the Pirates, because no one was quite sure when, or if, Jim Gott's elbow injury would allow him to return to the active roster. Veterans Walt Terrell and Ted Power were added to help shore up the pitching staff, as Terrell could fill the role of fourth or fifth starter in the rotation, and Power could spot start or pitch in any kind of bullpen situation, whether it be short, middle, or long relief.

The Pirates even went out and got some help for Mike LaValliere in the off-season by trading Jeff Robinson and a minor league pitcher to the Yankees for right-handed hitting catcher Don Slaught. Sluggo, as his teammates refer to him, was a welcome addition to the Pirates' roster, because he could handle himself behind the plate and hit for average, with just the right touch of power.

Most publications picked the Pirates to finish no higher than second place, but optimism ran high as the club left its Bradenton, Florida, spring training headquarters and flew to New York for Game 1 of the long and often stressful ordeal known as the regular season.

≈

Before the Pirates had ever thought of Dwight Gooden's first pitch to Wally Backman on that sunny April afternoon in Shea Stadium, they had gone through some of their first celebrated cases in the off-season of the relatively new negotiations in baseball known as salary arbitration.

Salary arbitration happens when a player with at least three years of major league experience under his belt can present his salary demands to the club, and if the club does not agree with those figures, it can decide to settle with that player through arbitration. At this point, a federal judge listens to the player and his agent tell why he is worth the money he is seeking, while the team and its representatives actually present an argument against the player, in hopes the judge will decide on the team's offer as the final figure of settlement.

Both sides don't particularly care for the process, but it is most often the only manner in which a common ground can be figured upon if there is a stalemate in the negotiations. In either case, the player comes out a winner, because the team's offer is still usually higher than what the player made the year before. So even if the player loses, he still, in most cases, comes out with a hefty raise from the season before.

In a lot of cases, the proceedings end with bitter feelings, because if management loses, there is a feeling that the player is not worth the money he is being paid. If the player loses arbitration, he often feels scorned because of the negative things said about him during the proceedings by the team he feels he has given his heart and soul for.

Through all the hurt feelings, however, and the negative publicity that surrounds each case, arbitration seems to operate successfully in baseball. If it didn't, the process would be abolished by the owners at one of their annual winter meeting sessions.

Many times a team can avoid salary arbitration by agreeing on a contract with a player before the case ever reaches court. The Pirates were successful in that regard following the 1988 season by signing their three big outfielders to contracts with various terms.

Van Slyke inked a three-year deal that would carry him through 1991, while Bonilla signed a one-year agreement for 1989 that would pay him $730,000, and Bonds also signed a one-year deal for $360,000.

Bonilla hit .281 in 1989 with 24 home runs and 86 runs batted in, and he also led the team with 37 doubles. Bonds batted .248 with 19 homers and 58 RBIs, but these were figures that came from the lead-off position in the order. He was second with 34 doubles, and he led the team with 32 stolen bases.

Both players, along with Drabek, chose the arbitration process following the 1989 season because they found it difficult to agree with the Pirates on long-term contracts. Drabek was 14-12 in 1989 and had a team-best 2.80 earned run average. His figures were good enough for the judge who decided the case, as Drabek was awarded a $1.1 million settlement for 1990. Bonds and Bonilla, however both lost their cases.

An arbitration loss in these cases meant that Bonds would make $850,000 in 1990, and Bonilla would have to settle for $1.25 million. Despite their raises, the gauntlet had clearly been thrown down by the Pirates in the eyes of Bonds and Bonilla. Free agency was still a couple of years away for both players, but both said they would remember their first experience with salary arbitration when their respective free agency years came around.

Filled with mostly happy, and a few unhappy faces, the Pittsburgh Pirates were signed, sealed, and delivered for 1990 and were prepared to dive into the new season with legitimate thoughts of winning the National League Eastern division championship.

The Pirates matched their ace, Drabek, against Gooden in that opening-day encounter. Gooden had developed a new respect for the Pirates during a time not long before this when he referred to them as an easy win on the Mets' schedule. That was after he ran away with the Cy Young award in 1985, and after the Mets toasted the Pirates 17 out of the 18 times they played each other in 1986.

The Pirates were inspired by Gooden's words, which were posted on bulletin boards all around the clubhouse and earmarked for future reference. On opening day, 1990, the Pittsburgh Pirates were a much different ball club than the one in '86, but they treated Gooden with nowhere near the respect they gave him during the Mets' championship season. They jumped on him early and often and didn't let him get past the third inning. Drabek and the Pirates won the opener, 12-3, and followed by winning two out of three in the series.

Pittsburgh was 4-5 and in a tie for fourth place very early in the season, but a four-game winning streak catapulted the Pirates to first— a position they would hold for much of the rest of the season.

Part of that four-game winning streak was an unusual quirk in the schedule that had the Pirates start a 13-game road trip with a single in St. Louis, then play a three-game set in Chicago and back to St. Louis for another single game. Then it was on to the west coast for an eight- game swing through San Francisco, San Diego, and Los Angeles.

It was a trip that may have helped the Pirates find themselves after the several years of reconstruction the organization had been through. They banded together as a team behind Drabek, who won the first game in St. Louis, 5-0, and built momentum by sweeping the Cubs in three straight. The Cardinals momentarily interrupted the Pirates' streak the second time through St. Louis, but Drabek hit his first major league home run at Candlestick Park and raised his record to 3-1 by shutting down the Giants 4-1, in the west coast opener.

Relief pitcher Bob Patterson helped the Pirates win the second game in San Francisco, 7-4, in 12 innings, and John Smiley went the distance in a 2-1 victory as the Pirates swept the series. Pittsburgh raised its record to 14-6 by taking three from San Diego, before hitting a little snag in Los Angeles, where the Dodgers took both games against the Pirates.

Still, they had endured the toughest road trip they would have all season, and came away with a 10-3 record. The Pirates followed their successful road trip with an 8-1 homestand, which gave them a 22-9 record and kept them in first place.

A 2-7 road trip through Cincinnati, Atlanta, and Houston dampened the festivities just a bit, but the Pirates found success at home again by winning nine out of 12, including a memorable Memorial Day win over the Dodgers in which the Pirates trailed 5-1 going into the bottom of the ninth, but rallied for a 6-5 victory.

The Pirates dropped to second place briefly on June 23, in a loss to Zane Smith and the Montreal Expos. The loss was ironic, because just two months later Smith would be traded to the Pirates in a move that would ultimately point the Pirates in their intended direction.

The end of June saw the Pirates heading back to the west coast, and again it would be a trip that weighed heavily on the Pirates' fortunes for the rest of the season. It started with a loss in San Francisco, but the club bounced back to take two out of three from the Giants. It was in the very next game, a 14-inning affair in San Diego, that another young pitcher would step to the forefront and lay his claim as a member of the Pirates' rapidly improving pitching staff.

&

These Pirates were built mostly on youth that gained experience over time: Bonds, Bonilla, Bream, Lind, King, Bell, Drabek, Smiley. They all sharpened their skills under Jim Leyland's watchful eye and grew together to make the Pirates the contenders they had so quickly become.

In their early days together, mistakes often led to losses, because the mistakes were usually the kind that young teams with young players find difficult to overcome. The 1986 and early 1987 Pirates found losing an easy thing to learn, but unlike the teams of '84 and '85, they did not find losing easy to accept.

This group realized they could learn how to win, and when they did that, the mistakes and ill fortunes that often led to losses would eventually turn in their favor.

One of the team's newer young players was a rookie relief pitcher who made a brief appearance with the Pirates in September of 1989, but stayed with the club for good following his May 19 call-up from Class AAA Buffalo in 1990. Stan Belinda is a "local boy makes good" story, having grown up in nearby State College, Pennsylvania, where he also attended high school.

"I grew up a Pirates fan," Belinda said in the midst of the Pirates' 1992 season. "So it was a big thrill to get drafted by them. It's a perfect place for me to play." Pittsburgh is a perfect place for Belinda to play baseball, because he is a quiet young man who shies away from life in the big city. It is about a three-hour drive from Pittsburgh to Port Matilda, Pennsylvania, where Belinda and his wife, Lori, reside in the off-season. Belinda grew up in a town known more for Penn State University and its highly successful major college football program, but baseball was always his first choice.

"I just always enjoyed baseball," Belinda said. "It's tough because it seems that never a day goes by there without hearing something about the Penn State football team, but there's not much there besides that. I was happy because I got to play baseball, and I was grateful that the Pirates noticed me."

It would have been hard not to notice Belinda's hard-throwing, sidewinder type of delivery when the Pirates selected him 10th in the June, 1986, free agent draft. He, like several other young Pirates, moved rapidly through the Pirates farm system to get to the big leagues.

Belinda saved seven games for Bradenton in the Gulf Coast Rookie League his first season before being promoted to Class A Watertown, where he had two more saves near the end of the season. He spent the entire 1987 season at Class A Macon where he was 6-4 with 16 saves and a 2.09 earned run average. In 1988, Belinda limited opposing batters to a .205 average and was 6-4 with 14 saves for Salem, including 3-0 and six saves over his final 30 appearances.

Belinda began the 1989 season at Class AA Harrisburg, where he finished third in the league with 13 saves despite being promoted to Class AAA Buffalo on July 17. He was 2-2 with nine saves and a 0.95 ERA in 19 appearances for Buffalo, and opposing batters had a cumulative .137 average against Belinda as he did not allow an earned run in his last 10 appearances for the Bisons. Jim Leyland got a good look at Belinda when he was called up to the Pirates for the month of September, and although he appeared in only eight games and had no saves, Leyland knew it would be only a matter of time before Belinda would be with the Pirates to stay.

The time that so many young pitchers yearn for came in mid-May 1990 for Belinda, and since he had had a taste of the majors the season before, he knew this was his opportunity to take a major bite out of the pie that the Pirates might share at the end of the year.

His first major league victory came on June 5, a 6-5 win over the Cubs. Then it was time for his first save, which came on June 24, as he saved a 5-3 win for Neal Heaton. There are many firsts in a major leaguer's career, and Belinda was slowly and methodically collecting his. But the Pirates may remember him for an accomplishment that gave him neither a win or a save, but kept them from dropping a very important game in San Diego.

It was July 2, and the Pirates had battled the Padres to a 3-3 tie into extra innings. Trouble brewed for the Pirates in the bottom of the 11th inning, as the Padres loaded the bases with no outs. Leyland called on Belinda, because he liked the idea that the Padres hadn't seen him yet, and maybe his sidewinding style would throw them off just a bit.

The situation called for nerves of steel in a game that neither team could afford to lose—especially the Pirates, who felt they would need every game if they had any hopes of winning a division title. Belinda delivered for the Pirates by striking out the side in a classic stare 'em down, shoot 'em down fashion. It wasn't finesse that got Belinda by the Padres, but sheer power with a rocket fastball that seemed to shoot from the right-hander's hip pocket. The Pirates improved to 45-30 by defeating the Padres 4-3, in 14 innings, and kept their hold on first place in the division.

"That was a special moment for me," Belinda said. "It's a time to look back on and remember, because it may have been a point where I became a major part of the team. It's an exhilarating feeling, where pure adrenaline is flowing. I knew what I wanted to do in that situation, and I did it. Unfortunately, it doesn't always work out that way."

There have been times when Belinda could not nail down a Pirate victory. Like the game three weeks later in Montreal, when the Pirates took a 7-5 lead over the Expos in the top of the 10th inning, but saw rookie centerfielder Marquis Grissom hit a three-run homer off Belinda in the bottom of the inning to win it for the Expos.

Belinda also faced a horrendous stretch in 1992, when the Pirates were in the midst of losing 11 out of 12 games. It started after the Pirates snapped a six-game losing streak with a 6-4 win in Los Angeles. It was 6-1 going into the bottom of the ninth, but Belinda gave up a three-run, pinch-hit homer that pulled the Dodgers within reach. The next night he wasn't as lucky as Dodger rookie Eric Karros sent Belinda's 3-2 pitch into the Los Angeles night to rally the Dodgers from a 4-1, ninth-inning deficit to a 5-4 victory.

Four days later, in an afternoon game to close this most miserable of all Pirate west coast trips, the Pirates took a one-run lead into the bottom of the ninth, but lost it when San Diego's Craig Shipley hit a line-drive single off Belinda to drive in the winning run.

"Those are the kind of outings the media and the fans seem to remember the most," Belinda said. "It's nice when someone comes up to you and says, 'I remember when you struck out the side in San Diego in 1990,' but that doesn't happen too often. When you do something wrong as a relief pitcher, it seems to get highlighted."

Still, Belinda figures to be a key to the Pirates' future, and he knows he is pitching for one of the best managers in the game today.

"Jim Leyland realizes that we're human and not machines," he said. "And he knows that bad things are bound to happen to every pitcher at some point. All he stresses is for us to give our best effort. If we win, that's great. But if we lose, but still gave everything we had, why be mad? He just feels there's no sense in it, and that makes it easier for us, as pitchers, to handle.

"He hates to lose, but he won't *ask* you to win. A lot of managers hate to lose, but they might come up to you before a game and say, 'We want you to win.' That's just not Jimmy's style."

It is also not Leyland's style to give up on a pitcher—or any player for that matter —just because he has a couple of bad outings.

"In 1990, Skip [Leyland] put me right back out there if I had a bad game," said Belinda, who was 3-4 in 55 appearances during his rookie season, with eight saves and a 3.55 ERA. "That showed me a lot more than telling me, 'Oh, that's okay, don't worry about it.' He threw me right back to the wolves, and I usually came back and did a good job."

Some players believe that seeing a pitcher the second time around is usually to the hitter's advantage, because now he may have a better idea of what to expect. Today's players can also use videotape to study a pitcher's form and delivery in several different speeds. It also depends on the type of pitcher you're dealing with, and in Belinda's case, his may have become an easy style to pick up on.

"If you look in our clubhouse on a day when we might be facing a rookie pitcher, you'll see guys standing all around the portable VCR trying to see any film they can get their hands on of the guy," Belinda said. "They try to pick up his tendencies and see how he selects his pitches in the pitch count. I think that might be where I've run into problems, because players pretty much know where my delivery is coming from."

But Belinda also knows he has someone to turn to in Leyland and Pirates pitching coach, Ray Miller, who can help him correct the minor quirks that tend to put major dents into a pitcher's delivery.

"Ray watches the films also," Belinda said. "And he lets me know if my mechanics are off, or if something is way wrong with me. He always keeps me on the right path."

And because of Miller and Leyland, Belinda knows he is able to stay at the level of baseball he had worked so hard as a youngster trying to reach.

"Everybody's goal in the minor leagues is to reach the highest level, and this is the highest level as we know it," he said. "At the time, I was just thrilled to be here, but I also told myself I wanted to make a contribution to the team and hopefully stay here. Fortunately, I did all right and helped contribute to a playoff season."

As the season wore on, it did indeed seem the Pirates were destined to win their first division title since they won the World Series in 1979. Players who were either injured or slumping in 1989 were contributing in 1990, and those who were hot the season before, stayed hot.

Bobby Bonilla followed his successful 1989 season with even better numbers, as he set career highs in hits (175), home runs (32), RBIs (120), and runs scored (112). He also led the National League in extra-base hits (78,) and sacrifice flies (15), and hit .420 (29-for-69) during a 17-game hitting streak from August 2 through August 17. Bonilla, who made the National League All-Star Team for the third straight year, hit .357 during August while totaling nine home runs and 23 RBIs.

Bonilla was second in the league in RBIs, runs scored, doubles (39), total bases (324), and was the N.L. Player of the Month for April when he hit .279, with seven homers and 21 RBIs, and finished second in the balloting for the National League's Most Valuable Player Award at the conclusion of the season.

It would have been a nice accomplishment to win such an award, but Bonilla did little complaining because it was his best friend and teammate who won it. Barry Bonds had been the Pirates' lead-off batter for most of his career, but when Jim Leyland decided to bat him fifth in the order about a month into the season, Bonds became one of the hottest hitters in the league.

He finished 1990 with a .301 batting average after hitting just .248 the season before. Batting behind Van Slyke and Bonilla in the order also meant more opportunities for run production, and Bonds certainly didn't disappoint the Pirates. Not only was his average a career best, but so were his totals in home runs (33), RBIs (114), and stolen bases (52). He became the first player in Pirate history to have 30 or more home runs and 30 or more stolen bases in the same season— his father, Bobby, accomplished the feat five times as a major leaguer—and Barry became just the second player in major league history to hit 30 or more home runs and steal 50 or more bases.

Bonds was named the N.L. Player of the Week for April 23-29 after hitting .588 (10-for-17) with three home runs and six

RBIs, and was N.L. Player of the Month in July when he carried a .326 average with five homers and 22 RBIs. He led the National League with a .565 slugging percentage and was second in walks with 93. Bonds also hit his 100th career home run on July 12 and homered at least once against every N.L. opponent.

Defense can sometimes be overshadowed by offense, but Bonds was clearly recognized in left field. His 14 assists tied him with Kevin McReynolds of the Mets for the league lead, and fans and teammates acknowledged him for turning so many drives down the left-field line into either outs at second or long singles. Few players—even the speedsters—elected to challenge Bonds and his strong left arm.

He earned his first Gold Glove Award for his accomplishments in the field, as well as his first trip to the All-Star Game, and won both National League Player of the Year and Major League Player of the Year honors, which are handed out by *The Sporting News*.

The awards didn't stop with the accomplishments of Bonilla and Bonds for the Pirates. Doug Drabek won the National League Cy Young Award after he became the Pirates' first 20-game winner since John Candelaria went 20-5 in 1977. Drabek, who was 22-6 in 1990, led the league in wins and winning percentage (.786), and was the first Pirate pitcher to lead the league in wins since Bob Friend went 22-14 in 1958. He was also the first Pirate pitcher to win a Cy Young since Vernon Law went 20-9 in the Pirates' world championship 1960 season.

Drabek led the pitching staff in wins, starts (33), complete games (9), innings pitched (231.1), and strikeouts (131), was second in the league in complete games, and sixth in earned run average (2.76). He was 11-0 and had a 2.15 ERA against Western division opponents and had lost only twice in his last 18 starts. Drabek pitched the first one-hitter of his career on August 3 at Philadelphia. He was one out away from a no-hitter when Phillies' pinch-hitter Sil Campuasano lined a two-out, ninth-inning single to right center field to break it up.

Drabek had records of 14-12 and 15-7 his two previous seasons with the Pirates, but several of those losses were by 1-0 and 2-1 scores. Through it all, he never complained about lack of support, whether the Pirates were making a run at the division title or just playing out the string, much like they were forced to do in 1989.

"You're not supposed to have favorites," Pirate pitching coach Ray Miller said. "But Doug Drabek is probably the most coachable person I've ever had. When he got here [to Pittsburgh], he threw a hard fastball, a four-seam fastball, and a slider. We went down to the bullpen and worked on a curve ball for about a month, and he came out with one of the best curves in the game.

"I'll always remember when Barry Larkin [a shortstop for the Cincinnati Reds] once said, 'Doug Drabek has the biggest heart I've ever seen in a pitcher.' What that means is whether Doug has his good stuff or bad stuff, it's always going to be a battle to beat him."

In many ways, 1990 was Doug Drabek's reward, both financially— with his salary arbitration victory— and statistically, where he left all other National League pitchers in the dust. He was named N.L. Pitcher of the Month for both July and August, which was the first time a National League pitcher had won such back-to-back honors since 1977. His season was highlighted not by his 20th victory, which came on September 19 against the Cubs, but by his three-hit shutout of the St. Louis Cardinals on September 30, which clinched the Eastern division title for the Pirates.

Drabek's post-season awards were highlighted when he was selected as the recipient of the 1990 Roberto Clemente Award by the Pittsburgh Chapter of the Baseball Writer's Association of America. The award has been given annually since 1973, and it is given to the Pirate player who best exemplifies the standard of excellence established by the late, great Pirate outfielder, Roberto Clemente.

"When I first came to Pittsburgh, Jim Leyland and all the other coaches gave me a good feeling about coming to the ballpark and playing here," said Drabek, who was 3-0 against both Philadelphia and Atlanta in 1990 and also defeated San Francisco and Chicago three times each. "Everything was as relaxed as possible, and we were just a bunch of young guys that got along very well. It gave you the feeling that if we stuck together and kept the same kind of positive attitude, everything would come together for the Pirates."

That positive attitude finally did come together for the Pirates in 1990, and it was done with the right mixture of talent, plus the wisdom and patience of a manager who never stopped believing in his players and refused to take any of the credit himself.

Jim Leyland capped his fifth season of managing the Pittsburgh Pirates by guiding them to a 95-67 record and a National League Eastern division title. He also capped a sea of post-season awards earned by the Pirates when he was named N.L. Manager of the Year by both the Baseball Writers Association of America and *The Sporting News*, which is the managers' poll. Leyland was also named Dapper Dan Man of the Year, an award given annually to a Pittsburgh sports figure in recognition of outstanding achievement on a national level.

Through his career, Leyland has been given the label of genius by such notables as his former mentor, Oakland A's manager, Tony LaRussa, whom Leyland coached third base for while with the Chicago White Sox. LaRussa once said that Leyland would someday make a better manager than LaRussa himself. Leyland is known for his great rapport with players and the ability to make the right decisions in often the most critical situations. But he is also the type of person to shy away from such praise. He prefers, instead, to give the credit to his players, the ones who put themselves out on the field each and every day.

"I've always felt the players deserve the credit when the team wins, and a manager should take the blame when the team loses," Leyland said. "The manager is the leader of the ship, and if things aren't going right, you have to be able to step up and take the responsibility. When things are going right, obviously you have people executing properly, and they deserve recognition for doing so.

"People don't come to the game to see the manager, they come to see the players. I've always remembered how tough it is to play the game, and I think that has helped me in managing. The players have their responsibilities and so does the manager. It's my responsibility to see that the team hustles and is prepared for each game. If things don't go well, I have to be able to take the blame for it. If the players had to take the blame, then they would be the ones being fired and not the managers. But it just doesn't work that way."

"He'll go down with his ballclub, but he won't go up with it," Bonds said. "That's just Jim Leyland. He won't try to take the glory for what his team has done. He'd rather let his players have it because they were the ones making the plays. But he makes the key decisions, and he's the best there is at that."

"There's no question in my mind that Jim Leyland's the best manager in the game today," Pirate shortstop Jay Bell said. "He makes moves the way he sees them, and you may question one of his moves, but time and time again that move will pay off for the team. He's the type of manager that commands respect, but doesn't demand it. He's very human, and he loves his players and treats them all like his sons. He handles forty or so different personalities about as well as I've ever seen."

*

Another thing Jim Leyland does well is handle the personalities that are handed to him in the middle of the season. Whether they are veteran major leaguers traded from other teams or rookies from the Pirates farm system, he accepts them as part of the team and tells them the same things he tells his everyday players— "come prepared; play hard; have fun."

One of the first notable newcomers to the Pirates roster was left-handed pitcher, Randy Tomlin, who had posted a 9-6 record and 2.28 earned run average through much of the season at Class AA Harrisburg. Tomlin appeared in only three games for Class AAA Buffalo when the Pirates purchased his contract on August 6, because they needed an extra arm to start the first game of a twi-night doubleheader in Philadelphia.

Tomlin was expected to be sent right back to the minors after his appearance, which is the normal procedure in the major leagues when a team is in need of a fill-in starter. The Pirates were starting a five-game series with the Phillies because of a rainout earlier in the season, and though they were still in a dogfight with the Mets for the division title, Tomlin's start would give Leyland and pitching coach Ray Miller a chance to look at his mechanics as well as his poise under pressure.

It was an exciting evening for Tomlin, much like any first appearance in a major league uniform would be for a baseball player. But unlike any player making his first big league start, Tomlin did not appear nervous. He was in the minors only the day before, but when Tomlin found out from Harrisburg pitching coach, Spin Williams, that he'd be starting for the Pirates in a doubleheader against Philadelphia, he simply shrugged his shoulders and convinced himself he'd be ready to accept the challenge.

"Of course I was excited," Tomlin said of his major- league debut. "It was an opportunity to pitch in the big leagues and right in the middle of a pennant race. I just wanted to do as well as I could and help the team win."

And hopefully have a chance to *stay* in the big leagues.

"Yeah, that was in my thoughts also," he said with a quiet smile. "Spin told me that I could very well be sent back down right after the game, but he also said, 'Hey, you never know. If you do a good job, maybe they'll keep you around for a while.'"

Since his debut, Tomlin has never left the Pirates. He pitched masterfully in his first major league start, using a strange pitching style that neither Leyland nor Miller had ever seen before. As he goes through his motion, Tomlin rotates his upper body to the left and then brings his left (throwing) arm through as though he were stepping off the mound and delivering the ball from first base.

The motion threw off a lot of Philadelphia hitters that evening and has continued to confuse teams ever since. The Pirates made things easy for Tomlin in that first outing by staking him to a big lead, as he shut the Phillies out through eight innings and cruised to a 10-1 victory.

"When I first went out there, I kept telling myself it's the same game I'd been playing all my life," Tomlin said. "I couldn't worry about who I was pitching against or who the batters were that I'd be facing. I just had to throw strikes and not let anything take me out of my game plan."

No one on the team really says much to a rookie making his debut like Tomlin did that evening. Veterans simply feel the rookie knows what he is up against, and he doesn't need them telling him about this certain hitter or that one. Sometimes the manager will explain the club's intentions, and the pitching coach will always go over the kid's strengths, weaknesses, and pitch selection. After that, however, the rookie is on his own to prepare in whatever way he is most comfortable.

"Ray [Miller] offered some advice," Tomlin said. "He told me just to pitch the way I had been and let the guys play behind me. I may have been a little surprised that I went as long as I did [into the ninth], but I was throwing strikes and getting the outs. The big lead we had made it a lot easier, and Jimmy just decided to let me keep going."

After his debut, media members everywhere wanted to know where Tomlin picked up this unorthodox delivery. The press marveled at the way it literally froze several of the Phillies batters, who had trouble picking up sight on the ball until it was almost on top of home plate.

"Everybody has their different styles," Tomlin simply shrugged. "Nobody taught it to me. It's just what has come naturally to me and has made me very comfortable over the years. I'm able to get a lot of movement on the ball, and if it helps me get the hitters out, I'll keep doing it."

There are two things that Miller tells every young Pirate pitcher who has just been called up from the minors. One, give credit to your defense. And two, give credit to your minor league pitching coach.

"Minor league coaches have done a great job with our prospects fundamentally," Miller said. "I know this league pretty well, and after a kid's been here a while and he learns how to pitch to certain guys on a regular basis, then maybe I can share in some of the credit. But Spin Williams is the guy who has helped many of our minor league pitchers. He works his butt off with the kids, and if a kid comes up here and says, 'Boy, Ray Miller really helped me out. He's the best I've ever had.' That's not true. Spin's the one that spent all the time with him."

Tomlin was quick to heed Miller's advice and has done so ever since.

"There's no doubt that Spin Williams helped me to prepare for the moment when I'd get my first major league start," he said. "He worked a lot with my mechanics and helped me to define my game in a way that would get me to the big leagues.

"And when you give credit to your defense, you're not doing it just to push the attention away from yourself. Those guys on the field deserve it, because a pitcher needs them more than anybody. I'm a ground-ball pitcher and I don't get a lot of strikeouts. But when you have a defense like ours, you don't need a lot of strikeouts, and I certainly don't need to be in the spotlight."

When Tomlin won his debut, however, in the spotlight was exactly where he found himself. Over 50 members of the print and television media crowded around the 24-year-old's locker to try to catch a whisper of what it felt like to win a game for a team reaching for a possible pennant.

They strained to catch a word and tried their best to move in closer, but the mild-mannered Tomlin spoke in the only voice he knew. He is aggressive and competitive on the field, but in the clubhouse, he is the exact opposite. Just as much as he loves the challenge of striking out a Darryl Strawberry or Howard Johnson, Tomlin prefers the opposite direction if he sees a microphone or video camera coming his way.

"I think I can keep a good mental attitude and play the best I can on the field," said Tomlin, whom teammates began calling "Whispers," because of his hushed tone of voice. "But I've never been as talkative or outgoing away from the field. I don't always handle things with the media very well. I mean, I don't mind them asking questions. That's their job and I know that. But sometimes it can be intimidating. After my first game the reporters were all yelling at me to speak up. I tried, but it was an unfamiliar situation to me, and I don't know if I ever did get loud enough for them. If it was up to me, I'd just as soon prefer the media pay their attention to someone else."

Tomlin didn't mind talking to the Pittsburgh media for the rest of the 1990 season, however, because it meant he would remain in a Pirate uniform. Leyland and Miller were so impressed with the softspoken pitcher and his strange but successful form, they decided to put him in the permanent rotation. Tomlin made 11 more starts for the Pirates and finished the season with a 4-4 record and a 2.55 ERA in 122.2 innings pitched.

The Pirates weren't finished shaping their roster as it was just two days after Tomlin's debut that general manager Larry Doughty made his most significant move of his year-and-a-half tenure. Some said he was selling the farm, but his reasoning was hard to argue with. "We have a chance to win a pennant," Doughty said at the time. "You don't get that many opportunities, so when it comes around, you better go after it."

Doughty sent left-handed relief specialist, Scott Ruskin, and top minor league prospects, Moises Alou and Willie Greene, to the Montreal Expos for left-handed pitcher Zane Smith.

Ruskin was 2-2 in 44 relief appearances during his rookie season in 1990 and helped the Pirates to their fast start with clutch middle- inning work, two saves, and a 3.02 ERA. Alou made a couple of cameo appearances with the Pirates, and Greene was still in the farm system, but both were to figure heavily in the Pirates' near future.

Smith had been in the big leagues since 1985, when he made the Atlanta Braves roster out of spring training. He was 45-66 lifetime, and had suffered through his worst season in 1989 when he finished 1-13. He was 1-12 with the Braves and 0-1 out of the bullpen after being traded to Montreal on July 12. Smith's only win that season came against the Expos on May 6, and he wound up losing his last nine decisions.

Pirates fans had mixed feelings about the trade because they knew of Smith's disastrous 1989 and weren't very impressed with his 6-7 1990 record at the time of the trade. What many didn't know, however, was that Smith had undergone surgery to remove bone chips from his left elbow near the end of the 1988 season, and there were a lot of lingering effects that changed his pitching technique in '89.

The Pirates liked what they saw in Smith in 1990, and even though he was under .500 at the time of the trade, Larry Doughty felt Smith might become the key addition to the Pirates roster if there was any hope of wresting the division title away from the Mets.

Smith was carrying a 3.23 ERA at the time of the trade, but Doughty and Jim Leyland realized that the Expos had only scored 11 runs in Smith's seven losses. He was a pitcher they felt could keep the Pirates in games. One who could force the ground ball outs and fit in well with what was rapidly becoming one of the best defensive infields in major league baseball.

"We needed one more piece to complete the puzzle," Pirates pitching coach Ray Miller said at the time of the trade. "Earl Weaver used to say, 'Lefties always develop late.' Well, Zane Smith came at just the right time for us."

The Pirates hoped to prove that Smith was a better pitcher than his record indicated, and that maybe it was the poor infield conditions in Atlanta's Fulton County Stadium that contributed to his less-than-stellar numbers. The Braves were also not known for having the most talented infield when Smith pitched for them, and when a pitcher lacks confidence in the players behind him, he can often try to be too fine with his pitches. When he joined the Pirates, he heard the old, familiar song from Leyland and Miller. "Throw strikes and let the defense do the work for you."

That's exactly what he did, and the defense did exactly what it was supposed to do behind him. Smith won his first start with the Pirates, 6-4 over the Braves, and went 4-0 in his first five starts, while posting a 1.42 ERA. He finished the season 6-2 with the Pirates and had a 1.30 ERA in 10 starts. Smith's acquisition made Pirates fans forget all about Doughty's ill-advised trade for Rey Quinones the season before, as well as the poorly-timed deal that almost brought an over-the-hill Alan Ashby to the Pirates from Houston for Glenn Wilson. The one thing Pirate fans will remember the most about the 1990 season was a game that involved Zane Smith and a series that may go down as one of the most exciting, and definitely the most anticipated, in Pirates history.

It was September 5, and the Pirates were 78-56 and leading the National League East by a half-game over the Mets, who just happened to be in town for a three-game series that ultimately could have turned the table in either team's direction. Smith was scheduled to face New York's Frank Viola in the first game of a twi-night doubleheader, and 49,793 fans turned out to lend a hand in pulling the Pirates closer to a title.

Keith Miller led off the first inning for the Mets with a sharp single to centerfield, but Smith got out of the inning with no further damage. Viola danced around trouble in various innings and somehow managed to leave several Pirate baserunners stranded in scoring position. Smith was in fine form —maybe his best ever— and the Mets were having trouble putting even the slightest dent in him.

The game was scoreless through eight innings, and Viola appeared to be upset when he was lifted for a pinch hitter in the ninth. Although normal strategy would have called for such a move in the late innings, both pitchers did not want to give way to their respective bullpens. Smith put the Mets down in order in the ninth, and New York sent relief ace John Franco in to try to force extra innings.

Franco is normally New York's closer and the move seemed odd because at the moment, the Mets had no lead for him to protect. The Pirates had Bell, Van Slyke, and Bonilla due up in the bottom of the ninth, and Franco quickly got in trouble when Bell led off with a single. Van Slyke and Bonilla both followed by reaching base, and that left it up to Barry Bonds. Smith had given up just the one hit—the lead-off single to Miller in the first—and Bonds made the one-hitter stand by lofting a fly ball over a drawn-in outfield to drive in the winning run.

The second game matched another pair of lefties— Neal Heaton for the Pirates, Bob Ojeda for the Mets— and the Pirates jumped out quickly thanks to a home run by third baseman Jeff King. Heaton turned in another fine performance by a Pirate left-hander, and King victimized Ojeda with another home run as Pittsburgh defeated the Mets, 3-1. The Pirates were 2-1/2 games ahead of the Mets following the doubleheader sweep, and New York suddenly seemed desperate for a win in the final game of the series, or its chances of overtaking the Pirates might go right out the window.

It was Tomlin who got the call for the Pirates in the series finale, and the Mets again appeared to be baffled by a Pirate lefty as they could not solve Tomlin, and dropped a 7-1 decision. Mets rookie, Julio Valera never had a chance against the Pirates, who had waited for the opportunity to knock off the Mets in a series for a long time, although no one would come right out and say so.

"I don't really look at rivalries," Jim Leyland said. "I think that stuff's good advertising for the ballclub and the fans, but our players realize that every game is important, and there are always 11 other clubs in the division who want to come out and beat you just as badly as you want to beat them.

"It was a big series, no question about it. And it was a nice sweep for the Pittsburgh Pirates. If you look back on it, that might have been one of the most pivotal points in the season."

"Yeah, it was a time where we finally got them [the Mets]," Bonds said. "We just tried to stay focused on the fact that we didn't win anything yet, but winning those three games really sparked us. It gave us the feeling like we finally belonged, and that we had finally taken our place as the team we knew we were building for."

If the Pirates weren't sure about belonging at the top of the division standings at that point, they would find out in the 159th game of the season on September 30 at St. Louis' Busch Memorial Stadium. Doug Drabek had won his 20th decision just 11 days earlier, but now he faced perhaps an even more formidable task. The one that could finally rid the Pirates of the distasteful memories of only a few years earlier. Memories of three straight last-place finishes with disinterested players and unsatisfied egos. Memories of drug trials and an uncertainty about where the team would play its games in the coming years. All of these dark clouds could be whisked away if the Pirates were to win this normally meaningless regular-season game against the Cardinals.

It was vintage Drabek in his final start of the season as he mowed down the Cardinals through eight innings. The Pirates staked him to a 2-0 lead, and it would have to hold as they went to the bottom of the ninth. It was an unusual situation for the Pirates, one the organization hadn't experienced in 11 years, and one that very few players on the current team had ever been in.

But there they were. Three outs away from a division championship. The first two Cardinal batters went down easy, and now it was up to light-hitting Jose Oquendo. What does a defensive player think about when he has a chance to record the pennant-clinching out? What thoughts run through his mind as the ball leaves the pitcher's hand, seeming to take forever to reach the plate?

"I used to play imaginary games as a kid in Connecticut," said Pirates radio and television commentator Steve Blass, who was on the mound when the Pirates won the seventh and deciding game of the 1971 World Series. "I used to make believe it was the seventh game of the World Series, and I pretended what I would do when I got that last out."

When it actually happened, Blass said that all he remembered was going blank. That was right before he jumped into the arms of Pirate first baseman Bob Robertson, who had taken the throw on the infield out from shortstop Jackie Hernandez. "I still get excited about it," Blass said. "Because it was a moment that most kids dream about since they're six years old, and I had a chance to live it."

The film of 1990 shows Oquendo hitting a slow bouncer two steps to the left of Pirate second baseman Jose Lind, who takes his time and fires a bulls-eye to the outstretched first baseman's mitt that is set firmly on the big hand of Sid Bream. As Bream catches the ball, his arms thrust upward in victory, and Drabek is seen running deliriously toward first base and jumping into Bream's wide-open arms.

"It still gives me goose bumps just to think about that moment," Bream says now. Even though it is two years later, and he is wearing the uniform of the Atlanta Braves for the second year in a row, he will not forget the moment of ecstasy that was something special to every member of the 1990 Pirates. "We had worked a long, hard time to reach that point, and you don't always know if you'll even get there. But when we did, it was a credit to Jim Leyland, to the players, to ownership, and to the fans, who stuck by us through all the hard times. I'll never forget the special feeling we all had and how we just kind of shared it with each other the rest of the day."

"I remember the moment vividly," third baseman Jeff King said. "I'm not an emotional guy, but I looked back at the struggles and pressures I faced when I was drafted, and it became an emotional moment. I looked at the things the Good Lord had done for my life, and I just felt a very special feeling."

The Pirates closed out the 1990 season with another three-game series at home against the Mets. New York took two out of the three games, but with the division title firmly under their belts, the Pirates looked toward preparing for the National League Championship Series against the Cincinnati Reds. One way to do so was by giving most of the starters a day of rest in the season finale and letting a former Pirate fan favorite have his final day in the sun.

Jerry Reuss was a solid left-handed starter for the Pirates in the mid-70s, and although he had been with several different teams after the Pirates traded him, he agreed to a minor-league contract midway through the 1990 season, which brought him back to the Pirates for one more curtain call. Jim Leyland was aware of Reuss' retirement announcement just a few days earlier, and decided to give him the starting assignment in the Pirates' final game of the regular season.

It was a nice touch to a touching season, and although Reuss did not leave the field victorious, the fans —and players from both teams— gave him a long and loud standing ovation when he was pulled by Leyland in the sixth inning. That, in itself, seemed to speak volumes of the way people remembered him in Pittsburgh.

The Pirates finished the season four games in front of the New York Mets at 95-67. They broke the attendance record they had set just two years earlier as they welcomed 2,049,908 fans to Three Rivers Stadium. It was the first time in team history that the Pirates had cracked the two-million mark in attendance, and Leyland couldn't have been happier.

"It said a lot for the people of Pittsburgh," he said. "They believed in our group of ball players and supported us through the good times and the bad. That made a difference to everyone, knowing they had the fans out there cheering them on."

As much as Larry Doughty was lauded for his acquisition of Zane Smith, he took a tremendous amount of heat for a move that some believed cost him his job at the conclusion of the 1991 season. In late August 1990, Doughty felt secure in putting a pair of top minor league prospects on waivers—outfielders Wes Chamberlain and Julio Peguero—with thoughts of making them a part of the roster once they cleared.

It was Doughty's assumption that if any team tried to claim either one of the players, he could pull them off the wire and keep them in the Pirates' farm system. But Doughty misunderstood the waiver rule, and when the Philadelphia Phillies claimed both players, they were lost to the Pirates. Phillies general manager, Lee Thomas, did not have to supply the Pirates with any sort of compensation, but he gave up veteran first baseman Carmelo Martinez as part of the deal. The Pirates acquired a player who was capable of hitting the long ball and could also spell Bream at first, but they lost two more prospects from an already-depleted farm system.

But the move was behind him now, and though the Pirates' front office was embarrassed by Doughty's lack of knowledge regarding the waiver rule, they had to move on. The Pirates rolled through September under speculation that if they didn't win the division, it would probably cost Doughty his job and even if they did win it, his head might still roll. In the meantime, however, the playoffs approached, and the city of Pittsburgh wallowed in the fact that, at last, their beloved Pirates —the team with the most division championships since the inception of divisional play in 1969—was battling for another National League pennant.

For the fifth time since league championship play began, it would be the Pittsburgh Pirates versus the Cincinnati Reds to decide who would represent the National League in the World Series. The Reds had won three of the four previous playoff encounters with the Pirates and were slight favorites going into the 1990 NLCS, simply because they had displayed a slightly better bullpen throughout the season.

The Pirates split the season series with the Reds, losing four of the six games played at Three Rivers Stadium, but winning four out of six at Cincinnati's Riverfront Stadium. Some felt the Pirates had momentum in their favor because they had gone into Cincinnati in mid-August and swept a big four-game series. But that was nearly two months earlier, and the Reds had been playing good baseball themselves to close out the regular season.

There was no rest day between the last game of the regular season and the opening game of the playoffs, as is normally the custom, because of the owner's lockout of the players at the beginning of spring training. The delayed start of workouts in February pushed the start of the regular season back almost a week, therefore pushing makeup games to the end of the season.

Jim Leyland announced a surprise starter for Game 1 after much speculation that it would be his ace all season, Doug Drabek. Feeling better about giving Drabek one more day's rest, Leyland called on his reliable veteran, Bob Walk, to start the opening game, and Walk, as had most often been the case over his career, came through for his manager.

The Pirates staked Walk to an early 1-0 lead, but Cincinnati moved ahead and led 3-1 into the fourth inning. With the Pirates' big bats (Van Slyke, Bonilla, and Bonds) being stifled for much of the evening, Sid Bream came to the rescue in the top of the fourth by smacking a home run with Bonds on base to tie it at 3-3. The Pirates scored the eventual winning run in the seventh when Reds' leftfielder Eric Davis misplayed Van Slyke's fly ball and turned it into a ground-rule double, which scored Redus from second.

Cincinnati had a chance to win in the bottom of the ninth, but relief pitcher Bob Patterson made a nice play on Ron Oester's sacrifice bunt to get Todd Benzinger at third base. With Davis at second and pinch-runner Bill Bates on first, the Reds tried a double steal with Chris Sabo at the plate. Pirate catcher Mike LaValliere threw to second to get Bates, who got a late jump on the pitch, and Sabo was out swinging at a third strike.

Things looked good for the Pirates as they held a one-game lead with their ace, Drabek, set to start Game 2. Drabek turned out to be every bit the battler that Barry Larkin had described earlier, while defense became the focus in the series on both sides. The Pirates, for instance, had Van Slyke on second base with no outs in the top of the sixth and Bonilla on first. Bonds hit a fly ball to rightfield that was caught by Cincinnati's Paul O'Neill, and when Van Slyke tried to tag and advance to third, O'Neill's throw was right on target for the second out of the inning.

"You really don't think about anything on a play like that," O'Neill said afterward. "I was just trying to keep the ball low enough so it could be cut off if Bonilla tried to go to second. When the adrenaline starts flowing a little bit, I guess you get a little bit extra on your throws."

Tom Browning was equally effective on the mound as Cincinnati pitching continued to silence the Pirates' heavy hitters. The only offense Pittsburgh could muster was a fifth-inning solo home run by the light-hitting Jose Lind. Relief pitcher Randy Myers closed out the Pirates in the ninth for the first of his three saves in the series as the Reds defeated Drabek and the Pirates, 2-1, and evened things at one game apiece.

The series was about to shift back to Pittsburgh for Games 3,4, and 5, but the Pirates were concerned with the condition of third baseman Jeff King, who injured his back while diving into second base as a baserunner in the second inning.

"I didn't feel the exact point that my back went out," King said. "When I got back to the dugout, it felt like something was wrong, and I told our trainer I felt like I hurt my back. Someone made the third out right away, and I had to go back in the field. But when I took a ground ball to warm up, I realized I couldn't bend over. So I walked off the field, because I felt there was something very wrong."

Pirates' trainer Kent Biggerstaff kept a watchful eye on King over the two days of rest both teams had before Game 3. He put King through a series of sessions on an inversion table, which literally turns a person upside-down for a period of time to help keep the pressure off the part of the back that is ailing. As the series shifted to Pittsburgh for the next three games, King felt confident he would be ready to give it a go.

Zane Smith would get his first shot at a playoff start in Game 3 against Cincinnati left-hander Danny Jackson, who hadn't faced the Pirates in over two years. Smith had finished hot for the Pirates after his acquisition in August, and it was the opinion of many that he was the key factor that helped the Pirates get by the Mets and win the division title. Whatever the case, he was a pitcher who had the respect of the Cincinnati Reds.

"Zane is tough because he doesn't really have a pattern," Reds leftfielder Eric Davis said. "He changes speeds well and has three or four different pitches he can get over for strikes. You have to be patient with him, but at the same time you have to be aggressive, because he knows how to throw strikes."

"I think the change of scenery did Zane Smith a world of good," Reds shortstop Barry Larkin said. "When you have a club like the Pirates fielding behind you, your pitching is probably the same as it always was, but you'll get some more wins because of the plays they're making for you."

Pittsburgh was making the plays for Smith in Game 3, but unfortunately Smith didn't do much to help himself. After putting away the Reds in the first inning, he got two quick outs to start the second. But catcher Joe Oliver singled to center, and centerfielder Billy Hatcher, who was traded to the Reds from the Pirates in March, hit a two-run homer to give the Reds a 2-0 lead.

The Bucs rallied against Jackson in the bottom of the fourth as Jay Bell lined a double down the leftfield line, Van Slyke walked after falling behind 0-2 in the count, and Bonilla laced an RBI single up the middle. After Bonds popped out to Larkin, Carmelo Martinez doubled to left to drive in Van Slyke with the tying run.

The Three Rivers Stadium crowd was back into it, but Smith quickly put the fans to sleep again by giving up a three-run homer to second baseman Mariano Duncan in the top of the fifth, which put the Reds ahead again, 5-2. The Pirates had their chance to rally in the bottom of the fifth, but they left the bases loaded without getting a run across.

Each team added a run, but the Reds' relief corp, known as "The Nasty Boys" (Norm Charlton, Rob Dibble, and Randy

Myers) were too much for the Pirates as Dibble kept them in check through the middle innings, and Myers picked up his second straight save in the Reds' 6-3 victory.

The Pirates were suddenly in a pivotal position, because a win in Game 4 would even the series once again and take it to a best-of-three. But a loss would put them at a 3-1 disadvantage, and no team had ever come back from such a deficit in NLCS play.

While Cincinnati was getting the clutch pitching, Pittsburgh batters were often tripping over themselves on the way to the plate. Pirate pitching was in equally excellent form, but there was little run support to show for their efforts.

The Pirates were mired in a deep slumber, and nothing seemed to get them going. Van Slyke came into Game 4 batting 2-for-11 with one RBI. Bonilla was 3-for-12, and Bonds was 2-for-10. Together, the Pirates' top three hitters were a combined 6-for-33 with one RBI. While those three seemed to be having the toughest times in the series, the Pirates overall were hitting .120 with runners in scoring position, and had left 22 men on base. They were also 0-for-5 with runners on third and less than two outs and 0-for-4 with the bases loaded. If the situation didn't change soon, it appeared the series wouldn't even have a chance to go back to Cincinnati.

Wally Backman got the Pirates started early as he led off the bottom of the first with a double over Eric Davis' head in left field. Jay Bell tried twice unsuccessfully to sacrifice Backman to third, and finally got the job done after fouling off several pitches by grounding out to second. The Reds were well aware of Bell's new-found ability to bunt in 1990. Bell led the major leagues in sacrifice bunts with 39, which also established a new Pirate team record. His total was more than four *teams* in the American League, and the Pirates reaped benefits from his figures because 25 of his 39 sacrifices led to runs.

"Bunting was actually something I worked on during my first short spring here [in Pittsburgh]," Bell said. "Fortunately, it's been something Jim [Leyland] has relied on, and I've felt very comfortable doing it. It was a big part of our offense in '90 and '91 because with Andy, Bobby, and Barry batting behind me, they were driving in a lot of runs. I would never have believed my being able to bunt would have helped as much as it did."

Even though Bell didn't get the bunt down this time, his mission was accomplished by pushing Backman to third. Van Slyke came through with the RBI by grounding out to first to give the Pirates a 1-0 lead.

Walk pitched well through the first three innings as most of the 50,461 fans in attendance supported his every move. Cincinnati rightfielder Paul O'Neill, who had been a thorn in the Pirates' side through much of the series, cracked a solo home run to lead off the Reds fourth and that was followed with back-to-back singles from Eric Davis and Hal Morris. When Davis moved to third on the hit-and-run single by Morris, Chris Sabo drove him home with a sacrifice fly to give the Reds a 2-1 lead.

Pittsburgh battled back against Rijo in the bottom of the fourth, when Van Slyke led off with a single and later scored on a two-out double by Sid Bream. Bonilla followed Van Slyke by popping up to shortstop, and Bonds struck out to lower his series average to .167. The Pirates had a chance to take the lead after the Reds intentionally walked Mike LaValliere. Jose Lind drove a single up the middle, but Hatcher's throw was right on target to cut down Bream for the third out of the inning.

The score stayed at 2-2 until the top of the seventh, when Morris singled to lead off the inning, and Sabo followed with a two-run homer to give the Reds a 4-2 lead. Bell got a run back for the Pirates in the bottom of the eighth when he led off with a solo home run, but again the Pirates squandered opportunities to cash in more runs.

Randy Myers replaced Rijo after Bell's home run, and quickly disposed of Van Slyke. Bonilla followed with a long drive to straight away center that Hatcher could not catch up to. The sound of the ball and Hatcher slamming into the wall at the same time echoed throughout the stadium and was replayed on the CBS television broadcast on several occasions.

As Bonilla headed into second for the sure double, he noticed Hatcher laying on the artificial turf and decided to go for three. What he failed to see, however, was Davis backing up perfectly on the play and throwing a strike to Sabo to nail Bonilla at third. It is said in baseball that you should never make the first or third out of an inning at third base, but this was the second out, and it was aggressive running, which the Pirates had had little opportunity for previously in the series.

When Bonds followed with a single to right, the crowd groaned even more, because Bonilla would have surely scored from second, had he been satisfied with a double, and the game would have been tied. But everyone on both teams—especially Bonilla—knew that he had made the right decision by trying for the extra base.

"In a situation like that, you're going to have to throw me out," he said the next day. "Everyone said that Eric Davis made the play of the year by backing up Billy Hatcher on the play. You hope some of the breaks will start to go your way eventually, but we can't take anything away from the Reds. They've made the big plays, especially in the outfield, where it's so difficult."

Bonilla felt the frustration of seeing his aggressive base running turn against him, while Bonds was feeling the pressure of not being able to produce in a seven-game series after turning in numbers all season that were about to land him his first MVP trophy.

"There is pressure," Bonds said in between games. "You can't lie about that. It gets to you, because you want to go out and do something for your team and for the fans, but things just aren't falling. It's frustrating, but it just seems like Cincinnati hasn't done anything wrong."

Bonds' words weren't far from the truth, and with a 3-1 series lead, the Reds needed to play to that near perfection for just one more game to wrap up their first National League championship since 1976. To get there, though, they would have to go through Drabek, who had pitched so well in Game 2, only to come up short. His mound opponent would once again be Tom Browning, who went six innings in the Reds' 2-1 Game 2 victory.

The Reds tried to jump on Drabek early, as Barry Larkin led off with a double down the leftfield line, moved to third on an error, and scored on a sacrifice fly to give Cincinnati a 1-0 lead.

Pittsburgh showed it still had some life left in the series in the bottom of the first, as Bell walked with one out and scored on Van Slyke's triple over O'Neill's head in rightfield. Bonilla walked to put runners on the corners and Bonds, who was 3-for-14 in the series to this point, plated Van Slyke with the go-ahead run by grounding into a fielder's choice.

The Pirates added a run in the bottom of the fourth when Bonds walked to lead off the inning and moved to third on a hit-

and-run single by R.J. Reynolds. Catcher Don Slaught drove in Bonds with a sacrifice fly to give the Pirates a 3-1 lead. The lead could have been greater, but the lack of aggressive base running left the Pirates without a run in the seventh inning.

Drabek helped himself with a one-out single and moved to third on Bream's pinch-hit single to right. Both runners were aggressive on the base hit because Drabek never hesitated about moving to third, and Bream hustled into second behind the throw to try to tag Drabek. The Pirates had two runners in scoring position with one out, but when Bell grounded out on a tough play to Mariano Duncan at second, Drabek held firm at third instead of scoring easily on the play.

Drabek looked at third base coach Gene Lamont with confusion, but it was too late to do anything about it, and both runners were left stranded when Van Slyke struck out to end the inning.

The Reds inched closer in the top of the eighth when Larkin's RBI double scored Luis Quinones from second to make it 3-2 Pirates, and the events of the top of the ninth would keep everyone on pins and needles, Reds and Pirates fans alike.

It started with a lead-off single by O'Neill. Eric Davis then got a break when his ground ball down the line hit the third base bag and left third baseman Bonilla with no play anywhere. Hal Morris laid down a perfect sacrifice bunt to advance both runners, and Leyland decided to pull Drabek in favor of left-handed reliever, Bob Patterson.

The Reds had the right-handed-hitting Sabo due up, but the Pirates' strategy was to walk him intentionally and pitch to seldom-used backup catcher, Jeff Reed. Cincinnati manager Lou Piniella was forced to stay with Reed, despite his .198 career average against lefties, because he had already removed his only other regular catcher, Joe Oliver, as well as Quinones, his emergency catcher. The situation left very capable pinch-hitters Glenn Braggs and Billy Hatcher on the bench, and left Leyland with a much easier feeling in the Pirates dugout.

Pittsburgh needed a double play in the worst way, no matter who was batting for the Reds and had their middle infield set up for just exactly that. Bonilla and Bream were playing up on the corners to force the run at home, but when Reed hit a sharp grounder just to Bonilla's left, he was in perfect position to snatch it, throw a strike to Lind covering second, and Lind was able to turn the double play to end the Pirates' win in dramatic fashion.

It was a nail-biter from beginning to end, but the Pirates would take the win, because it meant they would return to Cincinnati for a chance to take the series to seven games. Once again, Drabek had pitched masterfully and showed a national television audience, as well as 61 other countries from around the world— many of which don't even know who or what a Cy Young is—why he was deserving of such an award.

"I just wanted to keep us in the series and give us a chance into the later innings," the humble Texan said after the game. "Bob Patterson got the key double play, and the guys made the plays in the field and got just enough runs to keep us alive."

The normal rotation called for a Danny Jackson-Zane Smith matchup in Game 6, and Lou Piniella wasted little time in announcing that Jackson would indeed be his starter. Jim Leyland did not show at the off- day media gathering, but he did send Smith to presumably discuss what he would have to do as the Pirates' starting pitcher to keep the team alive.

As game time approached, however, Leyland threw a curve ball of his own by announcing that Ted Power would start in place of Smith, with hopes of going as long as possible. Power had not started a game all year for the Pirates and hadn't made an official start since September 27, 1989, when he was with the St. Louis Cardinals.

The Pirates were using a little psychology in using a pitcher who had been a reliever all season for them. They hoped it would give the Reds something to think about and maybe even change their lineup a little bit.

"What we're doing is simply trying to do everything we can to win a game," pitching coach Ray Miller said during batting practice. "You could see Zane Smith as early as the first inning or any time, but we're trying to turn their lineup over just a little."

In a way, the Pirates succeeded in getting Piniella to change his lineup. When Cincinnati faced Smith in Game 3, its lineup of position players featured seven right-handed batters and a switch-hitter and looked like this:

1. Larkin, SS
2. Duncan, 2B
3. Sabo, 3B

4. Davis, LF
5. Braggs, RF
6. Benzinger, 1B
7. Oliver, C
8. Hatcher, CF

Benzinger was the only switch-hitter in Piniella's Game 3 lineup, and it probably would have been the same had Leyland stuck with Smith as his starter in Game 6.

Because of the pitching change, Piniella did some shifting with his lineup and replaced Glenn Braggs in rightfield with Paul O'Neill. The only players who stayed in their same spots in the order were Larkin, Davis, and Benzinger, while Hatcher moved to the second position and Duncan was switched to bat seventh. O'Neill hit third and Sabo fifth, while Joe Oliver was slotted into the eighth position.

No one knew if the changes would have any effect on the outcome of the game, but it made some of the players a little bit weary of all the attention that managers place on hitter-to-pitcher matchups.

"This lefty-lefty, righty-righty thing has taken over baseball in the last couple of years," O'Neill told CBS before the game. "All managers worry about are the statistic sheets, but with a game this big to both teams, nothing will really matter except going out and trying to win this game."

One thing that amazed the media was the fact that Pittsburgh was still in the series despite the lack of offense produced by its three best hitters. The "Pittsburgh Power Shortage," as the cumulative slump was labeled, had gone into the sixth game with a combined average of .214. Van Slyke was a modest 5-for-21; Bonilla, 4-for-18; and Bonds, a paltry 3-for-17. Together, they had produced no home runs and had driven in just five runs in five games. Pittsburgh fans everywhere wondered when they were going to turn it on after having such fabulous regular seasons.

The Pirates came away empty in the top of the first, but Larkin provided the Reds with some early offense by hustling out an infield single. The hustle continued as Larkin stole second on a 1-2 pitch from Power and continued to third when Slaught's throw went into center field.

Larkin held at third when Hatcher grounded out to Carmelo Martinez at first, but he managed to score when Eric Davis grounded into a force play following a walk to O'Neill. The Pirates should have had the double play, but Lind couldn't get the ball out of his glove after a perfect feed from Bell.

Power lasted into the third inning, but when Larkin reached base with one out, and Hatcher moved him to third on the Reds umpteenth successful hit-and-run play, Leyland decided it was time to bring in Smith. Television replays showed Larkin should have been called out before Hatcher's single, after Power had surprised him with a quick pick-off attempt. Larkin's hand never made it past Martinez' foot to touch the bag, but first-base umpire Harry Wendelstedt thought he got back safely. Smith inherited the first-and-third situation and came away unscathed, as the Pirates maintained their 1-0 deficit.

The Pirates tied it in the top of the fifth when Bonds negotiated a two-out walk and scored on Martinez' triple over O'Neill's head in right field. Martinez was left at third, however, when Slaught struck out to end the inning.

Earlier in the game, Jeff King was forced to come out when the pain in his back, which he injured diving back to second in Game 2, flared once again. Despite the constant training room attention and the heat packs between innings, the pain worsened to the point of severe spasms and genuine concern on the part of the Pirates' medical staff.

"This is no longer at a point where we worry about whether he can play in a game or not," Pirates trainer Kent Biggerstaff said. "This is a time where we worry about his career and his long-term future."

With King gone, Leyland pulled Bonilla in to play third base again, and sent R.J. Reynolds to rightfield. The move almost became significant, because on Reynold's first chance in the outfield—a sinking liner hit by Davis in the bottom of the sixth — he lost the ball in the lights, and Davis wound up on second base with what was ruled a single and an error on Reynolds.

Still worse for the Pirates was the fact that Paul O'Neill was standing on third after the play, because he led off the sixth with a single to center. Smith regrouped, got Sabo to pop up in the infield, and then intentionally walked the switch-hitting Benzinger. Mariano Duncan, who had hit a three-run homer off

Smith in Game 3, was the next batter, but Smith won the duel this time by striking out Duncan on a 2-2 fastball. Joe Oliver popped out to Lind for the third out, and the Pirates had dodged the bullet temporarily.

Pittsburgh started a threat of its own in the top of the seventh, when Bonilla and Bonds led off the inning with walks. Piniella replaced Jackson, his starter, with reliever Norm Charlton, and the left-hander got a big out when Martinez popped out to Sabo on a failed sacrifice bunt attempt.

The second-guessers began to chirp in both fan and media circles at that point, because Martinez was a player who had not tried a bunt in a game situation in over two years. While the strategy did call for a sacrifice, the Pirates had several pitchers to waste as pinch-hitters in that obvious situation, plus a light hitter, but an excellent bunter in utility infielder Rafael Belliard.

Martinez's at bat was wasted nonetheless, and although Bonilla advanced on Slaught's fly ball to center, he was stranded there when Lind flew out to O'Neill to end the threat.

The Pirates' opportunity to take the lead went by the boards in the top of the seventh, but the Reds made the most of theirs in the bottom of the inning, as pinch-hitter Ron Oester led off with a single and moved to third on Hatcher's one-out single to right. Piniella sent up right-handed pinch-hitter Luis Quinones to bat for O'Neill, and he delivered an RBI single to right after fouling several of Smith's 2-2 deliveries.

Stan Belinda replaced Smith, who had worked four innings and given up one run and six hits, but was in line now to suffer his second NLCS loss in as many outings. Belinda retired Davis and Sabo to keep the Reds from inflicting further damage on the Pirates, as Cincinnati had taken a 2-1 lead.

All through this series, the Pirates had tried to warn themselves — and heed the warnings from others—that it would be unwise to face a one or two-run deficit in the late innings. That's because any one of the big three Cincinnati relief corp can come in and shut the door on you. Randy Myers had saved two of the Reds' wins thus far, and Rob Dibble had saved the other. Dibble was pure heat on the mound, and his size was sometimes an intimidating factor to those facing him for the first time.

Myers also possessed speed in his left (throwing) arm and was well-equipped to retire a series of batters for the final outs in the late innings. Norm Charlton made up the final part of this trio of excellent relief pitchers, and as Myers made his way in from the bullpen to start the eighth inning, the Pirates would have to rally against one of the very pitchers they had hoped to avoid.

Neither team mustered a threat in the eighth, so it came down to the ninth inning, and one last attempt to salvage a victory that would let the Pirates play at least one more day. Bonilla popped up to Larkin for the first out of the inning, but Bonds worked Myers to a full count and walked after fouling off a couple of pitches. Myers was overthrowing as he went to a 2-0 count on Martinez, so Oliver went out to settle him down. He threw a pair of strikes past Martinez before again going to a full count, and after paying rather deliberate attention to Bonds at first, Myers let go of a pitch that left him almost wishing he could have it back.

The pitch was right up in the letters for Martinez and just over the outside corner of the plate— basically right where he liked it— and when he swung, 56,079 voices silenced as the ball headed for the rightfield wall. Glenn Braggs, O'Neill's defensive replacement in right, back-pedaled on the ball and never took his eyes off of it.

Suddenly, thoughts of Bill Mazeroski and Willie Stargell came to mind for many Pittsburgh fans who would compare this ball hit by Martinez to famous Pirate home runs from years gone by. But this was the one that almost was. Braggs backed up as far as he could against the rightfield wall and timed a perfect leap that stretched his glove above the top of the wall and snatched the ball out of the air.

How cruel fate can sometimes be. What the Pirates wouldn't have given for just a couple more inches of flight on a baseball that could at least have given them the opportunity to have one more day in 1990 to play the game that was their livelihood.

Myers was reprieved by Braggs's oversized glove, and he struck out Slaught to prove he would not slip again. The celebration was on in Cincinnati, as players and coaches hugged each other, while the Pirates watched mournfully and agonized over the thoughts of what might have been. Myers (3 saves) and Dibble (1 save) were named co-MVPs in the series, and both were looking forward to facing the heavy hitters of the Oakland A's, who had won the American League championship just a day earlier.

The Pirates would head home and wonder how such a successful regular season could turn so sour in just six games. They would wonder how their three most reliable hitters all year could suddenly fall into a collective slump. Van Slyke finished the series 5-for-24 (.208) with three RBIs. And his were the best numbers. Bonilla batted .190 (4-for-21) and had one RBI. Bonds hit .167 (3-for-18) and also had just one RBI. Together, the Pirates' big trio could gather just three extra-base hits, which was what light-hitting Jose Lind had all by himself.

"We knew the Pirates had a good offense and that they did everything well," Reds' pitcher Danny Jackson said. "We felt we'd have to go out and manufacture runs, play better than them and execute. We felt we did that, but the Pirates had some breaks go against them.

"With our three relievers, we felt we were going to win the game if we got into the seventh, eighth, or ninth inning with a lead. The Pirates didn't do anything less than what was expected of them. Our pitchers just did a good job of keeping their first two hitters off base because when their big three hitters came up, there was no one for them to drive in."

"I came here for a purpose," Bonds said. "It just didn't happen this time, but I know I'll be back. It's something that frustrates you for a while, but afterwards you go home, have a cup of coffee, and forget about it. Or else it'll affect you for a long time to come."

The 1990 Pittsburgh Pirates had grown to be a loose and upbeat ball club. The pain and disappointment of losing the National League Championship Series would wither away with the passing of time, and they could look toward next season with hopes of building on their success.

Players in any sport continually chant the familiar phrase, "We'll be back," when they lose a tough game or drop a championship series. It's the competitive spirit in all of us. But, listening to Barry Bonds' words, one could sense a certain truth about them, a certain feeling of belief. When CBS signed off on the Pirates for 1990 after that Game 6 loss, somehow it seemed not long before baseball would be singing the praises of Jim Leyland once again, and network television would be describing another Pirates' quest for World Series treasure.

# 1991: A Brave Encounter

There is a common belief in all sports that the only thing tougher than becoming a champion is repeating as one. A division championship hadn't been repeated by any National League team since 1977-78, when both the Phillies and Dodgers won their respective divisions back to back.

Repeating was more realistic in the past because there was more loyalty within the team. The New York Yankees of the 1920s dominated because they stuck together with players like Babe Ruth and Lou Gehrig. Even in the early 1970s, the Pittsburgh Pirates won three N.L. East titles in a row with Roberto Clemente and Willie Stargell leading the way.

But along came free agency, and players were suddenly open to the highest bidder. Loyalty became a thing of the past in many players' eyes, and they were willing to listen to the most generous salary offers made to them.

Besides the Pirates, the Philadelphia Phillies were the only other team to win three consecutive division championships in the National League (1976-78) since 1969, when divisional play began. The Phillies were the last team to repeat a division championship, but the 1991 Pirates figured to have a good chance because they had stayed relatively unchanged from the season before.

The Pirates had the 1990 Cy Young Award winner returning in Doug Drabek, and Barry Bonds would make a run at his
second straight Most Valuable Player trophy. They also had the
big bats of Bobby Bonilla and Andy Van Slyke, reliable pitching
with John Smiley, Zane Smith, Randy Tomlin, and Bob Walk
joining Drabek in the rotation, and a defense that could hold its
own against any in the league.

The defense would be a little more suspect in '91 because
of the loss of first baseman Sid Bream, who signed a three-year
contract with the Atlanta Braves. It was a tearful farewell for
Bream, who came to the Pirates at the end of the 1985 season and
was a major part of the reconstruction that made the Pirates the
contenders they were as they headed into the current season.

Bream hit .270 in 1990 and was a genuine threat in the
Pirates' lineup, where he usually batted sixth behind Bonds. His
15 home runs and 67 RBIs let opposing pitchers know that it
wasn't always wise to pitch around Bonds to take their chances
with the next batter. In the field, Bream is what a manager might
call a pitcher's best friend. Few first basemen in Pirates history
made the plays he made, as he swept low throws out of the dirt
time and time again and made plays at first base look routine.

Bream played 142 games at first base in 1990 and made
only eight errors in 1,083 chances for a .993 fielding percentage.
He was valuable to the Pirates, but at what cost? Money didn't
seem to be the main factor in Bream's decision to leave. In fact,
he was willing to take less to stay with the Pirates. But what he
wanted most, the Pirates weren't willing to give.

Bream owned a home in Wexford, Pennsylvania, just
outside of Pittsburgh, and he still lives there in the off-season. He
loves the area and wanted to build security there for himself and
his family. He didn't want to worry about being moved around
in the future, so his main request to the Pirates was to add a no-
trade clause in his contract.

The Pirates refused. They knew of his value and his desire
to be loyal to the ballclub. But they also knew of his three major
knee operations over the last two years, and that was of major
concern to them. The Pirates also felt they just could not give a
player—*any* player— the right to say when and if he would be
traded if he did not meet the guidelines of major league baseball.
The team elected to take its chances and irate Pirate fans found

out on December 5, 1990, that they were losing one of their favorite players.

Larry Doughty had saved his job, despite the waiver-wire snafu the season before that cost the Pirates two of their top minor league prospects, but he was taking further heat from the fans who had loved and adored Sid Bream for the past five years. In fairness to Doughty, however, fans must realize that his decisions are based on corporate decisions; club president Carl Barger and chairman of the board Doug Danforth both agreed that giving in to Bream's no-trade request was a no-can-do situation.

The Pirates could not deny they missed Bream's defense, however. They tried seven different players at first base in 1991, and none could equal his acrobatic pickups on the close plays. Rookie Orlando Merced became the most frequently used player at the position, and he performed quite admirably with a .988 fielding percentage in 105 games and 983 chances. Gary Redus played 47 games at first base and had a .990 percentage in 406 chances.

ひ

Pittsburgh did not offer Wally Backman a contract to return in 1991, and R.J. Reynolds, who came with Bream in the 1985 trade with the Dodgers, headed to Japan to play baseball. The Pirates traded minor league outfielder Steve Carter to the Cubs near the end of spring training for reserve outfielder Gary Varsho, and they signed free agent Curtis Wilkerson to a one-year contract as a utility infielder.

The roster appeared set for 1991, but there was that now-annual matter of salary arbitration to think about. The Pirates refused to negotiate with eight of their 10 arbitration-eligible players the winter before and appeared set for a similar standoff in '91.

Bonds and Bonilla both made remarks in the off-season that they wouldn't forget the Pirates' unwillingness to negotiate with them from the previous season when they became eligible for free agency in the very near future.

"We were upset and our feelings were hurt," Bonds told *Beaver County Times* sportswriter John Perrotto at the time. "There's been some anger. They told me and Bobby we were franchise players, and then said 'we don't want to talk to you.' They lied to us."

Barger had a reason for the Pirates' hesitancy toward offering the big money to their big players, and said the Pirates were willing to change their stance on negotiating this time around.

"The reason we decided to let them go to hearings last year was because the free agent market was so volatile," Barger told Perrotto. "The way money was being thrown around, it was hard to establish exactly what market value was on players. It was a sound business decision on our part to take our chances in arbitration. We'll explore a strategy this year, and hopefully we'll reduce, if not eliminate, arbitration."

It didn't happen that way. The Pirates avoided arbitration with one of their bigger name players by signing Zane Smith to a three-year deal, and although Van Slyke's contract was scheduled to run out at the end of '91, he agreed to a three-year extension that would run through 1994 and pay him a total of $12.65 million.

There were still the big three salaries to contend with: Bonds, Bonilla, and Drabek. Drabek won his case the winter before, while Bonds and Bonilla both lost. After their accomplishments in 1990, Pirate management feared all three players would come out on top this time around, which would have represented about one-third of the Pirates' total payroll.

Drabek, 22-6 the season before, won his arbitration case and was awarded a $3.335 million contract for 1991. It was the highest arbitration settlement figure in major league baseball to date, but management feared Bonilla's and Bonds' figures could go even higher if they were rewarded favorably. Unbelievably, however, both players lost their cases and were awarded the club's figure. Bonilla made $2.4 million in 1991, while Bonds pulled in $2.3 million.

Bonilla, who would be eligible for free agency following the '91 season, refused to negotiate with the Pirates once the season got underway, and when his agent, Dennis Gilbert, turned down a five-year, $23 million offer from the Pirates near

Hall of Famer Willie "Pops" Stargell teamed with Roberto Clemente in 1971 and Dave Parker in 1979 to lead the Pirates to stunning come-from-behind World Series Championships.

A six-time All Star and future Hall of Famer, Dave Parker helped lead the Pirates to a World Series Championship in 1979. After leaving Pittsburgh amidst the early rumors of a drug scandal, Parker went on to star for the Cincinnati Reds and the Oakland Athletics.

Years after his tragic death, Roberto Clemente still inspires awe and respect throughout all of baseball. Shown here collecting his 3,000th hit, Clemente was enshrined in Cooperstown only a few months after his death, when Major League Baseball waived the required five-year wait for induction.

*The Beginning of a New Era. At a news conference in Pittsburgh on November 20, 1985, former White Sox third base coach, Jim Leyland, was introduced as the new manager of the Pirates.*

*Catchers Don Slaught and Mike LaValliere limber up during the middle of the 1990 season, as the Pirates begin their march to the first of three straight division championships.*

David Arrigo/Pittsburgh Pirates

*As Pirates fans watched pitcher Doug Drabek jump into the arms of teammate Sid Bream to celebrate the Pirates' 1990 National League Eastern Division crown, little did they know that Bream would shatter their World Series dreams in 1992 with his ninth-inning, game-winning slide for the Atlanta Braves.*

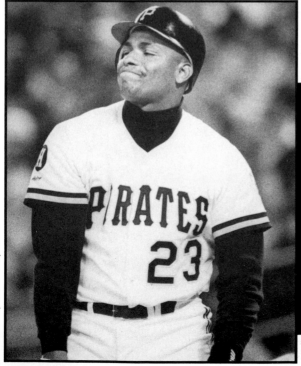

Beaver County Times—Sally Maxon

*During his six seasons with the Pirates, Bobby Bonilla became one of the most feared hitters in baseball, joining only a handful of players to ever hit an upper-deck home run at Three Rivers Stadium. After the 1991 season, Bonilla took his bat to the "greener" pastures of New York's Shea Stadium.*

Manager Jim Leyland celebrates the Pirates' 1991 National League Eastern Division Crown.

Second baseman Jose Lind's sure-handed fielding earned him a Gold Glove for the 1992 season, but his error in the ninth inning of Game 7 of the 1992 playoffs opened the door for the Atlanta Braves' dramatic comeback.

Beaver County Times—Greg Lynch

*Pitcher Randy Tomlin and catcher Don Slaught celebrate Tomlin's shutout against the Cincinnati Reds during Tomlin's first full season with the Pirates in 1991.*

*Bobby Bonilla, manager Jim Leyland, and the rest of the Pirates congratulate Barry Bonds after Bonds scored the winning run to cap another late-inning rally by the Pirates.*

Beaver County Times—Greg Lynch

*Pitcher Doug Drabek's intense determination and gutsy attitude earned him the 1990 Cy Young award, and made him one of the most dominating pitchers in baseball. Drabek has returned to his home state of Texas to pitch for the 1993 Houston Astros.*

*The winner of five Gold Gloves, Andy Van Slyke has covered centerfield in Three Rivers Stadium like few ever have. With the departure of Bonds and Bonilla, Van Slyke is the lone remaining Pirate from one of baseball's most talented outfields.*

*Jay Bell was originally called up to the major leagues on the strength of his hitting, and he responded by homering in his first big-league at-bat. Since then, he has become one of the finest fielding shortstops in the league.*

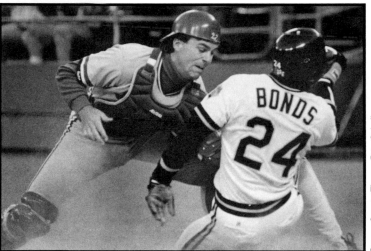

Throughout his MVP career in Pittsburgh, Bonds has thrilled Pirates fans with his electric style of play. Every at-bat brought the possibility of another home run (left) and his aggressive style of base running often resulted in a number of dramatic finishes (below). In 1993, Bonds will be displaying his grace and talent in San Francisco's Candlestick Park.

The 1992 Pirates are introduced to the fans at Three Rivers stadium as the team prepares to face the Montreal Expos in the season opener.

John Swart/AP

*During the 1992 National League Championship Series, the Pirates rose to the brink of World Series glory (left) as rookie knuckleball pitcher Tim Wakefield is congratulated by catcher Don Slaught after the Pirates' 13-4 pasting of the Atlanta Braves in Game 6 of the playoffs. However, the Pirates' World Series hopes came to an abrupt end after the Braves rallied for three runs in the ninth inning of Game 7 to stun the Pirates. (below) A dejected Barry Bonds sits alone in the Pirates' locker room after the loss.*

Doug Mills/AP

the end of the season, it appeared that Bonilla would be playing elsewhere in 1992.

"I'll say flat out we'd like not to have any animosity," Barger said. "We don't expect any players to sit back and love management, but if we can be consistent with basically sound business judgments and reach a settlement, we'd love that."

ꙮ

Repeating as division champion seemed more distant as some Pirates were heading into the 1991 season with feelings of unhappiness, but Bonds and Bonilla both insisted they wouldn't let their bitterness toward management interfere with their play on the field.

Bobby Bonilla has always been the kind of player who can separate life on and off the field. He always has a smile on his face and has been one of the city's fan-favorites since he became a full-time player in 1987. He is always gracious with the media and has given much of his time and donations to local Pittsburgh charities that often benefit the children of the city. He also enjoys his hometown roots in Brooklyn, and spends much of his time in the off-season doing the same things with kids in Brooklyn that he does during the season in Pittsburgh.

Barry Bonds is an equally charitable person. He is good with kids and is very generous with his time away from the field. But the public doesn't always see that. What the public most often sees of Barry Bonds is him snubbing a fan seeking an autograph after a tough game, or when he makes an ill-advised remark about a teammate or some other team official.

Those who know him best simply say, "That's just Barry," which means they are used to his actions and don't really take offense from whatever he says or does. The fans perceive him as stuck up and overpaid when he says no to an autograph request, but 90 percent of those fans would probably rather see him stay with the Pirates than go elsewhere and play. Bonds' actions on the field speak louder than his words, but his words usually get most of the attention.

Following the 1990 National League Championship Series, Bonds questioned Jeff King's desire when King was forced to leave two games and sit out the rest of the series because of problems that resulted from diving back to second base on an attempted pick-off in Game 2 of the series.

King spent much of the off-season consulting doctors from all over the country and would eventually spend much of the 1991 season on the disabled list because of the injury, wondering whether surgery would be the answer. He played in only 33 games and hit .239, with four home runs, 18 RBIs, and a lot of pain.

"I never questioned Jeff King's integrity or desire to play the game," Bonds said. "All I did was openly wonder how someone could pull himself out in such big games. I didn't know how badly he was hurt, and if I had, I wouldn't have said anything. I never meant any personal harm to him in any way."

King, who is quiet and very self-contained, preferred to let the matter drop and, much like his teammates, looked at it as another example of Barry being Barry.

"It was unfortunate that he [Bonds] made the comments that he did," King said during the 1992 season. "The thing that hurt the most was the way that some of the writers, the guys you get to know the best during the course of a season, handled it. Of all people, they should know that what Barry was saying was totally ridiculous. . . and to go out and print it . . . It was really just something to sell a lot of newspapers."

When the clouds of controversy started hanging over spring training of the new season, they somehow managed again to settle right over the area where Bonds was standing. It started when Bonds had a personal friend on the field taking pictures, but would not let a photographer with credentials photograph him as he warmed up.

A member of the Pirates' public relations department informed Bonds of the photographer's credentials and said that if one photographer could not take pictures, neither could his friend. As Bonds discussed the matter with the member of the Pirates' staff, outfield coach Bill Virdon stepped in. A small argument developed, and when Jim Leyland stepped in, television cameras began to roll.

Most of Leyland's words were inaudible because of the camera's distance from the player and manager, but Leyland was heard at one point saying, "I'm the manager here, and if you don't like what's going on around here, you can take your ass and get out."

It was suddenly national news. Everyone from the local Pittsburgh TV stations to ESPN and CNN carried the footage. Words could not be heard between the two, but the words were not important. All people saw was a manager yelling at one of his players, but because that player was Barry Bonds, the session seemed to take extra precedence.

"I understand the media has a job to do and when they see something like that going on, well that's news, and they have to report it," Leyland said. "Because of that, I don't think it was blown out of proportion. But when Barry Bonds is in a slump, or when he hits three or four home runs in a game, and the media somehow mixes in an argument we had in spring training two years ago, that's when it becomes old hat.

"I've had disagreements with other players, but there weren't twenty television cameras around, and nobody really ever knows about those. But because of that situation, people think of Barry as some problem child, and that's just not true. I messed up because I started yelling without knowing the whole story and Barry messed up by talking to a coach the way he did. We just figured, he got hot, I got hot, let's turn the page. That's it."

"It's really a closed subject," Bonds said when asked about the incident. "The media always brings it up, but it's really past tense to me and Jim Leyland. Tempers flared and things got blown out of proportion. It wasn't the first time something happened between a player and his manager, and it won't be the last. We dealt with it and, honest to God, we laughed about it five minutes later."

Some felt the spring training incident would tear the Pirates up and divide them. But others felt it would bring them closer together. The national television audience that watched the sensationalized replay of the Bonds and Leyland disagreement saw a verbal altercation with one of the game's best players as the main attraction.

If they looked a little closer, however, they may have also noticed the game's finest manager taking control of a tense situation and commanding the respect that all managers should have from their players, whether the player fills a lesser role or is the defending Most Valuable Player of the league.

"I think Leyland gained a lot of respect that day," *Pittsburgh Post Gazette* sportswriter Paul Meyer said. "He realized the distracting qualities of such an incident and handled it before it got way out of hand. As for Barry, he isn't a bad guy at all. He says a lot of things that don't come out the way he means them. The Jeff King thing for instance, he came out the next day and said he just meant the team needed Jeff King in there.

"Barry is at his worst in a group interview, such as the playoffs or an All-Star game. He can talk for ten minutes, but if you're not there for the whole interview, it's easy to take something he said as outrageous and write a story about it. He says things that he may mean at the time, but he doesn't always have a lot of tact. But he says what he feels and I'll say one thing for him, he has never, ever requested that anything he says stay off the record."

In spring training of 1987, the New York Mets had a similar altercation. This one was more a clash of egos between Darryl Strawberry and Keith Hernandez, two of the team's higher profile players who led the Mets to a world championship the year before. That, like Bonds-Leyland, was shown on every sports segment in the country, and it seemingly did have an effect on the team's second-place finish to St. Louis in '87.

Many felt the Mets never regained the camaraderie that had carried them the season before and is so vital to a team's success. You stay together, travel together, and share the same dugout and clubhouse. If personalities clash, so do the final results in most cases.

That was one case, however, and the Pirates were another. Bonds and Leyland put their differences behind them and never gave the matter another thought. The Pittsburgh Pirates were ready for another season and had serious thoughts of repeating as National League East champions.

≈

The Pirates opened the season at home against the Montreal Expos. For the second straight year, Drabek was tabbed by Leyland as his opening-day starter, and it was a ritual that Drabek would never get tired of.

"When your manager has the confidence and faith to name you his opening-day starter, it gives you a good feeling," Drabek said. "I think it's something you have to earn, because it means your manager believes you can go out and get your team started off on the right foot."

Drabek was set to face the Expos' Dennis Martinez, who had become one of the toughest opponents the Pirates had faced over the years. Martinez was into his game early, and the Pirate bats were silent as the Expos blanked Drabek and the Bucs, 7-0, in front of a record home-opening crowd of 54,274.

Drabek didn't get the start he would have liked, but the Pirates came back to win three in a row and later won nine out of 11 in one stretch to move into first place by a game-and-a-half at 15-7. While Drabek struggled to an 0-3 start and didn't get his first win until April 24, left-hander John Smiley picked up the slack and cruised to a 4-0 start.

Smiley had compiled a 40-34 record in four full seasons with the Pirates before 1991 and had never won more than 13 games in one season. He was a raw talent when Pirate pitching coach Ray Miller took him under his wing and taught him everything he knew.

"Smiley was an example of the young, hard thrower that you have to help learn the ropes," said Miller, who has coached seven 20-game winners in his career and three Cy Young Award winners. "We had to teach him the basics and walk him through everything from A to Z. John didn't like being a celebrity, and he wasn't fond of talking to the media when he first came up. We had to start him from scratch both physically and mentally— right down to what he said to the press."

Smiley took his lessons well and developed into the pitcher both Miller and Leyland hoped he would by 1991. The 26-year-old had developed a solid curve to go along with his hard fastball, and he had grown a tremendous amount of confidence for perhaps the first time in his career in his 6-foot-4, 200-pound frame.

Smiley didn't suffer his first loss until May 4, but he ventured on another four-game winning streak from May 10 to June 1 and was 8-1 with a 3.02 earned run average after his first 10 starts. The streak included a one-hitter against the Mets on April 17, and despite a four-game losing streak in June, Smiley earned a spot on the N.L. All Star team.

Better things were ahead for Smiley, and the same held true for the rest of the Pirates. They played determined all season, and their efforts were best summed up by shortstop Jay Bell: "One thing I think we've shown all along is that we play a full nine innings," he said. "We don't give up."

No words ever rang truer than on a cold afternoon in April —the season just a dozen games old, but the fire in the Pirates' eyes was burning brighter than ever. Pittsburgh trailed the Chicago Cubs, 7-5, in the bottom of the ninth, but rallied with a pair of runs to send the game into extra innings.

In the top of the 11th, Andre Dawson cracked a grand slam —his second in three games against the Pirates— to highlight a five-run inning and give the Cubs a 12-7 lead. By now, only a handful of the 10,860 fans who paid their way in remained, but the ones who left missed one of the greatest Pirates rallies ever. It started with a walk and snowballed from there.Four hits, two walks, and a sacrifice fly later, the game was tied. Don Slaught then made sure there were no more extra innings by lacing a shot to straight-away center that bounced off the wall and scored Barry Bonds with the winning run.

The outcome reminded many people of the Memorial Day rally over the Dodgers the season before, when the Pirates rallied from a 5-1 deficit in the bottom of the ninth to win, 6-5. Whatever it did, it made believers out of the skeptics who said the Pirates would self-destruct before the end of May.

The Pirates took sole possession of first place on April 27 and never let it go. They were 30-15 by the end of May, and their lead had grown to four games in the National League East. They gained two more games in June and were 48-31 at the All-Star break.

If someone would have told Jim Leyland that his ball club would be in first place despite a 1-6 start by his ace, Doug Drabek, he would have found that hard to believe. Leyland has always had faith in his pitchers, but Drabek had become the glue that held the Pirates' staff together. If his efforts were to go downhill, it would appear that the Pirates' fortunes would go right along with him.

But while Drabek was finding himself again, the rest of the Pirates' pitching staff was picking up the slack. Randy Tomlin, ready to notch a full season under his belt, finished 8-7 in 31 games and posted a 2.98 ERA. Zane Smith raised his career record as a Pirate to 22-12 by finishing 16-10 in '91, with a 3.20 ERA in 35 starts. Veteran Bob Walk spent different parts of the season on the disabled list, but still registered his fifth straight winning season by finishing 9-2.

And then there was Smiley. He was 9-6 at the All-Star break with a 3.40 ERA in 16 appearances. He had gotten the Pirates off to a good start, but many expected someone else, such as Drabek, to take the controls and carry the Pirates to another division title.

Drabek recovered from his 1-6 start and won five of his next six decisions between May 26 and June 17, a period in which he allowed just 10 earned runs in 49 innings for a 1.84 ERA. He tossed his second career one-hitter on May 27, as the Pirates beat the Cardinals, 8-0, and went 3-1 in August to help the Pirates build their lead in the division to eight games.

While Drabek was pitching himself back into his customary form, Smiley was carrying himself to heights he had never reached before. He lost only two more games after the All-Star break and carried a 19-8 record into the last game of the season —a meaningless season-ender for most players, but a game of significance for someone who has a shot at his first 20-win season ever.

The Pirates went 18- 11 in September, and it was Drabek —who would finish a respectable 15-14 for the season after his disastrous 1-6 start—who would nail down the division-clinching win for the second year in a row. The Pirates won their 91st game of the season on September 22 when Drabek defeated the Phillies, 2-1, at Three Rivers Stadium. The site of the victory was significant because this time the Pittsburgh fans had a chance to celebrate right along with the team.

Drabek pumped his fist and jumped into Don Slaught's arms when he recorded a strikeout for the last out, and the rest of the team swarmed the field to bask in the glory of another title that no one gave the Pirates much chance of winning. Bonilla and Bonds hugged each other, while the fans stood and cheered endlessly. Jim Leyland congratulated his coaching staff and hugged any player he could wrap his arms around.

Then came the sight that was played over the highlight reels again and again that evening — a sight no one would have ever believed possible had they remembered the circumstances that took place in March. Bonds sought out his manager among the crowd of Pirate uniforms and threw his arms around him for what seemed like an eternity. He then grabbed another player and hoisted Leyland upon his shoulders and proclaimed him to be the best, as he pointed a No. 1-sign with his index finger at the hordes of television cameras recording the celebration.

"This is what we worked for all year," a tearful Leyland said in his office after the game. "All the critics said we'd self-destruct, but we proved them wrong."

The celebration continued with champagne showers in the Pirates clubhouse and Leyland himself took part by smoking a cigar and singing a country-western tune in honor of Pirates' long-time equipment manager John Hallahan, who died earlier in the season after serving over 60 years with the Pirates.

The emotion Jim Leyland displays is always genuine. His heart goes out to those in need, and he will almost always offer a handshake, or an autograph, or a photo opportunity to a fan waiting outside the gates of Three Rivers Stadium. The tears on this Sunday afternoon were tears of joy over a celebration that not many thought the Pirates would ever see. When Leyland looks back on the times he has cried over the joyous opportunities, he remembers something his wife, Katie, told him.

"She said when I first came to Pittsburgh, people called me, 'Jim who?' Now she says they're going to start calling me, 'Jim Boo-Hoo.'"

Bonds had gotten off to a slow start and was hitting just .170 with two home runs and 14 runs batted in through the first month of the season. He finished strong, however, and wound up at .292 with 25 homers and 116 RBIs. He also won his second straight Gold Glove Award with 13 outfield assists, which was the second highest total in the league.

Bonilla led the team with a .302 average and added 18 home runs and 100 RBIs in what was to be his last season as a member of the Pittsburgh Pirates. Van Slyke hit .265 with 17 home runs and 83 RBIs, but struck out 85 times, which was the highest total on the team. Van Slyke was tremendous once again defensively, as he won his fourth consecutive Gold Glove Award in center field. He played in 135 games and finished with a .996 fielding percentage, with just one error in 281 chances.

Bonds finished second in the balloting for the National

League Most Valuable Player Award, just 15 points behind Atlanta third baseman Terry Pendleton, who led the Braves to the N.L. West title with a .319 average, 22 home runs, and 86 RBIs. Bonilla finished a not-so-distant third.

The Pirates struggled somewhat at third base after King went on the disabled list and was gone for much of the season. They tried utility man Curtis Wilkerson, but he was more of a middle-infielder. They tried minor-league third baseman Joe Redfield, but he batted just .111 in 11 games with the Pirates.

For a while, there was an answer to the Pirates' dilemma at third base when rookie John Wehner got the call from Class AAA Buffalo. The 24-year-old Pittsburgh native started the season at Class AA Carolina and was promoted to Buffalo on June 14. He hit .304 at Buffalo and was promoted on July 14, faster than anyone would have guessed. But he stepped in immediately and gave the Pirates the lift they most surely needed.

"Getting a chance to play in the majors was something I had always dreamed of," said Wehner, who hit .340 (36-for-106) for the Pirates in 37 games and had a .936 fielding percentage at third base. "It's easily the best experience I've ever been through. Jim Leyland made it easy for me by just telling me to do what I could. There was no pressure on me at all."

Although he did not possess power (no home runs, six RBIs), Wehner was doing the job defensively at third base, and the Pirates knew they could look to their other big hitters to drive in the runs. But as the Pirates headed west for their final trip to the coast, bad news approached them again.

The third base position seemed cursed in 1991, as Wehner developed a ruptured disc in his back in mid-August, and he too was lost to the Pirates for the rest of the season. The Pirates held a five-game lead over St. Louis at the time of the trip, and Larry Doughty figured his team would need help if it was going to maintain that edge.

Doughty shopped around while the Pirates won the first two games of the trip in Los Angeles. On August 30, he traded minor league pitchers Kurt Miller and Hector Fajardo to the Texas Rangers for veteran third baseman Steve Buechele. It was another example of the Pirates depleting their farm system, but a move Doughty was forced to make.

Buechele figured to be a genuine home run threat batting sixth in the order behind Van Slyke, Bonilla, and Bonds, and his

.991 fielding percentage in 1991 set a new American League record for third basemen. Buechele hit .306 with six home runs and 17 RBIs in May for the Rangers and hit .313 during a career-high eight-game hitting streak in early August. He started 0-for-7 with the Pirates and finished the season at .246 with four home runs and 19 RBIs. Buechele hit a combined .262, with 22 homers and 85 RBIs in 152 games with Texas and Pittsburgh.

While Buechele was the only major acquisition for the Pirates in 1991, the organization lost one of its driving forces when club president Carl Barger stepped down on July 8 to take a similar position with the Florida Marlins, one of the league's two new expansion teams for 1993.

Barger stepped to the front in Pittsburgh sports along with Malcolm Prine and then-Pittsburgh Mayor Richard Caliguiri in 1985 and helped form the public-private coalition that bought the team from the Galbreath family, which ultimately saved baseball in Pittsburgh. He was a lifelong resident of the city, but was intrigued by the challenge of building a team from the ground up. Barger was also close friends with Marlins' owner H. Wayne Huizenga, who owned Blockbuster Entertainment and offered Barger a minority ownership in the Marlins as well as a seat on the board of directors for the entertainment company. That friendship played an important role in Barger's decision to leave the Pirates.

"I grew up with the Pirates," said Barger, who was 58 at the time he took the position with the Marlins. "But this was a challenge I couldn't turn down. It's a chance to take over a team and start from scratch. I know I'll miss the Pirates, but it's a move that is in my best interests."

The Pirates rolled through July, August, and September and nailed down their second straight division title with 13 games to spare. The final days of the regular season gave Jim Leyland a chance to rest a few of his starters, get a look at some up-and-coming young players, and keep his starting rotation as sharp as possible.

John Smiley won his 19th game on the first of October, the same day the Pirates surpassed the two-million mark in attendance for the second straight year. Suddenly a milestone was within his reach, and it didn't take a genius to figure out that Leyland would give Smiley the opportunity to reach that milestone.

Twenty-game winners are rare these days, because there aren't as many ironman pitchers in baseball as there were even 20 years ago. Today's game features specialty pitchers who enter games in certain situations, and the starter no longer is asked to go the distance in every outing. Most teams now also feature five-man rotations instead of four, and that cuts down on the number of starts a pitcher gets in a season. The less starts he has, the less opportunities there are for 20 wins.

Leyland is a believer in the five-man rotation system, but when the Pirates had an off-day in between Smiley's 19th victory and the last game of the season, he knew he could give the 6-foot-4 southpaw a shot at his own brass ring. It was October 6, the last day of the regular season, and the Expos were in town. The game should have been played in Montreal, but Olympic Stadium suffered severe damage when one of its cement walls came crashing down about a month earlier and left major holes in its structure. The Expos were forced to play the last month-and-a-half of an already dismal season on the road.

There was no suspense. No game-winning home run in the bottom of the ninth. No breathtaking gasps that were held with every pitch. Smiley simply shut down the Expos, and the Pirates supported him with enough offense to produce a 7-0 shutout and a 20-win season.

Smiley was at his best following the All-Star break as he made 17 appearances and finished 11-2 for the rest of the season with a 2.79 ERA. He was a most-impressive 13-3 against Eastern division teams and closed the season with seven straight wins. He finished the regular season with a 3.08 ERA and totaled 129 strikeouts and only 44 walks in 207.2 innings. His 1.9 walks per nine innings pitched was fourth best in the league.

Smiley tied Atlanta's Tom Glavine for the league lead in victories, and he became the first left-hander to win 20 games for the Pirates since John Candelaria went 20-5 in 1977. His .714 winning percentage tied him with Cincinnati's Jose Rijo for the league lead, and he finished third in the balloting for the Cy Young Award behind Glavine and St. Louis' Lee Smith.

"John had an outstanding season," pitching coach Ray Miller said. "The kind every pitcher dreams about as a kid. He worked his butt off for those twenty wins, and I'll never forget the happiness I felt for him."

Smiley was equally happy to win 20 games, but the playoffs were ahead, and  as much as the so-called experts expected the Pirates to fold their tents in  spring training, they would never have predicted the outcome in the N.L. West.

While the Pirates were running away with the East, the West was coming down  to the wire. As expected, the Dodgers, who had signed free agent Darryl Strawberry in the off-season from the Mets, were in the hunt, but their rivals were the upstart Atlanta Braves, who had finally put together a defense to go with their highly talented pitching staff.

The Pirates finished 14 games ahead of the Cardinals at 98-64 and watched the race in the West with genuine curiosity. They were 40-32 against the West overall and hadn't fared particularly well against either of the teams in the  hunt for the division championship. They were 5-7 against the Dodgers during  the regular season, including 3-3 in Los Angeles, and 3- 9 against the Braves.

There were many factors for the Pirate players to consider in who they would have chosen to play if they had such an opportunity. First, there was  the travel. Atlanta was certainly a lot closer than Los Angeles, and that  might make a difference when the later games came around.

But if their opponent had to be Atlanta, the Pirates knew of one ugly statistic that would stare them in the face until they proved otherwise. Pittsburgh was 0-6 at Atlanta-Fulton County Stadium during the regular season,  and as much as they tried, they could not find a way to win there. The only  favorable thing about playing Atlanta would be its lack of experience. The Pirates were in this situation the year before, and the Braves hadn't played in an NLCS since 1982. The Dodgers, on the other hand, were there in 1988  and still had some of the faces on their current team that won the World  Series that year.

When asked by members of the Pittsburgh media who they would rather play, most of the Pirates said it wouldn't matter or that their opinion was  immaterial, because they were in and they would have to play the series no  matter who their opponent would be. Very few offered a direct answer, but those who did said they would like to play Atlanta because they would be  happy to see Sid Bream and Rafael Belliard—who had also joined the Braves as a free agent during the off- season—play in another National League  Championship Series with them.

Those who pulled for Atlanta got their wish as the Braves won eight in a row down the stretch and clinched the N.L. West title on the next-to-last day of the regular season. Atlanta turned a 65-97 1990 record into a 94-68 mark in 1991 and won the division by one game over the Dodgers. This, just a year after finishing in last place in the division, while Cincinnati defeated the Pirates in the NLCS and the Oakland A's in the World Series.

The Braves, who—along with Minnesota—became the first team since Louisville (1889-90) of the American Association to go from last to first in one year's time, had grown considerably in such a short span. General Manager John Schuerholz had brought together a strong pitching staff for manager Bobby Cox, and even when the Braves were finishing last or next to last in previous years, there was a glimmer of hope that was brought on by the durable arms of young men like Glavine, John Smoltz, Pete Smith, and Steve Avery, as well as veteran left-hander Charlie Leibrandt.

Atlanta's biggest problem was its defense. When Zane Smith pitched for the Braves, he was 1-12 in 1989 before being traded to Montreal. While he had problems from elbow surgery from the season before, he also knew his pitches had to be pretty well placed because Atlanta consistently led the league in errors. People wondered why he became so successful when he was traded to the Pirates in 1990, and he simply answered that he didn't have to be as fine with his pitches, and he could count on his defense behind him.

Schuerholz knew the Braves needed some help because this was a pitching staff that shouldn't be wasted on marginal fielding. Fielding expertise is why the Braves wooed Bream so heavily in the off-season, plus they knew he could hit very well against right-handed pitching. And when Belliard didn't seem welcome in Pittsburgh anymore, Schuerholz signed him to a contract with the Braves because, although he was a very light hitter, he had defensive skills that the Braves hadn't seen at shortstop in a while.

Bream hit .253 in his first season with the Braves with 11 home runs and 45 RBIs, while Belliard hit a respectable .249 and played up to Schuerholz's and Cox's expectations in the field. A memorable moment for Bream in '91 came during Atlanta's first trip to Pittsburgh in early May. The Braves trailed, 5-1, in the late innings and Bream was called on to pinch-hit. The almost 24,000 fans at Three Rivers Stadium gave Bream a standing ovation when he stepped to the plate, and he greeted Pirate reliever Bill Landrum with a solo home run to straight-away centerfield. The fans cheered him even more as he circled the bases because to many, it was an unhappy day when Sid Bream left the Pittsburgh Pirates.

Atlanta also benefited from a spring training trade that brought them speedy outfielder Otis Nixon from Montreal, and the Braves trade for relief ace Alejandro Pena from the Mets in late August helped nail down two victories and 11 saves during the stretch run.

The biggest move by Schuerholz, however, may have been the off-season signing of free agent Terry Pendleton. He was a cornerstone of the Cardinals' infield at third base since mid-1984, but when his contract was up at the end of 1990, the Braves felt whatever they could get him for would be the right price to tighten up their rapidly improving defense.

"Atlanta was a team much like we were in '88," Bob Walk said. "They were a young team, and they got themselves in a pennant race. They probably should have fallen apart at the end of the season like we did, but they didn't. They stayed together and proved they belonged in the playoffs."

The Atlanta Braves, a team that had dubbed themselves "America's Team" for so many years on owner Ted Turner's superstation television network, would now get the chance to live up to that role. Their playoff run made believers out of many baseball fans around the country and brought loads of Braves fans out of the closets, where they had hidden for so many years from the last-place finishes and the general stigma of being a Braves fan.

A stadium that had seen more empty seats than full for the last several years during the baseball season was suddenly filled daily to its near-52,000 capacity, and the Pittsburgh Pirates were about to find out first-hand what had become the ritual in Atlanta—the tomahawk chop.

за.

The 1991 National League Championship Series was billed as a youth versus experience playoff, and the Pittsburgh Pirates were the early favorites to use their experience as an advantage over the raw, but talented Atlanta Braves.

The first and last two games were to be played in Pittsburgh's Three Rivers Stadium, while the middle three would be played at Atlanta-Fulton County Stadium. There was much interest from the media about the Braves' new legion of fans and their interesting approach to the way they supported their team.

As the pennant race wound to a close in the N.L. West, Atlanta fans were seen continually pistoning their arms at the elbows with their fingers perfectly straightened. At the same time, they chanted what appeared to be the familiar Indian war cry, which is often heard on the old Cowboy and Indian movies that are so prevalent on Saturday morning television.

It became known as the "tomahawk chop," but the custom had been acted out by fans of the Florida State University Seminoles long before the Atlanta Braves became successful. The chop wouldn't be so bad in Pittsburgh, where the Pirates hoped they could gain a quick edge on the Braves in the first two games, but when they got to Atlanta, it would be like something the Pirates had never seen before in a baseball stadium.

First things first, however, as there was the matter of playing Games 1 and 2 in Pittsburgh. The Pirates would send the 1990 Cy Young Award winner in Drabek to the mound against the eventual 1991 winner, Tom Glavine. Drabek lost his first five decisions at Three Rivers Stadium in 1991, but came back to finish 9-3 in his last 14 starts there. He has always been considered a second-half pitcher, which is why Leyland had little doubt as to who would start the series for the Pirates.

"Dougie will keep you in just about every ball game," Leyland said. "He's a competitor and he'll give you everything he has. He's the guy we want out there for the key matchups."

The Pirates were matched against Glavine, who recorded his first 20-win season , and at age 25 seemed destined for many more. Glavine was 20-11 for the Braves during the regular season after finishing 10-12 in 1990. He pitched a total of 246.2 innings, and had 192 strikeouts to go along with his 2.55 ERA. Glavine was especially hot in the early part of the season when he allowed just seven earned runs in his first 28 starts, but he struggled down the stretch somewhat, as he allowed 13 earned runs in his last six starts.

Pittsburgh was a determined team going into the series with the Braves. The sting of falling short to the Reds the season before in the playoffs still remained in the Pirates' minds, and they wanted to prove they were capable of reaching the next level.

A local television station did a pre-game special from Three Rivers Stadium right before the start of Game 1, and the music of the rock group, U2, seemed to lament the feeling of every Pittsburgh fan as the city braced itself for another playoff ride. "Still Haven't Found What I'm Looking For," summed up the mission of the 1991 Pittsburgh Pirates and from the looks of the first inning, it appeared they were more than determined to find the championship ring they missed out on a season ago.

Drabek put the Braves down 1-2-3 in the top of the first, and Glavine appeared to be headed for the same kind of inning after disposing of Gary Redus and Jay Bell in the Pirates' half of the first. Andy Van Slyke worked Glavine to a full count, however, and then sent the payoff pitch into the rightfield seats to give the Pirates a 1-0 lead.

Much had been made about the silence the Cincinnati Reds pitching staff had put on the Pirate bats in the 1990 NLCS. Especially Van Slyke, Bonilla, and Bonds, who were the Pirates' main source of power in 1990, but batted a collective .191 in the playoffs, with no home runs and just five RBIs. The fans were especially delighted to see that Van Slyke had started this series off on the right foot and the record crowd of 57,347 hoped that Bonilla and Bonds could swing right along with that momentum.

Glavine appeared shaken following Van Slyke's home run and walked Bonilla on four straight pitches that weren't even close to the strike zone. Bonds followed with a sharp line drive that skipped the turf in front of shortstop Rafael Belliard and bounced wickedly off the heel of his glove. The play was poorly ruled an error, but the Pirates had runners on first and third with two outs, and Steve Buechele at the plate.

Buechele worked Glavine to another full count and finally walked after fouling off a couple of pitches. Glavine was on the ropes early, but the Pirates let him off the hook when Don Slaught grounded out to Pendleton to end the threat.

Drabek continued strong, and Bell set the Pittsburgh offense rolling again in the bottom of the third. Bell sent a lead-off single up the middle off Glavine and came around to score on Van Slyke's double to right centerfield. Bonilla drove in Van Slyke with a base hit to left, and the Pirates had a 3-0 lead over the Braves. Bonds walked on a 3-2 pitch, but the inning stalled when Buechele and Slaught struck out, and Jose Lind bounced back to Glavine.

The Braves ran themselves out of a possible big inning in the top of the fourth when second baseman Mark Lemke led off with a sharp bouncer that skipped through Redus' legs at first and bounced into the rightfield corner. Lemke was sure to reach second, but when he figured to take a chance and try for the extra base, a Bonilla-to-Bell-to-Buechele relay nailed him at third.

The media questioned Lemke's judgement with his team down by three, but television replays showed the Pirates needed two perfect relay throws, and that was exactly what they got. Buechele never had to move his glove as he received Bell's throw from just behind second base, and Lemke's hand slid right in as the ball arrived. If Buechele would have had to move an inch in either direction, Lemke would have been safe.

Lemke's aggressive, but ill-timed strategy may have cost the Braves, because the next batter, Pendleton, walked on four pitches, and David Justice followed with a single to center. Ron Gant and Bream both flew out to left to end the inning, but the Braves would almost certainly have had at least one run home if Lemke would have stayed at second.

Sometimes one inning can tell the story of an entire series. Not that the future suddenly turns up on the stadium scoreboard and tells who wins and loses, but a certain event in an inning can change the course of a manager's strategy, and ultimately can throw a series in a different direction.

In the bottom of the sixth inning, the Pirates still clung to their 3-0 lead, but looked to add to it when Buechele stroked a lead-off double down the leftfield line. Slaught popped up to Belliard for the first out, but Buechele advanced to third when Lind grounded out to second base. The Braves' outfield played Drabek very shallow, and he made them pay by driving a double to the wall over Gant's head in centerfield.

Buechele scored easily, but Drabek went against all the rules that a pitcher running the bases should follow. As he neared second base, Drabek saw Gant just picking up the ball on the warning track. Figuring he could reach third easily, Drabek kicked his legs into high gear and kept on running. Belliard's relay throw from Gant beat Drabek easily for the third out of the inning, but when Drabek was slow in getting up, there was sudden concern in the Pirate dugout.

At first, it was believed Drabek injured his knee or ankle when he slid into the bag, but Pirate trainer Kent Biggerstaff later confirmed that the pitcher jammed his left hamstring when he hit the bag rounding second. Drabek went to the mound for the seventh inning and threw a couple of warmup pitches while Biggerstaff stood by his side, but there was pain as he kicked in his motion and he was forced to leave.

Drabek, who struck out five and allowed just three hits and two walks, acknowledged the crowd's ovation for him, but he and the Pirates were more concerned with the long-term consequences of his injury. Bob Walk replaced Drabek and allowed just a solo home run to Justice in the ninth inning as the Pirates captured the first game, 5-1.

"We don't believe [Drabek's] injury is too severe," Biggerstaff said in the Pirate clubhouse. "We'll be able to determine more tomorrow after we see how much bleeding and spasms he experiences overnight."

Walking was very difficult for Drabek the next day, and if he had any hope of making his next scheduled start in Game 4, he knew he'd have to spend much of his time in the training room. He would be subject to heat treatments, rubdowns, time in the whirlpool, and a little bit of prayer. Then maybe, just maybe, he would be able to take his turn in the playoff rotation.

The Pirates' chances of sweeping the first two games in Pittsburgh rested on the left arm of Zane Smith, who turned in another fine season after signing a three-year contract in the off-season to stay with the Pirates. Smith was 16-10 during the regular season and would face another Atlanta left-hander who was equally as effective for the Braves.

Twenty-one-year-old Steve Avery was 18-8 in his first full season with the Braves, and his 137 strikeout total was the third-highest on the Braves' pitching staff. Avery was a pleasant surprise for Atlanta manager Bobby Cox, who never expected the young left-hander to improve so quickly after his 3-11 1990 record in 21 appearances.

The Pirates broke the attendance record they had set the night before, as 57,533 fans packed into Three Rivers in hopes of seeing their team head to Atlanta with a 2-0 series lead. Smith started the game much like Drabek did the evening before, by setting the Braves down in order in the first inning.

Cox wasn't sure how his starting pitcher would react to the playoff surroundings and the overwhelming atmosphere sometimes created. He was making his first appearance in a league championship series—away from home—at a time when most young men his age are deciding what aftershave to use.

Avery didn't appear nervous when he threw his first pitch to Gary Redus. When he fell behind in the count and lost Redus on a 3-1 pitch, the crowd sensed that maybe there was a tense edge about him, and it was time to pounce. Avery quickly got ahead of Bell and slipped a called third strike past him on a nice curve that caught the outside corner. Amazingly, Avery punched out Van Slyke and Bonilla in the same fashion, and the Pittsburgh crowd was left stunned at the kid's sudden composure.

Atlanta mounted a rally of its own in the top of the second when Brian Hunter and Greg Olson led off with back-to-back singles. Lemke lined a one-hop single to right to load the bases, but Smith pitched out of the jam by inducing Belliard to ground into a force play, Buechele-to-Slaught. He then struck out Avery and forced Lonnie Smith to ground out to Bell.

Bonds lined a single off Avery's leg in the bottom of the second, but Buechele, Slaught, and Lind all went peacefully to remove any Pirate scoring threat. Avery stayed in control for the next three innings as he retired 11 straight Pirate batters. Lind broke up the string with a two-out single in the bottom of the fifth, but the Pirates couldn't put anything together.

It wasn't until the sixth inning that either team asserted itself. Justice lined a lead off single to rightfield and moved to second on Olson's one-out ground ball to second. Smith ran the count to 3-2 on Lemke, who then hit a high hopper to Buechele at third.

Buechele kept one eye on Justice coming to third and tried to keep his other eye on the ball as it bounced next to the bag.

Buechele took a gamble and tried to sweep the ball out of the air and tag Justice all in one motion, but the ball went skittering past his glove and down the leftfield line. There was no bad hop on the play, which was ruled a hit for Lemke. It was just a case of Buechele trying to come down with his glove while the ball was bouncing up from the ground.

Justice scored easily on the play, and Lemke managed to get to second despite his confusion as to whether the ball got past Buechele or not. Avery's confidence grew with each passing inning, and his teammates appeared ready to make their 1-0 lead stand up.

The Pirates had their cracks at Avery, but he remained strong and stared down every challenge. Bonilla led off the bottom of the seventh with an infield single, but was erased on Bonds' 4-6-3 double play. Redus punched a two-out single to left in the bottom of the eighth and promptly stole second. Bell sent a ground ball back through the middle that would have easily scored Redus had it gotten through to center field. Lemke made a great diving stop, however, and held Bell to an infield single, but more importantly, forced Redus to hold at third. Avery then pitched out of the jam by coaxing Van Slyke to ground into a force play for the third out.

Bonilla added to the dramatics by driving a double down the leftfield line to start the bottom of the ninth. Bonds worked Avery to a 3-1 count, but popped out to Belliard on a high and tight fastball that would have been ball four. Avery had pitched 8-1/3 innings and struck out nine Pirates, while allowing six hits and just two walks. But the Braves hadn't traded for Alejandro Pena to leave him sitting in the bullpen.

Cox could see his pitcher tiring just a bit, and with the right-handed-hitting Buechele stepping to the plate, it may have been better to bring in Pena, who was not only a right-hander, but someone Buechele had never faced, because he came from the American League in late August and had never faced the Braves.

Pena threw a strike to Buechele, but his next pitch bounced past Olson to the backstop and allowed Bonilla to move to third base with just one out. Buechele worked the count to 2-2 before chopping one right back to Pena, who looked Bonilla back to third and threw out Buechele for the second out.

The next move called for a pinch-hitter for Slaught and it was figured Leyland would go with left-handed-hitting catcher

Mike LaValliere. LaValliere hit .298 during the regular season and was a .284 career hitter against the Braves, including .300 in 1991. But Leyland sent up the switch-hitting Curtis Wilkerson instead, who hit just .188 during the regular season, but was 2-for-5 in his career against Pena.

It took three pitches for Pena to dispose of Wilkerson. The first two were swinging strikes, the last one was called. The series was tied at one game apiece, and the Braves were going home sorry they didn't sweep the Pirates, but still content with the split.

The Atlanta players felt good about coming home. They had gained a split in Pittsburgh and could avoid a return trip if they could sweep their three games with the Pirates in Atlanta. There wasn't any reason for the Braves to think they couldn't do that since they had won all six games at home against the Pirates during the regular season. The Pirates, however, had other ideas and were quick to point out that the playoffs are a new season and previous records should be left in the past.

The Braves were sending one of their most durable starters to the mound in John Smoltz. Besides being the only right-handed starter in Bobby Cox's rotation, Smoltz tied left-hander Charlie Leibrandt for the second highest number of innings pitched with 229.2. He finished the regular season 14-13 and had a 3.80 ERA. Smoltz would face John Smiley, the Pirates' second 20-game winner in as many years, and the ace of the Pirates' staff for 1991.

If the Atlanta Braves depended on anything in 1991, it was their starting pitching. They lived and died with the efforts of Glavine, Avery, Smoltz, and Leibrandt and with good reason. The four combined for 141 starts and accounted for 67 of the Braves' 94 wins.

"If anything were to beat Pittsburgh that year, it would have been the Braves' pitching," *Pittsburgh Post Gazette* sportswriter Paul Meyer said. "Atlanta had a tremendous staff and could come at you with four of the best in the league."

As promised, Atlanta fans were out in full force with their tomahawks poised to celebrate any and all Braves rallies. Among the 50,905 fans packed into Fulton County Stadium were Braves' owner Ted Turner and his wife, actress and exercise video queen, Jane Fonda. Seated next to them were their guests, former

President Jimmy Carter and his wife, Rosalyn. Many of the Pirates thought they had seen everything, until they saw a former president of the United States rocking his arm back and forth with a sponge tomahawk in his hand.

Pirate first baseman Orlando Merced, making his first start of the series,  silenced the crowd momentarily when he lashed at Smoltz's first pitch and sent  it  barreling over the rightfield wall for a home run. Smoltz had given up only 16 home runs all season and had not allowed one in his last 96 innings. The Pirates had gotten the start they had hoped for in Atlanta and took a 1-0 lead into the bottom of the first.

One of the things that is undoubtedly listed in all the scouting reports on Atlanta is to get out of the first inning without giving up any runs. The  Braves led the major leagues in 1991 first-inning runs with 124 and were liable to bust out at any given time.

Smiley appeared as though he would avoid such a fate as he retired Lonnie Smith and Terry Pendleton for two quick outs. Ron Gant kept the inning alive  for the Braves by driving a two-out double into leftfield, and he came around  to score the tying run on David Justice's RBI-double. Brian Hunter, who had started 64 games at first base as a Braves rookie in '91, drove the third  straight double of the inning down the leftfield line to give the Braves a 2-1 lead, and Greg Olson drove Smiley's well-placed changeup over the left field wall for a two-run homer and a 4-1 Braves lead.

The Pirates went quietly in the top of the second, while the Braves looked for more in the bottom of the inning. With two outs, Smith was hit in the left wrist by a Smiley fastball, and when Smiley had him picked off first just a couple of pitches later, Merced's throw to second sailed into leftfield and allowed Smith to go to third. Pendleton made the Pirates pay for Merced's throwing error by rapping a single to center, and the Braves' lead improved to 5-1.

The talk was spreading once again about the ineffectiveness of the Pirates' Big Three in post-season play. Van Slyke was 0-for-9 since his home run and  double in his first two at bats of the series, and Bonds was 1-for-7 so far  with two stolen bases. Bonilla was 4-for-8, but he had just one RBI, despite  the several opportunities he had to drive in runs.

One opportunity came in the top of the third when Bell lined a two-out double over the third base bag, and Van Slyke worked a walk on a 3-1 pitch from Smoltz. Bonilla left the runners stranded, however, when he popped up to Pendleton for the third out.

As the Pirates headed for the bottom of the third, Leyland had seen enough of Smiley and elected to bring in Bill Landrum, who with 17 saves in '91, was normally a late-inning pitcher. Greg Olson continued his torrid hitting in the series with a two-out single and later scored on Rafael Belliard's base hit to give the Braves a 6-1 lead.

Olson changed the complexion of the inning when he followed his hit by stealing second off Landrum. That forced the Pirates to intentionally walk Mark Lemke in order to face the light-hitting Belliard, but Leyland's strategy backfired when Belliard singled up the middle.

Bonds got his second hit of the series by leading off the Pirates' fourth with a single. He later stole second and scored on Jose Lind's one-out single, which followed a walk to Mike LaValliere. Leyland sent up reserve outfielder Gary Varsho to pinch hit for Landrum despite his 0-for-10 performance against the Braves in '91, and he promptly struck out to make it 0-for-11.

The Pirates came up empty again in the top of the sixth despite Steve Buechele's lead-off double. LaValliere popped out to short leftfield, Lind grounded out, and so did pinch-hitter Curtis Wilkerson as Buechele was left stranded at third.

Pittsburgh finally chipped away again at the Braves' lead in the seventh as Bell crashed a solo home run to leftfield to make it 6-3. Smoltz was then lifted in favor of left-handed reliever Mike Stanton, who promptly walked Van Slyke on a 3-1 pitch. After Van Slyke took second on a wild pitch, Bonilla and Bonds could not produce once again as both grounded out to end any further scoring threats.

Ron Gant gains most of his power for the Braves when he can pull the ball to leftfield. Of the 126 hits he had to the outfield in 1991, 100 were hit to leftfield, 17 to center, and just nine to right. Gant gave the Braves a four-run cushion again in the bottom of the seventh by cracking a solo homer to leftfield as the Braves added to their lead, 7-3.

Atlanta had managed to score just two runs in the first two games in Pittsburgh and its 1-2-3 hitters were a combined .091.

In Game 3, the tables turned as the Braves' top three batters hit a combined .364, and the entire Braves lineup went 6-for-8 with runners in scoring position.

Buechele and Slaught led off the top of the eighth with back-to-back singles, and after Lind struck out, pinch-hitter Lloyd McClendon walked to load the bases. Alejandro Pena, who had allowed just one hit in the last 25 batters he faced with runners in scoring position, came on to try to nail down his second save of the series.

Merced worked the count from Pena to 3-1, but popped the next pitch almost to the backstop where Olson caught it for the second out of the inning. Bell was the Pirates' last chance to mount a serious threat, but Pena caught him looking for the third out of the inning, and the Braves maintained their four-run lead.

Atlanta put the game well out of reach in the bottom of the eighth when Olson walked on four pitches to greet reliever Rosario Rodriguez. Lemke also walked, and Belliard laid down a perfect sacrifice to advance the runners for Sid Bream. It was a nice feeling for Pirate fans back in May when they saw Bream hit a solo home run in his first trip to Three Rivers Stadium following his signing with the Braves. But Pirate fans didn't need to see Bream send Rodriguez' 1-0 pitch into the Atlanta skyline for a three-run homer.

Talk about driving the stake in just a little further. Even Leyland wasn't very happy about that one.

"That game was a case where pitching let us down," he said at the time. "I was happy for Sid when he hit the home run back in May since it was at Three Rivers and all, but I'm not happy about the way it happened here today. Our pitchers had a job to do, and not one of them did it very well. I'm not going to reflect any more on what Sid Bream does because for right now, he's on the other side, and I'm not about to say how happy I am for his home run. I'm unhappy with our pitching staff, and if we don't do a better job against the hitters they have, the series will be over sooner than we think."

The Pirates went down quietly in the ninth, and the Braves had pulled in front two games to one with two more games still to be played in front of their hometown crowd.

The national media saw signs of 1990 in the Pittsburgh Pirates. Too many men left on base. No clutch hitting with runners in scoring position. No relief pitching. Was it a question of the big-name players coming up not so big in the playoffs? Were the Pirates "gagging," as some of the headlines referred to it?

"Getting beat 10-3 is not a question of gagging," Van Slyke said after the Pirates' third-game disaster. "But that's what people are going to think of us. Atlanta just kicked our butts and our pitching hasn't held up very well. We'll have to step it up a bit."

As expected, Doug Drabek could not play in Game 4 because of the severe hamstring injury he suffered while running the bases in Game 1. Left-hander Randy Tomlin, in his second year with the Pirates, got the call from Jim Leyland to make his first start ever in post-season play. The surprise announcement, however, came from Atlanta manager Bobby Cox, who decided he would forego the three-man rotation most commonly used in seven-game playoff series and use a fourth starter. That meant that Game 1 starter Tom Glavine would have to wait until the fifth game, while another Braves left-hander, Charlie Leibrandt, would get the call in Game 4.

The move appeared to be a good one, strategically, for Cox. Glavine got knocked around pretty good in his Game 1 outing, and it was felt that if Leibrandt could lift the Braves to a 3-1 series lead, Glavine would have the opportunity—with one more day's rest—to wrap up the series at home in Game 5.

Cox also undoubtedly looked at the stat sheets and the matchups that Leibrandt would most likely be facing. Bell was a .214 lifetime hitter against Leibrandt, while Van Slyke was a mere .143. Bonds came in at .200 for his career against the 35-year-old southpaw, and Slaught was at .192. On the plus side for the Pirates, Gary Redus was a career .333 hitter against Leibrandt, while Lind batted .300, Bonilla, .455, and Buechele, who had faced Leibrandt a few times in the American League, hit .344 against him. But the matchups seemed to favor Leibrandt and the Braves, because most of the Pirates' big hitters were struggling, and the ones who weren't were the ones he had done well against.

Leibrandt set the Pirates down in order in the top of the first, and the tomahawk-crazy crowd chanted in unison for the Braves to continue their first-inning success that they had enjoyed all season. Lonnie Smith started quickly on Tomlin by driving a ground-rule double into leftfield.

Terry Pendleton then flew out to Bonilla near the right-field line, which allowed Smith to tag to third, and Ron Gant drove Smith home by grounding out to Bell. The Pirates would have been thankful to get out of the inning having allowed just one run, but Tomlin appeared shaken after giving up a two-out single to David Justice. Brian Hunter moved Justice to second with a base hit and Greg Olson, who had owned Pirate pitching up to now, continued his pace with an RBI-single to left, which gave the Braves a 2-0 lead.

One of the reasons Atlanta was getting the job done was because of its consistency in Game 3 and— so far in Game 4— to drive home runners in scoring position. The Braves were now 7-for-12 in that situation over their last 10 innings, while the Pirates were a paltry 9-for-74 (.122) with runners in scoring position over the course of nine post-season games in the last two years.

The Pirates improved that mark slightly in the top of the second when Bonilla led off with a walk and advanced to second on Buechele's one-out single to left. Slaught, who had only one RBI and a career .227 average in post-season play coming into the series, scored Bonilla with a single to left, and the Braves lead was cut to 2-1.

Pittsburgh tied it in the top of the fifth when Redus reached base on a two-out single and hustled to third on a single to rightfield by Bell. Justice made a poor decision in trying to throw out the fleet-footed Redus at third, and the decision seemed even worse when Justice's throw got past Pendleton and allowed Redus to score the tying run.

The Pirates continued to squander scoring opportunities, while Tomlin had settled in nicely after his rough first inning to silence the Atlanta hitters. In the sixth, the Pirates had runners on first and second with one out, but couldn't get anything across. They left 11 runners on base in Game 3 and nine through seven innings of Game 4.

In the top of the eighth, Bonds got just his third hit of the series by hustling out an infield single to lead off the inning. Buechele, who was 3-for-3 in the game, sacrificed Bonds to second, but Slaught and Lind could not get him home.

Bob Walk, who was 9-2 during the regular season and had pitched three strong innings in relief of Drabek in Game 1, relieved Tomlin in the seventh inning and got some marvelous defensive support to keep the Pirates in the game. Smith led off the Braves' seventh with a bloop-single to center that Van Slyke's attempted dive just missed snaring. Smith, however, tried to stretch the hit to a double, but Lind backed up nicely on the play and threw a strike to Bell to nail Smith at second.

Justice sent a sharp line drive to the gap in left centerfield in the bottom of the eighth, but Bonds made a great diving catch to keep Justice off the bases and the Braves from breaking the tie. Defense came through again in the ninth for the Pirates, as Buechele darted quickly to his right and snared Olson's wicked line drive that was headed down the third-base line. Reliever Stan Belinda then walked Mark Lemke, but after Belliard sacrificed Lemke to second, Belinda got pinch-hitter Jerry Willard to pop up to Redus for the third out.

The Pirates and Braves were going to extra innings for the first time in NLCS play since the Dodgers and Mets played extra innings in 1988, but it was the Pirates who seemed to play with a little more desperation.

"Well, that was a game we definitely needed," Leyland said. "We didn't want to be playing Game 5 on their home field and down 3-1 in the series. We wanted to get a jump on them and have a chance to be in front when the series came back to Pittsburgh."

The clutch hitting that seems to disappear when the words "Pirates" and "playoffs" are mixed in the same sentence, reappeared in the top of the 10th inning for the Pirates and did so at a most opportune time.

Bobby Cox brought in lefty Kent Mercker (who was 5-3 with six saves in '91), to face the Pirates in the 10th, and he graciously walked Van Slyke on four pitches. Bonilla worked the count to 3-2 before he flew out to Justice, and after Bonds flew out to Smith, Buechele completed his perfect night by walking on a 3-2 pitch.

With Slaught—a .295 hitter in 1991—due up, Cox elected to go with right-handed rookie, Mark Wohlers. Leyland countered with his left-handed-hitting catcher, LaValliere, who hit .298 in '91. Leyland should actually have considered Cox's strategy a favor, because Slaught had struggled against Atlanta pitching during his two years in the National League. Slaught hit just .231 lifetime against the Braves and was a miserable .063 in '91. LaValliere, on the other hand, was a career .284 hitter against Atlanta pitching and was 6-for-20 (.300) with one home run and five RBIs against the Braves during the 1991 regular season.

LaValliere took a ball from Wohlers and then laced a single up the middle to drive home Van Slyke with the go-ahead run. Belinda put the Braves down in the order in the ninth, and the Pirates not only pulled out a 3-2, 10-inning win, but they also tied the series at two games each and assured themselves of a return trip to Three Rivers Stadium.

Before they made the trip home, however, there was one more contest to be decided in Atlanta. The Pirates would send Zane Smith to the mound against Atlanta's Game 1 starter, Tom Glavine. Both had lost their first outings: Glavine losing 5-1, against Doug Drabek, and Smith 1-0, to Steve Avery in Game 2. Smith, whose career post-season record dropped to 0-3, struck out five, walked two, and allowed eight hits to the Braves in Game 2, while Glavine made his first playoff start ever in Game 1 and gave up four earned runs, six hits, three walks, and had four strikeouts.

Atlanta threatened first, as it had in every game but the first one, as Lonnie Smith opened the bottom of the first inning with a single to left. Jay Bell quickly erased him by turning Terry Pendleton's ground ball into a double play, but Ron Gant kept the inning alive with a single to left. Gant then stole second— his fourth stolen base of the series— but Smith left him stranded by freezing David Justice for a called third strike.

Bobby Bonilla led off the Pirates' second with a double to left center, and Barry Bonds advanced him to third with a fly ball to deep centerfield. Bonds led the National League in 1991 by driving in 40.3 percent of the runners in scoring position when he batted, but he was hitting just .188 to this point in the series with no runs batted in. The Pirates failed to score in the inning as Steve Buechele struck out, and Don Slaught flew out to Justice in right field.

Atlanta put Smith in the same situation he faced in Game 2 in the bottom of the second. Brian Hunter led off with a base hit and moved to second on Greg Olson's walk. Mark Lemke singled sharply to right to load the bases, and shortstop Rafael Belliard batted with no outs.

In Game 2, Smith got Belliard to ground into a force play at home, struck out Avery, and retired Lonnie Smith on a ground ball. This time, Zane struck out Belliard and worked the count full on Glavine. As Smith delivered the 3-2 pitch, Glavine showed bunt, and Slaught saw Hunter break for home out of the corner of his eye. Glavine missed the bunt as the pitch sailed low and away, while Slaught made a good stop and chased Hunter back to third for the third out.

With one scoring opportunity squandered, the Braves had another in the bottom of the fourth. Justice reached second to lead off the inning on a two-base throwing error by first baseman Gary Redus. Hunter hit a high chopper in front of the plate that he didn't immediately run on. As Slaught came out of the box to try to field the ball, he ran into Hunter, who then started to run. Home plate umpire Bob Davidson immediately threw up his right hand and signaled Hunter out for interfering with Slaught and ordered Justice to go back to second.

It was a confusing inning that was about to get worse, and if fans and the media were looking for controversy, this was the inning to find it. Olson was the next batter, and he hit a sinking liner that had Van Slyke charging hard from centerfield. Van Slyke reached down at his shoe tops and caught the ball firmly in the webbing of his glove, and television replays showed the ball did not hit the ground, despite Olson's protests to the contrary.

Justice was still on second when Lemke came to bat and although he was hitting a mere .154 in the series to that moment, Lemke rolled a single past a diving Buechele and into leftfield. Bonds came up cleanly with the throw, but hesitated before making a play on Justice at home. Justice beat Bonds' throw to Slaught and had apparently given the Braves a 1-0 lead.

As Justice clumsily rounded third, Bell alertly kept him in sight. When Justice reached the plate and Davidson's safe call was made, Bell screamed for the ball. Slaught didn't hear his pleas and tossed the ball to Smith. The Pirates dugout was begging Smith to give the ball to Bell, and he finally did so with a quizzical look on his face.

A good umpiring crew will help each other out, and in this case, that's exactly what the crew for this series did. Bell saw Justice round third base but miss the bag, and so did second base umpire Doug Harvey. It was Harvey's job to back up on the play, so when Bell finally got the ball from Smith and stepped on third for an appeal, Harvey made the out call. Television replays were inconclusive on whether Justice actually touched the base or not. The specks of dust that flew when his foot ran over the base really didn't suggest whether he touched the bag. But he gave no argument, and the Pirates were out of yet another jam.

The Pirates finally capitalized on a scoring opportunity in the top of the fifth, and it came from a couple of unlikely sources. Bonds continued his playoff slump by popping up to Belliard for the first out, but Buechele walked and went to second on Slaught's single to left. Slaught was only 1-for-12 in his career against Glavine, but came through in this important situation. Lind, who was 2-for-15 in the series up to that point, stroked a single to right centerfield that scored Buechele to give the Pirates a 1-0 lead.

Pendleton, who was in a 3-for-19 slump, made the third out of the Braves' fifth with Lonnie Smith at third, but the Pirates couldn't capitalize twice when Braves' manager Bobby Cox practically dared them to.

In the top of the sixth, Van Slyke doubled to right center with one out. Cox ordered Glavine to intentionally walk Bonilla and take his chances with Bonds, who was 3-for-18 in his career against Glavine and had the same average in the series, with no extra-base hits and no RBIs. Bonds went to a 2-2 count and was caught looking on a pitch that just hit the outside corner. Buechele grounded out to Pendleton, and the Pirates came away with nothing.

Pittsburgh faced the same situation in the eighth inning, as Bell reached second on a one-out double and moved to third on Van Slyke's ground ball to Hunter at first. Cox defied the odds again by intentionally walking Bonilla, but Bonds could not make the Braves pay as he lifted a harmless fly ball to Gant in centerfield.

The Braves were equally inept offensively, as Pendleton shook his slump momentarily by lacing a two-out triple over Bonilla's head in rightfield. With Gant due up, Leyland pulled Zane Smith in favor of reliever Roger Mason, who had appeared in just 24 games for the Pirates in the regular season and had posted a 3-2 record with three saves. Gant was 0-for-7 with runners on base in the series, but his solo home run in Game 3 reminded Leyland of the danger his bat possessed. Gant worked the count full on Mason, but left Pendleton at third by popping up to Buechele.

Leyland used some curious strategy of his own in the top of the ninth. Buechele reached first safely on Lemke's throwing error and moved to second on Slaught's sacrifice bunt. Lind's ground ball out moved Buechele to third, and everyone figured Mason would be lifted for a pinch-hitter.

For one thing, the Pirates had an opportunity to drive home an insurance run—something Mason appeared unlikely to do. The Braves also had the left-handed hitting Justice due up first in the bottom of the ninth, and with Leyland being the percentages-type manager that he is, it was figured he would bring in a left-hander like Bob Patterson to pitch to Justice. But Leyland let Mason bat, and after he struck out to end the inning, Mason was the man Leyland sent to the mound to try to finish it for the Pirates.

"I had confidence in him," Leyland said of Mason. "I knew he could get the job done. I think we have a few guys who can go out there and finish a game for us. I just liked him at the time."

Upon further investigation, there was some justification for Leyland's decision to leave Mason, a right-hander, in the game. Justice is one of those few left-handed batters who hits better against left-handed pitchers than right-handers. Justice was a career .311 hitter against lefties, but only .259 against righties. The strategy appeared to be right on target as Justice struck out looking at a 3-2 pitch.

But the Braves had not reached this point by quitting. Reserve outfielder Tommy Gregg was sent up to bat for Hunter, and he came through with a base hit to rightfield. Olson followed with a single to left, and the Braves suddenly had the winning run on base.

Mason remained on the mound to face Lemke, who was 2-for-3 in the game. Lemke hit a ground ball to Lind, who flipped a sure throw to Bell for the force-out at second. Lemke's hustle just beat Bell's throw to first to keep the inning alive. But with the tying run at third, Mason got Jeff Blauser to fly out to Bonilla to give the Pirates a 1-0 win and a 3-2 lead in the series.

Doug Drabek was back to give it a try in Game 6 after spending much of the time since Game 1 nursing his severe hamstring injury. His opponent was Steve Avery, who at age 21, became the second youngest pitcher to ever win a championship game when he beat the Pirates, 1-0, in Game 2.

Both teams struggled again offensively, but two of the best pitchers in the second half of the season were having a lot to do with that. Drabek and Avery seemed to match each other pitch for pitch, and as the game grew into its twilight, it looked once again like the first team to push a run across would come out victorious.

The Pirates had a couple of scoring opportunities wasted in the sixth and eighth innings because of double plays, and the Braves repeatedly left runners standing at third. Drabek left Lonnie Smith standing on third in the top of the eighth when Pendleton, who was 2-for-9 with runners in scoring position, flew out to Bonds in leftfield.

Avery set a new league championship series record with 17 scoreless innings when he set the Pirates down in the eighth. He gave up a one-out single to Buechele, but was still throwing at around 94 miles per hour as he retired Slaught and Lind to end the inning.

Atlanta had an NLCS record of consecutive scoreless innings going into the top of the ninth as the number had reached 26. The Braves had not scored since the first inning of Game 4, and their fans were wondering if they would ever score again. Gant drew a one-out walk from Drabek in the top of the ninth and stole second after Sid Bream flew out. It was Gant's sixth stolen base of the series, which established a new NLCS record.

Just when it appeared Drabek would pitch out of yet another jam, the Braves broke out of their scoring slump when Olson—who had hit .241 during the regular season but was hitting .333 in the series— lined a two-out double down the left-field line. Drabek retired Gregg for the last out, but he became a spectator in the bottom of the ninth and could only hope the Pirates would break out of their own scoring drought.

Cox wasted little time in calling on Pena, whose 13 saves in 13 opportunities since the trade that brought him to Atlanta, made him the ace of the Braves bullpen.

Reserve outfielder Gary Varsho led off the Pirates' ninth with a pinch-hit single to center and moved to second on Orlando Merced's sacrifice bunt. Bell hit a sharp line drive to rightfield, but Justice had him positioned perfectly and made the catch for the second out. It all came down to Van Slyke, who had not driven in a run since Game 1. Varsho made it to third when Pena threw a wild pitch, his second of the series, and Van Slyke managed to work the count full.

Pena had said from the beginning of the series that there would be no secrets about what he would throw. It would be a steady diet of fastballs, fastballs, fastballs, and it would be up to the batters to hit it. Up to now, the Pirates hadn't done very well, but Van Slyke stayed alive by fouling off five fastballs in a row.

Drabek looked on from the dugout. He had pitched as fine a ballgame as he could, and as he held his face in a towel, he hoped the game wouldn't come down to that one pitch that stayed up for Olson in the top of the ninth.

"I'll never forget the effort Drabek gave us in that game," Ray Miller said. "After he hurt himself in Game 1, his left leg was black and blue from his hip to his toes. He spent the next three days in the training room because he wanted to pitch again. We were hoping to get five innings from him, but there he was in the eighth and ninth, standing there with tears in his eyes, hoping we could score a run. That was the gutsiest performance in baseball I've ever seen."

Van Slyke readied himself once again in the batter's box, hoping to put one of Pena's fastball pitches in play; hoping to put the Pirates into the World Series. Two of the foul balls Van Slyke hit appeared as though they would do just that as they had home-run distance, but hooked harmlessly into the Pirates' bullpen.

The diet called for another fastball, but Pena fooled everybody with a changeup, his first of the entire series. The pitch clearly froze Van Slyke as he never took the bat off his shoulder and watched it hit the outside corner. Umpire Bruce Froemming threw up his right arm and called the third strike as Atlanta celebrated a huge victory.

Pena had earned his third save of the series, and Atlanta had evened it up once again to force a Game 7. It was the second 1-0 win for Avery, who was about as close to perfect as a pitcher can be. It was also the third 1-0 decision of the series, which marked the first time in 137 post-season series, including World-Series play, that such a feat had taken place.

The series, plus 162 games preceding it, had come down to just one game. One team would pack up for the season; another would prepare for the World Series.

"You dream about this for practically your whole life," Bonilla said of playing in a Game 7. "You never think it's going to take place, but now I'm actually in one. This one could end the season, or we could end up playing seven more. It's funny how you play six months of a season for two weeks of hell. But it's a lot of fun, and I'll never forget it."

The Pirates sent a well-rested John Smiley to the mound for the deciding game against his Game 3 counterpart John Smoltz, who won that decision in the only laugher of the series, 10-3. Smoltz was an interesting sidelight to the series because he had struggled so badly during the first half of the season, only to have a remarkable turnaround in the second half.

Smoltz fell nine games below .500 in the season's first half at 2-11. His earned run average suffered as well, as he could do no better than 5.16. He attributed his second-half turnaround to an Atlanta psychologist and whether that was the case or not, Smoltz went 12-2 over the rest of the season and came in with a 2.63 ERA. He became the first pitcher since 1918 to finish a season above .500 after dropping nine games below that level in the same season.

Smiley lasted just two innings in Game 3 and gave up four earned runs and five hits. He had allowed only five first-inning walks all season, which was the second-best mark in the National League, but he opened Game 7 by walking Lonnie Smith on a 3-2 pitch. Pendleton followed with a single under Lind's glove into centerfield, and that allowed Smith to make it to third.

Gant drove Smith home with a sacrifice fly to left that Bonds caught right in front of the wall. That gave the Braves a 1-0 lead and after Justice struck out, Smiley appeared in good shape to pitch out of the jam. Hunter erased those thoughts on the first pitch thrown to him, however, by planting the ball into the second-level club boxes in left field and the Braves had a 3-0 lead. Olson followed with a single to left, and Leyland had seen enough. He strolled dejectedly to the mound and signaled for right-hander Bob Walk from the Pirates bullpen.

John Smiley had won 20 games for the Pittsburgh Pirates in 1991 and had pitched in well over 200 innings. He pitched a grand total of 2-2/3 innings against the Braves in the 1991 NLCS and allowed seven earned runs, eight hits, and two home runs.

The only thing in the Pirates' favor now was the fact that it was still only the first inning. Walk pitched out of the inning without any further problems, and the Pirates knew they still had nine cracks at the Braves if their pitching could hold up.

Merced quickly gave the Pirates life in the bottom of the first as he rapped a single right back at Smoltz and into centerfield. Bell worked the count to 3-1, and he too singled to center. Van Slyke, who hit .265 during the regular season but was batting .190 for the series excited the less-than capacity crowd of 46,932 by rocketing a fly ball toward rightfield. Off the bat, the ball looked like it was heading for the seats, and the game would have been tied. But Justice calmly backed up and caught it with his back against the wall.

Merced advanced to third on the play, but Bonilla popped up to Lemke at second, and Bonds grounded out to kill the Pirates' threat. It was an inning wasted, another scoring opportunity down the drain. The Pirates' three top hitters had carried the team all season, but when they were counted on at the most important times in their careers, they had not come through. After the Pirates' first-inning threat was over, Van Slyke, Bonds, and Bonilla had stretched their hitless streak with runners on base to a combined 33 at bats.

Bonds, who was 0-for-15 in the series with runners in scoring position but 4-for-12 with the bases empty, got his first extra-base hit of the series with a one-out double in the Pirates' fourth. Buechele popped up for the second out, and after LaValliere reached safely on Lemke's throwing error, Lind bounced out to end another threat.

Hunter added an RBI-single in the fifth to give the Braves a 4-0 lead, and although Walk pitched strong relief into the sixth inning, the Pirates were left to merely play out the string. When Smoltz retired the Pirates 1-2-3 in the bottom of the ninth, the Atlanta Braves came storming out of their dugout to celebrate the continuation of a storybook season.

The Pittsburgh Pirates had their own stories to think about as well. Like how they played such terrific baseball for 162 games for a second straight season, but left their powerful offense behind when the post-season rolled around—again for the second season in a row.

"Cincinnati's pitching did it to them in 1990, and it appears Atlanta did it with pitching in '91," Paul Meyer said. "When you come home with a 3-2 series lead and don't score a run in the last two games, it has to be the pitching. Jim Leyland always reminds me that in 1987, the [Minnesota] Twins won the World Series with pitching and they won only five more games than the Pirates that year. Pitching will carry you a long way, and that was something the Braves had a lot of in '91."

Whatever the case, the Pirates had come within one game of culminating their long resurrection with a trip to the World Series. Instead they would watch on television once again, while the Braves lost a thrilling seven-game series to the Twins. It was only fitting that the deciding game ended in the bottom of the 10th as the Twins' Dan Gladden scored the winning run on a bases-loaded single. The final score: Minnesota 1, Atlanta 0.

# When Baseball
# Comes Second

On July 14, 1991, the Pirates were returning home on a USAir commercial flight from Cincinnati to Pittsburgh. They had just swept the Reds in a four-game weekend series, and the mood was festive as the team enjoyed the widening of their lead in the National League East to 3-1/2 games over the St. Louis Cardinals.

In first class, manager Jim Leyland discussed pitching matchups and the Pirates' upcoming three-game series with the Houston Astros at Three Rivers Stadium. The flight had just left Cincinnati when Leyland felt the first rumblings in his chest.

"I didn't know what to think," Leyland said of the pain that seemed to increase with every passing minute. "I told [third base coach and close friend] Gene Lamont, and he got [trainer] Kent Biggerstaff right away."

Suddenly, thoughts of excitement over the Pirates' sweep of the Reds went through Leyland's head. "Yeah, that's what I'm feeling," his mind reasoned. Thoughts of too much coffee and not enough food also raced through his mind. All the while, his chest pounded steadily and his heart beat faster by the minute.

The news of a possible heart attack was relayed to the cockpit by Biggerstaff, and the flight crew immediately radioed to the Columbus Airport that they needed to land immediately because of a passenger emergency and that paramedics would be requested.

News of the diversion reached the coach compartment of the aircraft, and when players slowly discovered the reason, they asked what they could do and most bowed their heads in prayer. Biggerstaff and Lamont never left Leyland's side, and when the plane made its unscheduled approach to the Columbus jetway, paramedics were on the scene as requested.

Heart attack is usually the first thought that comes to mind when someone suffers chest pains, and the medical personnel who met the plane treated Leyland's case no differently. Lamont and Biggerstaff accompanied Leyland to the hospital, while the USAir flight returned to its scheduled destination minus one manager, but full of concerned and somber passengers.

"It's scary because I had never experienced anything like that before," said Leyland, who was assured at the hospital that he had not suffered a heart attack. "I felt very different, and it made me feel even more scared. The airline was fantastic. The captain reacted quickly, and the personnel on the ground in Columbus treated us great. Fortunately, my heart was fine, and I don't really think about it any more."

The question Leyland gets asked most about his phantom heart attack experience is if he thinks the pains were a sign that he works too hard at what he does and maybe he should slow down and think of the life around him.

"I honestly don't think of it as a sign," he said. "At that time of the year, I'm usually tired, and I think a manager should be. If you're not tired you probably haven't been doing your work right. If I think about that incident, I just think it helps me to remember that the only thing we're assured of is yesterday."

❧

Too often, people get immersed in their jobs and don't take the time to see the other things in life that surround them. Whether a person's job is in medicine, law, teaching, street-cleaning, or sports, they sometimes get lost in their work and never notice the flowers growing in their back yards and birds singing on their window sills.

Jim Leyland spent 11 years of his life managing in the minor leagues, making the travel plans, driving the team bus, doing whatever it took to meet his players' needs. Baseball became everything to him, and there was little time for anything else. Leyland then spent four years in Chicago, coaching third base for Tony LaRussa's White Sox and watching every move LaRussa made in hopes of gathering information on what he could do when his day as a major league manager came.

Again there was no time for himself. When he came to Pittsburgh, Jim Leyland thought of finding a small apartment, convenient enough for a bachelor who thought of nothing every day but baseball and what he could do to right the ship of the Pittsburgh Pirates, which had sailed off course miserably for the past two seasons.

Leyland found a friend in a Pirate employee named Katie. She helped him find his Pittsburgh apartment and even helped him pick out the furniture. Gradually, the couple spent more and more time together as friends, and when Katie invited Jim to her parents' house for dinner one Easter Sunday, they realized their friendship was turning into something more.

"We just hit it off after that," Leyland said. "Baseball was, and always will be my livelihood, but meeting Katie let me know there are other things in life besides baseball. She's a helluva gal, and I know if the day comes when I no longer do have baseball, I'll still have her, and that makes me feel comfortable."

Jim and Katie Leyland were married in November, 1987, by Jim's brother, Tom, a Catholic priest. Katie went from front office employee to baseball wife in a very short time, but she knew the consequences of such a transaction and was willing to pay the price.

"It's tough on her," Jim Leyland said, "because we're gone so much during the season, but she's always been great about it. She's very supportive."

When your whole life has been baseball, "tough" is losing six or seven games in a row or blowing a lead in the bottom of the ninth inning. "Tough" doesn't begin to describe a baseball wife facing her husband after their child is stillborn.

"No one knows the answers as to why those things happen," Jim Leyland said. "There's no blame to put on anyone. You just have to have faith and let God take charge of the situation."

Katie and Jim discovered at the hospital that their first baby no longer had a heartbeat, despite the contractions she was feeling. She would have to go through with the delivery knowing full well there would be no positive result when it was all over. Suddenly, Katie became the strongest person Jim Leyland had ever known. "That was the toughest thing I had ever seen in my life," he said. "She knew there was nothing for her in the end, but she had to go through with the delivery anyway. I held him in my arms and he was beautiful . . . a beautiful baby boy. I'll never forget that."

Jim Leyland talks openly about the loss of his son, because he feels it is an experience that he and Katie should never forget. "You can't put it aside as though it never happened," he said. "If you pretend it never happened, then it becomes worse. It has happened to millions of people, and it's a tragedy, but holding my son is an experience I never want to forget and Katie and I have felt comfortable by just leaving everything in God's hands."

The couple left it in God's hands to try again a year later, and when Katie became pregnant once more, they rejoiced at the thought of this second opportunity and said every prayer they could think of in hopes for success this time around.

That success was born to Katie and Jim on October 11, 1991, and his name was Patrick James Leyland. While the Pirates were fighting the Atlanta Braves for the right to play in the World Series, Katie fought for her son's survival, and this time the Leylands came out victorious.

"Everything was going fine," Jim said. "But we were being cautious because everything was fine right up to the time we got to the hospital the first time and found the baby had no heartbeat. It all came at a great time, because we were in the playoffs and Katie was having the baby."

And for one of the few times in his life, Leyland found a reason to put baseball second to something else around him.

"Of course, Katie and the baby were on my mind every minute," he said. "I'll never forget the feeling I had in that delivery room when I saw that baby come out alive and healthy. It was a miracle, an absolute miracle. I'll never forget the doctor's words and how much sense they made: 'It's kind of weird' he told us, 'because four people usually go into the delivery room and five come out.' I kept thinking how true that really was."

Patrick was born on an off-day during the 1991 NLCS, but Leyland said he would have been with Katie no matter what day she had had the baby. "It just proves what a great baseball wife Katie is," he said. "She chose perfect timing by having the baby on an off-day."

&

After almost every Pirate home game, Jay Bell heads to a special place in Three Rivers Stadium that, for him, holds the very essence of his life. While most of the players are in the clubhouse digging into the post-game dinner spread, Bell is down the hall in a room adjacent to the Pirates' clubhouse.

For now, he is oblivious to the fans who are just outside the door to the press gate, which is no more than 10 yards from where he is standing. Bell has become a popular figure with Pirate fans over the last couple of years, and he is usually not one to turn his back on the public. His face is recognizable enough, but the fans have no problem realizing it is the Pirates' shortstop that is kneeling in front of an unknown doorway, his uniform still carrying the dirt of another day at the office.

"Jay! Jay Bell! Can I have your autograph?" one admirer calls to him. Soon other fans join in, while inside the room, a little girl plays with her toys, unaware of the world of professional baseball that surrounds her.

Bell does not acknowledge the fans who are limited to the outside doors by the watchful eyes of stadium security. When he leaves in street clothes, maybe then Bell will have time for an autograph. But for now, he has more important things on his mind.

"Bri-an-na," Bell calls in his softest voice to the little girl in the Pirates' family room. He says her name a couple more times and finally, Brianna looks in his direction. Her face lights up with a smile that stretches from ear to ear, and although she doesn't know much about baseball, Brianna Bell knows her daddy's face. Toys are suddenly pushed to the side, everything else can wait. Her arms stretch wide to the man in the uniform. Daddy's here, and that's all that matters.

Jay Bell knows the feeling of losing a child. It happened to him and his wife, Laura, in the early part of 1990. Laura was six months into her pregnancy when the miscarriage occurred, and together they shared the hurt and the uncertainty of possibly living a future without a family of their own. But they carried on because of their strong faith.

"The most important thing in my life is my relationship with Christ," Bell said. "Everything in life is vanity anyway, but my Christianity is very important to me. Losing a child was a tough thing for Laura and I to go through, but we believe there is some purpose for everything, and we knew we could make it through the uncertain times."

So many times, the complications in a pregnancy go undetected until it is too late to do anything about them. A child is lost, and the parents are left to wonder, "Why us?" Laura and Jay felt no different for a while, but they were comfortable in knowing they would be able to try again.

It was about a year later when the news came that Laura was pregnant again and although the couple was excited, they remained cautious because of the complications that arose the first time around.

"Laura did have similar complications the second time," Jay Bell said. "But we were much better prepared to handle them this time around. Now we have a beautiful little girl."

Brianna Bell survived the complications and was born August 5, 1991. Her fight to be a part of this world seems to mirror the competitive nature that is within her father. Jay Bell loves to play baseball, and he hates to lose. Before Brianna was born, he would literally scream at his bat to flush out the anger of a strikeout. Then the bat would usually be splintered against the wall of the runway adjacent to the Pirate dugout. He pressured himself for perfection and seldom accepted the fact that errors and strikeouts were a part of the game.

Then Brianna came along and changed all that.

"Strikeouts and errors don't even become a comparison when I think of her and hold her in my arms," Bell said. "She's definitely the joy of my life."

Jay Bell still hates to lose, but his days of throwing bats and yelling at himself until he's blue in the face are over. When he is on the field, his concentration is strictly on the game at hand. "If you let your mind wander, you'll more than likely take a line drive off your noggin," he quipped.

But now, if Bell makes an error in the field or takes a called third strike, he pictures the beauty that awaits him in a room just down the hallway, and all the mistakes in the world become second nature.

"Brianna has given me a new perspective on the way I look at things," Bell said. "That's why I make a detour to the family room after every game. I can't get enough of holding her in my arms and making sure that she'll be there when that game is over." ,

The game is his profession for now, and Bell is well aware of its importance. But someday the game will no longer be a part of his life. Baseball will pass him by, just as it has for many of the greatest names ever to wear a major league uniform. Some retire with grace, style and dignity. Others hang on to the game as if they have nothing else to cling to.

That is why Jay Bell stands outside an unknown doorway In the depths of Three Rivers Stadium every night, holding a little girl, rocking her gently in his strong arms and whispering words that only she can hear and smile to.

That is a time when baseball comes a distant second.

ॱ॰

The world according to Andy Van Slyke has not always been about baseball. He grew up in Utica, New York, which, because of the weather, didn't allow him much time for the sport. "Our high school only played 18 to 20 games a year, and half of those were in the snow," he said.

Instead it was basketball that Van Slyke picked up on, and as is his nature, wanted to become successful at. He was a small forward on the New Hartford High School team, where his three-foot vertical leap and plus-20 points per game average helped him land a spot in the New York Empire State Games.

Van Slyke also earned All-American honors in baseball as a senior, and when the St. Louis Cardinals made him their No. 1-selection in the June 1979, free agent draft, he made baseball his life. Since that time, he has won five Gold Glove awards for his play in centerfield, played in two All-Star games, and has hit consistently around .275 for his career.

He is the Pirates' team prankster and is not above the old shaving-cream-on-top-of-the-unsuspecting-player's-cap routine. He also wears the funny glasses with the grossly-protruding eyeballs with the best of them. He even did the weather segment on a local television station because of his profound interest in meteorology. That is how some players get through the everyday life of baseball and its often-routine habits.

Like most players, Van Slyke gets consumed by the game and loses himself in the thoughts of what can be done to break out of a slump, or what the tendencies of certain pitchers are and where he should position himself against certain batters when he's in the outfield.

At a time when baseball begins to take shape for another season, Van Slyke realized one day in spring training that baseball shouldn't always be a man's primary focus. It was February 28, 1992, and the Van Slykes were visiting Lauri's mother at her home in a Bradenton, Florida residential complex.

Andy was laying on the floor watching television in the living room, trying to forget the back pain that had become a spring training ritual for him by now. This year, however, the pain was considerably worse, something Van Slyke called a constant migraine headache in his back. It hurt to swing a bat, it was almost unbearable to tie his shoes or put on socks.

Some three blocks away, the Van Slyke children, A.J., Scott, and Jared, were enjoying a swim in the community pool and basking in the warm Florida sunshine. Lauri Van Slyke was nearby, but it was five-year-old Scott who reached into the hot tub for what he thought was a sunken doll or toy. What he pulled out, however, was the body of his three-year-old brother, Jared, blue and unconscious. A neighbor called 911, and Lauri's brother began administering CPR to the motionless child.

Eight-year-old A.J. jumped on his bike and raced back to his grandmother's house shrieking the first words that would come out of his mouth. "Jared drowned! Jared drowned!" he screamed.

The glaring pain of another baseball season was gone in an instant as Andy Van Slyke leapt to his feet and ran as fast as he could to the nearby swimming pool. His feet pounded on the hard pavement, but he had found the inner strength that everyone seems to find in a crisis.

"It's unbelievable what goes through your mind," Van Slyke recalled. "All I heard was, Jared drowned. And as I was running, all I kept thinking was, How come I don't feel any pain? How is it that I'm able to run like this? It was the strangest feeling, like my feet weren't even hitting the ground. I can't explain it, but if Jared had been five miles away that day, I still could have run it."

When he reached the ambulance door, Van Slyke shoved a paramedic aside and was relieved to see his son breathing. His eyes were open and rolling around his head, looking curiously at the medical gadgets surrounding him. Jared spent the night in a hospital and came home the next day, ready to live the life of a normal three-year-old again.

Andy Van Slyke is also a strong believer in Christ, and he knew that belief was what carried his family through that nightmarish ordeal, and would have carried him on should things have turned out differently.

"If Jared had died," he said, "It would have been like a nail being driven into by a two-by-four. There would have been terrible pain and anguish. If you pull the nail out, there is still a hole, but my belief in Jesus is such that he would have filled that hole."

≈

Andy Van Slyke is one of the most frequently requested Pirates when it comes to autographs, or interviews, or public appearances. If possible, he would no doubt be passed around the city of Pittsburgh 24 hours a day, signing baseball cards or taking pictures with the various charitable organizations around town.

During the regular season, a baseball player's time is very limited because his profession is one he must devote the majority of his time to. It is not the "show up at the ball park, put on a uniform, take a few swings and go home routine" a lot of people think it is. Van Slyke usually arrives at the clubhouse about four or five hours before game time. There is time spent in the training room for treatment to his back or whatever else is ailing him.

After a little time of relaxation or camaraderie with some of the other players and coaches, he begins to get dressed. He will put one sock on and  test the glove that is his best friend in baseball. Then he will put the other sock on, maybe his uniform pants as well, and take a couple of light practice swings with his bat. It is part of the routine that every player has.

Soon, he will be out on the field with the rest of his teammates going through the daily exercise regime that hometown fans never get to see. It is still about two-and-a-half hours before the first pitch, and Van Slyke is tossing a ball lightly with Jeff King or whomever will put up with his surprise knuckle ball tosses every once in a while. The home team takes batting practice first and when that is over, most of the players return to the clubhouse for the last hour or so before they take the field.

It is September 25, 1992, a cool, gray evening that seems better suited to football than baseball in Pittsburgh, but the Pirates are on the field taking batting practice in preparation for their 7:35 p.m. game with the New York Mets. The Pirates public relations department  hosts an honorary bat boy or girl for each game who gets to sit in the dugout for a portion of batting practice to meet and talk with some of the players as they pass by.

On this evening, the honor was bestowed on a young girl with a noticeably shy demeanor and a smile that would melt the hearts of many young suitors. Most of the kids get the opportunity because their parents' company is being  recognized that game for whatever reason, but this young lady, who was known only as Mandy, was in attendance because of a special wish she made.

The Pittsburgh Chapter of the Make-A-Wish Foundation helps kids with life-threatening illnesses fulfill a special request they may have in order that their days may be a little bit brighter. Fourteen-year-old Mandy sat patiently with  her father on the same bench that some of her heroes used every day. She tried her best to stay calm, but her blushing face and trembling fingers could not hide her excitement.

For the past nine months Mandy had been dealing with a form of cancer. In March of 1992, doctors discovered a malignant tumor on her back, and although they were able to remove it surgically, the doctors also had to remove two of Mandy's ribs and half of another one.  She also lost a large portion of muscle and tissue in her back and rib cage, and she continued to face chemotherapy treatments through April of 1993.

Chemotherapy is often known to wear a person out , but as the wonder of professional baseball surrounded her, Mandy was anything but exhausted. She loved the Pirates, and her uniform jersey with the number 18 on the back told everyone who her favorite player was.

"She's a big Pirates fan," Mandy's mother, Kathy said. "She and her dad usually go to several games a year, but this past season has obviously been kind of difficult."

When the Make-A-Wish Foundation informed Mandy that she was about to realize her dream of meeting Andy Van Slyke, she was under the impression that she would get to visit the dugout for a couple of minutes and maybe shake his hand or get an autograph. What she didn't expect was the limousine that escorted her and her parents to Three Rivers Stadium and the tickets the Pirates provided for the game, which were in Jim Leyland's own personal box.

"It was all so overwhelming," Kathy said as she recalled the evening. "Everyone went out of their way to see that Mandy was well taken care of."

Mandy seemed more than satisfied as she sat in the dugout and admired the field that was no more than 20 yards away from her. "What will you say to him when he comes out?" Mandy's father, Steve, asked her. "I don't know," she replied. "I have no idea what to say."

Patty Paytas, the Pirates' community relations director, offered suggestions to the obviously shy teenager. Things like asking him how he is or what his favorite movies are.

As they waited, Patty introduced Mandy to other players who passed by. Doug Drabek shook her hand, put his arm around her, and posed for a picture with her. Jim Leyland, Jay Bell, Jose Lind, and several others did the same. They signed her pennant. They signed a baseball. They gave her hugs and offered encouraging words. She thanked them all, and her eyes told them how much she loved them.

Mandy had spent practically all of her time in the dugout that afternoon looking over her shoulder, hoping to find the right words and wanting not to miss the person she had waited so long to meet. But when the opportunity finally came, she was lost in her thoughts, admiring the baseball that had rapidly been covered with signatures.

"Hi, I hope I didn't keep you waiting too long," a voice said from behind, as a long arm that presumably belonged with the voice slipped around Mandy's shoulders. She turned quickly in surprise and noticed the number 18, just like she had on her jersey. She was speechless. She began to cry softly.

Mandy's dream had come true, and with the help of the Pirates and the Make-A-Wish Foundation, Andy Van Slyke had made it all possible. He posed for pictures with her for what seemed like an entire roll of film, and he signed everything from baseball cards to the back of her Pirates jersey. She brought him gifts, including a pack of bubble gum, which he promptly opened and popped in his mouth.

He spent about 20 minutes with Mandy, discussing everything from school to boys to baseball. No one knows if she ever discovered what Andy's favorite movie was, but her smiling face spoke clearly of the joy she had found that day. Her hopes and expectations were fulfilled, and it became a day she would remember for the rest of her life.

*Hope* is the key word at the Make-A-Wish Foundation. Judith Augustine, who is a coordinator at the Foundation's Pittsburgh chapter, said experiences like Mandy's give hope to young people and encourage them to never give up, no matter how tough the road they must travel becomes.

"People commonly refer to cancer as a terminal illness," Augustine said. "But we will never use that word at Make-A-Wish. We may say an illness is 'life-threatening' but to say the word 'terminal' leads a child to believe there is no hope. Mandy is a person who has obviously shown that there is hope and there always will be."

Doctors have discovered no further cancer in Mandy, and it is their hope that when the chemotherapy treatments are finished in April of 1993, she will be able to lead a normal life, just like any other young teenage girl.

"She stays positive through all the treatments and all the doctors' visits she goes through," Mandy's mother said "She knows there will be further testing, but she won't let the difficult things get in the way. She'll go to more games as the seasons go on, and if she can't be there in person, she'll be watching the Pirates on TV."

Undoubtedly, Mandy will keep a watchful eye on centerfield and remember the day she met her favorite Pirate in person. She will never forget the joy that one day brought to her life.

The joy Andy Van Slyke felt was real also, and the smile he had on his face was no act. A young lady endeared herself to him that day, and he felt better knowing that he had something to do with making her day a little bit brighter. But it wasn't just Mandy's day he had brightened. It was her *life*. What stories she would have to tell to those who couldn't witness them: "I got my picture taken with Andy Van Slyke," she would say, "He signed my shirt and put his arm around me, and he chewed the bubble gum I gave him."

Sometimes, baseball isn't the only thing that matters in life. Even when you're a baseball player. Sometimes, all the home runs and diving catches in the world don't add up to the feeling one gets at the sight of a pretty girl's smiling face.

At one time or another, baseball seemed less important to a few members of the Pirates' coaching staff as well.

Hitting coach Milt May had an outstanding career as a major league catcher, including three full seasons with the Pirates. His father, Merrill "Pinky" May, was a former major league infielder with the Phillies. His son hoped to be a major leaguer someday.

The hopes of a star high school player were in jeopardy in December 1990, when Milton Scott May, Jr., was in a terrible automobile accident near the family's home in Bradenton, Florida. He suffered severe head injuries and lapsed into a coma. Doctors feared the worst, and whether or not Scott would play baseball again compared little to the thoughts and hopes for his survival.

Bobby Bonilla also made Bradenton his off-season home when he was with the Pirates, and when he learned the news of his young friend, it hit him hard. He spent much time at the hospital, holding Scott May's hand and willing him not to give up.

A couple of months passed and Scott did wake up. He would survive. And although it would take months of physical therapy and patience, the doctors felt he could return to as normal a life as possible. He still dreamed of playing baseball again, and Milt May would never doubt that his son could do it.

In spring training of 1991, when Scott was going through

the arduous task of rehabilitation, Bonilla wanted to pay tribute to him in some way. Scott wore number 23 for his high school baseball team, so when the Pirates' regular season came around, there was Bonilla starting in rightfield for the Pirates, and wearing number 23 on his jersey instead of his usual number 25. He wore it the entire season, and there was no one happier than Bonilla—except maybe Milt May—when Scott May threw out the ceremonial first pitch before Game 2 of the 1991 National League Championship Series.

"Sometimes you have to remember the people who have touched your life in some way," Bonilla said of his decision to change numbers. "You can't give up just because doctors around you are saying they're not sure. I knew he could make it back, and I didn't doubt him for a minute."

Rich Donnelly has been a member of the Pirates' coaching staff since Jim Leyland was named manager in 1986. He spent the first six years as bullpen coach, but realized his goal in 1992 when third base coach Gene Lamont took a job as manager of the Chicago White Sox, and Leyland named Donnelly as Lamont's replacement.

A third base coach has to be on his toes. He has to concentrate in every possible situation, and he must be able to react at a moment's notice. He must have one eye on the batter or baserunners, and the other eye on the manager in the dugout. His decisions are made in an instant, and once they are made, there is no looking back or second-guessing.

On April 16, 1992, Donnelly's daughter Amy turned 18. As each day passed, the Donnellys were thankful to have their only daughter with them. She was diagnosed with brain cancer in 1990, and since that time, life for Amy was no longer the way it should have been for a normal teenage girl. She has made countless visits to hospitals for radiation and chemotherapy treatments, but she never let the pain or despair show through.

"She's been brave through it all," her father said before a September afternoon of baseball in Three Rivers Stadium. "I tell you what, sometimes I look at her and wonder how she puts up with all that stuff, but then I realize it's because she's a fighter.

She just has it in her not to quit, and I think that's what keeps her going."

Other members of the Donnelly family did their best to keep Amy going as well. Her 20-year-old brother, Bubba, is a member of the Robert Morris College basketball team. The campus is situated in Coraopolis, Pennsylvania, a suburb of Pittsburgh, and Rich   never misses a game. Amy was often a visitor to her brother's games as well, but sometimes her illness prevented her. She spent part of her time during the school year in Texas where she received the treatments for her illness.

Bubba understood the times Amy couldn't make it, and she knew in her heart that Bubba, who is an excellent three-point shooter, played the games for her. One of Amy's biggest thrills was to see her brother play on national television in the 1992 NCAA basketball tournament. Robert Morris lost a first-round game to UCLA, but Amy was ecstatic to see her brother running up and down the court with the rest of his teammates in front of a national audience.

"Bubba thinks of her all the time out there," Rich said. "Everyone knows what she's up against, but we're all together and we're able to keep doing what we do as normally as possible."

Amy Donnelly's comeback from cancer was on the upswing when her father spoke of her courageous battle.  She fought a disease that millions dread to even speak of. On January 28, 1993, the battle ended. Rich Donnelly was called to Texas in mid-January because Amy had taken a turn for the worse. He was by her side when she passed away, and the only hope he could feel was that she would find a place where pain and suffering no longer existed.

Her heart, and many others, had suffered long enough.

❧

At the 1992 baseball winter meetings in Louisville, Kentucky, trades were rampant, and owners tossed money around like candy from a fire truck in a parade to those players— some outstanding, some marginal—who were eligible for free agency. Baseball, as expected, was the general topic on everyone's mind.

Pittsburgh Pirates and was mostly responsible for keeping baseball in Pittsburgh, was there in his role as president and minority owner of the expansion Florida Marlins. Like everyone else, he was there to discuss the issues of revenue sharing and salary caps. He discussed the signings of possible free agents with Marlins' general manager Dave Dombrowski, and met with friends that he hadn't seen in a while.

On the next to last day of the meetings, Carl Barger was dead. He attended an afternoon session of the meetings on December 9, and when he got up to leave, he fell to the floor. Dr. Bobby Brown, who was the American League president and also a doctor of cardiovascular surgery, was there immediately to perform cardiopulmonary resuscitation, but Barger died on the operating table at a nearby hospital. The cause of death was a severe loss of blood from a ruptured aneurysm in his abdomen. He fell unconscious in the hotel's meeting room and never awakened.

Carl Barger was a man who made whatever activity he was working on at the moment his life. He was born in 1932 and lived in Lewistown, Pennsylvania, which is about two hours from the outskirts of Pittsburgh. Barger grew up a Pirates fan and loved the game of baseball so much, he would often hitchhike from his home to old Forbes Field just to take in a game.

He played baseball and basketball at Shippensburg University in Pennsylvania and became Editor-in-Chief of the *Dickinson Law Review*, while attending law school there. He graduated summa cum laude from Dickinson and earned a Doctorate of Law degree in 1958. At that time he joined Eckert, Seamans, Cherin, & Mellott law firm, where he later became Managing Partner and practiced corporate law and corporate finance for both public and private companies.

Barger began his involvement with the Pirates in 1984 when his firm began to formulate the plans to keep the Pirates in Pittsburgh and from there baseball became his life. With the help of Malcolm Prine and former Mayor Richard Caliguiri, Barger succeeded in keeping baseball in Pittsburgh. Prine stayed on with the Pirates as team president, and Barger acted as secretary and general counselor. But when Prine left the Pirates at the end of the 1987 season due to personality conflicts with then-general manager Syd Thrift, Barger stepped in as president and held the position until his appointment with the Marlins in July 1991.

When Barger left the Pirates, Jim Leyland felt a tremendous loss because they had developed a close friendship. They played golf together and visited one another's houses frequently.

"Carl was one of the closest friends I had," Leyland said. "His death breaks my heart because of that friendship, but I also know how excited he was that, after such a long wait and so much work, he was going to get to see his team play."

"His team" was the Florida Marlins. After so many years as a fan and then an executive with the Pirates, Barger found leaving the city he practically grew up in to be one of the hardest things he had ever done.

"I grew up here," Barger said at the time of his departure to the Marlins. "Pittsburgh is my home. But this was a chance to start from the ground floor and see what we could do from scratch. The idea of building a team from its very beginning is very intriguing."

And that's how he spent his last 18 months. Building and signing. Negotiating with prospective employees. Interviewing managerial candidates. Developing a scouting staff and formulating the team's plans for the expansion draft, which was held in November 1992.

"This is what it's all about," he said as excitedly as a schoolboy on the eve of the draft.

Barger did not listen to the warning signs that signaled his failing health. He worked 16-hour days and failed in repeated attempts to quit smoking. His father died of heart failure at age 64, but that didn't stop him from pressing on. It didn't make him think about the consequences.

"I think it's a plus that I'm very emotionally attached to the team," Barger said in a *Miami Herald* story published just three weeks before his death. "I don't fall asleep; I collapse. But it's like they say about baseball— if I didn't love it so much, I'd hate it."

It may or may not have been a warning, but Barger passed out over breakfast one day at Leyland's house in 1991. Although it was a scary feeling, his collapse was attributed to a change in high blood pressure medicine.

Barger was to be married, but the date was not yet certain. As was typical of a hard-driven businessman, the time to wed would come when time and business allowed him to. Even though he moved to South Florida, Barger remained a partner in his Pittsburgh law firm and oversaw the recent opening of a Fort

Lauderdale office. He dedicated himself to his new surroundings, but he never lost sight of where he came from. Pittsburgh was his home for 33 years.

"You second-guess yourself sometimes when you're sitting alone in an office," Barger said in the *Herald* interview. "You understand a little bit more about the enormity of the job and what it's like to start from scratch."

H. Wayne Huizenga is the owner of the Florida Marlins as well as a chain of video stores known as Blockbuster Entertainment. He was Barger's friend for the last 20 years and the main reason Barger left the Pirates to undertake the task of building the Marlins. The two were frequent golf partners, and when Huizenga offered Barger the Marlins' first presidency, as well as a minority ownership in the club and a seat on the board of directors for the video chain, Barger accepted the position without a contract.

"People said I was crazy, and I'm a lawyer," Barger said. "But in my judgment, a contract would almost be an offense to our friendship."

Huizenga's emotions were equally heartfelt. "Mere words cannot convey the profound sense of sorrow and loss being experienced by those of us who loved Carl and worked with him," he said after letting the news of his friend's death sink in. "Carl was a unique human being in the very finest sense of the word. He spent his life pursuing the challenges that gave him the greatest joy and sense of accomplishment; and of those, developing the Florida Marlins was one of his greatest pleasures."

The challenges of baseball in its infant stages are gone now for Carl Barger. He will never get to see the fruits of his labor. But the Marlins and whatever legacy they build will always have a special attachment with the man who helped give them life and that attachment will more than likely go far beyond just the limits of baseball.

That was the way friendships were with Barger and whomever he came in contact with. Jim Leyland was one of those special people to Barger, and as Jim and Katie waited by the phone for further news of Barger's sudden collapse, Katie reflected on the friendship between the two.

"It's not about baseball anymore," she said. "Jim has a lot of friends in baseball. Jim and Carl were friends in life. And that goes a lot deeper."

Seconds later, the phone call came.

# *1992: "We Believe"*

Near the end of the 1991 season, Pirates general manager Larry Doughty was asked to make an assessment of the club's chances of signing potential free agents Barry Bonds and Bobby Bonilla. Bonds would not be eligible until the end of the '92 season, so Doughty said they would follow the normal procedures in dealing with his situation. That meant the two sides would discuss figures and determine whether a long or short-term agreement could be made, or whether they would end up in arbitration again.

Bonilla, however, had played out his option with the Pirates, and when the last pitch was thrown in Game 7 of the 1991 World Series, he was able to start listening to offers around the league.

"Bobby wants to investigate all his options," Doughty said when the question was put to him in Atlanta during the Pirates' playoff series against the Braves. "We know that for sure, and we'll just have to see what happens; who makes offers to him and what kind of figures they're discussing. Then we'll have to see what options we can take with him."

When spring training 1992, rolled around, neither Bonilla nor Doughty were in attendance at the Pirates' Bradenton training site. Bonilla entertained several offers from teams such as the

White Sox, California Angels, and Phillies before accepting a spectacular five-year, $29 million-offer from the New York Mets in early December. The best deal the Pirates could come up with was five years and $23 million, but it wasn't enough for him or his agent, Dennis Gilbert.

Bonilla left the Pirates with mixed emotions, because he loved the city and enjoyed being part of a team that went through a major rebuilding process and played its way through two consecutive National League Championship series. The main reason he stated for signing with the Mets was the opportunity to play in his hometown and the comfort he felt in knowing his father could come and see him play any time he wanted to.

Bonilla was a native of Brooklyn, and he grew up in a neighborhood where the road to drugs and trouble were easy avenues to take. He avoided them as a child, however, and knew in his heart there were better ways to live a successful life. By moving himself and his wife, Millie, back to New York, he felt he could better serve the youth of his old neighborhood, and maybe show them the positive things life has to offer.

Many of the Pirates were sorry to see Bonilla go, his good friend Bonds among them. But they understood the business the game had become, and most didn't blame him for seeking greener pastures.

"He did what he thought was right, just like I'll do what I think is right when the time comes," said Bonds as he entered the last month of the 1992 season. "I know Bobby Bonilla is happy, and I'm happy for him. I miss the fact that we're not teammates anymore, but you never know, we might be together again some day."

With Bonilla gone, the question for 1992 became not if Bonds would re-sign with the Pirates, but *where* he would end up in '93, and how much money would he make?

"I think a line has to be drawn at some point by the organization," Pirates broadcaster Lanny Frattare said. "The sentiment among the majority of Pirate fans was, 'why did they let Bonilla go?' Well, I think the Pirates made a good decision in Bonilla's case. If you make him a fair offer—and how can anyone say $23 million is not a fair offer—then you have to have the courage to say, 'OK, that's as far as we can go.' If that's not good enough, then you have to be able to look elsewhere."

The Pirates also decided to look elsewhere in the front office in 1992. On October 30, barely two weeks after the Pirates were eliminated from post-season play by the Atlanta Braves, Mark Sauer was named President and Chief Executive Officer of Pittsburgh Associates, the public-private coalition that owns and operates the Pittsburgh Pirates baseball club.

Sauer, who took over the position that was vacated by Carl Barger's departure to the Florida Marlins in July 1991, was a former front office executive with the St. Louis Cardinals, and before his appointment to the Pirates, was the President and Chief Executive Officer of Kiel Partners, the owners of the St. Louis Blues hockey club. He was also the developer of a new arena to be built in downtown St. Louis, was Vice Chairman of the Blues partnership, and served as member of the team's Board of Directors.

During his tenure with the Cardinals, Sauer was responsible for all marketing and administrative functions, and he was also involved in major decisions such as trades, player contracts, and payroll on the baseball side of the business. Sauer was immediately perceived by the fans and media as a no-nonsense, take-no-prisoners kind of businessman, and that approach worried more than a few people because of the possibility that he would clash with the Pirates' laid-back, fun approach to the game.

Sauer's first major decision with the Pirates came just a short time after Doughty re-signed free agent third baseman Steve Buechele to a four-year contract. Doughty seemed to be looking over his shoulder ever since his August 1990 blunder that lost the Pirates their top two minor league prospects to the Phillies due to a misunderstanding of the waiver-wire rules. The ax fell on Larry Doughty while the new year was still in its infancy, as Sauer fired Doughty on January 6, 1992, and decided to look elsewhere for direction of the team.

"It's part of the business," Doughty told reporters after learning of Sauer's decision. "There's not much else to say. I think I did the best I could, and our records have spoken for themselves. I'll take some time off and see if there are some other teams out there in need of a person with an eye for baseball talent."

Several names were thrown around as possible replacements for the general manager's position, including Doughty's assistant Cam Bonifay, who was hired at the beginning of the '91 season to avoid mistakes such as the waiver-wire snafu of 1990. Of the four finalists who were interviewed by Sauer and Pirates CEO and Chairman of the Board Doug Danforth, an interesting name surfaced as the leading candidate.

Ted Simmons was a former eight-time All-Star catcher with the St. Louis Cardinals and Milwaukee Brewers. He was currently serving as the Cardinals' Director of Player Development and had been in that position since October of 1988. Simmons had a tremendous 21-year playing career in the major leagues and during his 10 full seasons with the Cardinals, he batted .300 or better six times as a switch-hitter. He still holds the Cardinals' single-season record for home runs by a catcher with 26, and he had a career-high .332 batting average in 1975, which was the second-highest average in the National League and third-highest in the majors.

Simmons became adept at developing players, and his work with young St. Louis stars such as Todd Zeile, Ray Lankford, and Rheal Cormier proved that he had an eye for talent. Simmons approached Sauer at the beginning of the new year about his interest in the vacant Pirates' GM position, but both insisted their friendship and working relationship in St. Louis would have no bearing on the final decision.

Sauer interviewed each candidate carefully and cut the list down to Simmons and Bonifay by late January. Finally, after talking first with Bonifay and making sure he would stay on as assistant GM, Sauer appointed Simmons the Pirates' new general manager on February 5, 1992.

"I'm excited about this opportunity," Simmons said as he greeted the Pittsburgh media. "I feel this is a team that has been very well-kept by Larry Doughty, and I will do my best to keep it running smoothly. The Pirates have been successful in recent years, and we want to do our best to keep things that way."

Simmons was then off to Florida to meet and greet the members of the Pirates first hand. He read reports on all the players and spent much time getting to know them and discussing plans with manager Jim Leyland and his assistants. There were no immediate trades, and he was not willing to discuss the prospects of signing Bonds or pitchers Doug Drabek and John Smiley, who were also due for free agency at the conclusion of the 1992 season.

One thing Sauer and the Pirates managed to do before Doughty's departure was avoid any major arbitration cases. Bonds and Drabek could have gone, but both players and their agents agreed fairly easily to one-year contracts that pretty much sealed their plans to test the free-agent waters at the end of the season. Bonds agreed to play out 1992 for $4.7 million plus incentives that would ultimately boost him to $5.15 million and set a new club record for highest single-season salary. Drabek also got a raise in '92 as he signed for $4.5 million.

Simmons was quiet through the first month of his new position as he studied the Pirates' talent as well as some of the other teams' rosters in the Florida Grapefruit league. His first trade of significance came on March 10 when he sent left-handed pitcher Neal Heaton to the Kansas City Royals for outfielder Kirk Gibson. Heaton was 12-9 as a Pirate starter in 1990, but saw his record fall to 3-3 in '91 as he was limited to mostly middle and long relief. With Bob Patterson already in the bullpen and a couple of other young left-handers in the Pirates' farm system, Simmons figured the Pirates could use the outfield help, and Heaton was the most expendable.

Gibson had seen his better days on World Series championship teams in both Detroit (1984) and Los Angeles (1988), but he did possess perhaps the one thing the Pirates had lacked in their two previous NLCS appearances—leadership. In both years, no one really stepped to the front and said or did anything to lift the Pirates or make them believe they could win. Gibson was famous for his no-nonsense approach to the game and the one-hundred percent effort he put forth every time he stepped onto the field.

While Simmons' first trade had Pittsburgh fans talking, his second one left most screaming. A week after the Pirates acquired Gibson, Simmons pulled off what would be his biggest deal of the season by sending Smiley—and his $800,000 salary—to the Minnesota Twins for minor league prospects Denny Neagle and Midre Cummings.

Cummings was the Twins' number-one prospect, but GM Andy McPhail couldn't pass on the opportunity to grab a proven left-handed starter like Smiley. He would be able to file for free agency at the end of the season, but the Twins felt that Smiley might just be the kind of arm they needed if they had any hopes of repeating as world champions.

Cummings was immediately assigned to the Pirates' Class AA Carolina farm team, while Neagle was brought into the major league camp for a good look. He had spent only part of the 1991 season with the Twins, but Leyland felt the 23-year-old left-hander was ready for the majors when he reported to the Pirates' camp. Neagle pitched very well in a couple of the Pirates' spring training games and was as excited as anyone when he looked at Jim Leyland's final 25-man roster and saw that he had made the club.

"The trade was a big shock in the beginning," said Neagle, who was 4-6 in his first season with the Pirates. "It was a big deal and people talked about it all the time. All I wanted to do was pitch my best for the Pittsburgh Pirates."

There were the usual shock waves from fans when such a trade is announced. The radio and television sports talk shows had callers fuming: "First, we lose Bonilla 'cause the Pirates are too cheap, now this nut goes and trades away our only twenty-game winner. What is he doing?"

That was one example from the less than-overjoyed fans who were already calling for Ted Simmons' head.

The ultimate motive, as everyone perceived the move, was to cut costs and whittle down what had rapidly grown to be one of the highest payrolls in major league baseball. Simmons insisted that while the move would trim the Pirates' payroll, it would also pay long-term dividends to the Pirates because of the high value the club received in return for Smiley. Cummings was just a year or two away from the big leagues, and Neagle could be seasoned perfectly under the genius of Leyland and pitching coach Ray Miller.

"There was definitely pressure," Neagle said. "John Smiley was very well-liked by his teammates and the people of Pittsburgh. Jim and Ray just told me not to put pressure on myself, but it was hard not to. I wanted to show the fans they weren't just getting any Joe Schmo in the trade. I wanted to show they had someone who was going to help the team out.

"After a while, it got to the point where it was sickening to talk about it. I'd be lying if I said I didn't notice the articles in Pittsburgh that always said, 'Smiley has 11 wins for Twins,' or the way they always said the trade looked better for the Twins. As far as I'm concerned, I'm a rookie, and John Smiley has had his years here in Pittsburgh. He's done well for himself and I hope he continues to do well, but I think the most important thing for me to remember is to not go out to that mound and try to be John Smiley. I have to be myself."

It was true that Smiley was well-liked by his Pirate teammates, and many players agree that while trades are a part of the game—and business continues as usual—there is a human factor that is always present, and it's hard to say good-bye to a friend. Smiley was visibly shaken when he was told of the trade. He sat somberly in the Pirates' dugout at McKechnie Field in Bradenton, in street clothes, still not able to take in everything that had transpired. There were tears in his eyes as he waved off reporters who tried to get a comment from him.

Those reactions are common in baseball, even among the big leaguers, who are normally perceived as tough guys who never show emotion. They are sometimes thought of as conceited, moody, temperamental, and egotistical, and with some, that is a fairly close assessment. But major league baseball players also laugh and cry and hurt like other people, but they don't lead normal lives. They are in the spotlight much of the time, but when that spotlight is turned off, most players lead a life much like their neighbors who aren't involved in professional sports.

"I think that's what people don't think about," Mike LaValliere said. "We realize trades can happen at any time, but does that mean we shouldn't have our friends on the team? It's tough to see a guy like John Smiley walk out of that clubhouse for the last time because not only is he a twenty-game winner, he's your friend."

Friendships on the team were one reason the Pirates didn't take too kindly to Simmons' obvious cost-cutting measures. They had no problems with Cummings or Neagle, but there were feelings among the players that taking away Smiley, after having already lost Bonilla, was a sure sign that management was giving up on the Pirates' chances of repeating their division championships of 1990 and '91.

"Times, I think, definitely got a little turbulent when I made that trade," Simmons said. "People thought I was just being myself and they were saying, 'Oh God, we were right all along.' But I do know one thing. It took Oakland and the Mets five months to do what we did in spring training."

Simmons was referring to the big trades that Oakland and New York made in mid-August that were reportedly made to solidify a playoff position in Oakland and provide some youthful talent to the Mets' future. The A's unloaded rightfielder Jose Canseco and his $5 million a year salary to the Texas Rangers for All-Star outfielder Ruben Sierra and a couple of veteran pitchers (Jeff Russell and Bobby Witt), while the Mets picked up a couple of young prospects from the Toronto Blue Jays for 20-game winner David Cone. Ryan Thompson and Jeff Kent were just about ready for the big leagues when they came to the Mets, while Cone was in the last year of his contract and was about to earn a hefty raise no matter where he played in 1993.

The Mets figured they had enough four and five million dollar a year salaries and didn't want to pursue another, while Oakland management decided enough was enough in the often-unsettling relationship between Canseco and the eventual American League West champs. Canseco still had two years left on his contract after the '92 season, while Cone helped the Blue Jays win a World Series title and then signed with the Kansas City Royals in the off-season for 1993 and beyond.

"Those two trades are related to ours [with Smiley]," Simmons said near the end of the '92 season. "If you don't see that, then you don't follow baseball. People thought we were crazy when we traded for unknowns, but who knew Ryan Thompson or Jeff Kent in New York before the trade?

"I know my first major trade would be put under a microscope because you just don't take a 20-game winner, trade him for two relatively unknown people and expect to walk through the center of Dodge without someone drawing a pistol on you. I knew it would get the kind of reaction that it did, but five months later, the exact same scenario happened between New York and Toronto. The only difference was we made our move in spring training and we took  heat. When they made their move, everybody understood why."

Feelings got a little hotter when Simmons unloaded another big contract just  two days after the Smiley trade. Bill Landrum, who had stepped up so well in  1989 when Jim Gott was lost for the season with an elbow injury, was given  his unconditional release so the Pirates could make room for a young pitcher named Miguel Batista, whom they took from Montreal in the process known as  the Rule 5 free agent draft.

If a team leaves a player unprotected, such as the Expos did with Batista, another team can sign that player under the condition that he is kept on that team's major league roster the entire season. If, at any time, that player is designated for re-assignment to the minor leagues, he must be offered back to his original team for half of the fee that was originally paid for him, which is normally $50,000.

Batista was considered a bonafide prospect, but in the very long-term future. Simmons liked him, and felt the Pirates could use him in '92, but even Leyland felt Batista wasn't quite ready for the big time.

The move did a number of things, besides cause further hard feelings from the players. For one thing, it tied Leyland's hands because he knew, and said on a number of occasions, that Batista belonged on the Class A level, where he could get more work and time in, which were two aspects of the game he really needed. Secondly, it left Leyland unable to fill a valuable roster spot, whether it was with a more-seasoned veteran pitcher or a sixth outfielder, he could not use that luxury with Batista on the major league roster.

Leyland did not sit Batista in a corner during the first month of the season. He used him in mostly long and middle-relief to see how he handled the major league hitters. Batista took his lumps on a couple of occasions, but he also showed definite prospects of success. But how long could the Pirates wait for that success to come around?

Don Slaught had spent nearly the whole month of April on the disabled list, but after spending a couple of days on a rehabilitation assignment with Class AAA Buffalo, Slaught was given medical clearance to join the Pirates again. He was recalled from rehab on April 20, and three days later was reinstated from the disabled list. With nowhere else to turn, Simmons reluctantly agreed that Batista would need much more time than the Pirates could offer, and he was returned to Montreal as part of the Rule 5 draft agreement.

Landrum left the Pirates with bitter feelings because of the sudden way in which the news was delivered, plus the fact he claimed the Pirates could have made the decision a lot sooner so he would have had a better chance to sign with another ballclub. At this stage, with less than two weeks to go before the regular season, Landrum felt most teams' rosters would be set and they would not give him a look.

Most rosters were finalized with the exception of a final player decision  or two, but ironically, Landrum did catch on with another team that needed some veteran relief help. That team was the Montreal Expos.

❧

Montreal would figure quite heavily in the final outcome for Pittsburgh in 1992. For starters, the Expos and Pirates opened at Three Rivers Stadium  for the second consecutive season, and it was of little surprise that Doug Drabek would start on the mound for the Pirates against Montreal ace Dennis  Martinez.

Drabek's opening-day start marked the first time since Bob Friend in 1960-61-62 that the same pitcher had started three consecutive openers for the  Pirates. It was also the second straight year that Drabek would face Martinez,  and the Pirates hoped they could do better than last year's 7-0 opening-day loss to the veteran right-hander.

The Pirates gave Drabek all the support he would need in the second inning  as they pushed across the only runs of the game in the Pirates' 2-0 win. Jose Lind had two of the Pirates' four hits and scored a run, while Drabek held Montreal scoreless and allowed just six hits. The Pirates made it two in a  row two days later as Zane Smith won his first outing, 4-2. Barry Bonds belted his first home run of the season to lead the offense, and Stan Belinda  retired the Expos in the eighth and ninth innings for his first save.

Montreal turned a 4-2 ninth-inning lead into an 8-3 laugher as the Expos  captured the third game of the series. The Expos collected 14 hits and  snapped a 1-1 tie in the sixth inning by scoring a pair of runs off loser Bob Walk. Neagle made his Pirate debut in the seventh and allowed just one run,  but the Expos cashed in four times in the ninth off Vicente Palacios. Andy Van Slyke was 2-for-5 for the Pirates with two runs batted in.

Pittsburgh traveled to Philadelphia for a three-game week-end series and  took the opener, 3-2, behind Bonds' second home run, Randy Tomlin's first win,  and Belinda's second save. The

Phillies won the second game of the series, as Drabek was tagged for four runs in the Phillies' fourth inning.

Bonds had given the Pirates an early 1-0 lead with his third home run, but the Pirates, who had played error-free baseball through the first four games, committed three in this game and put Drabek in a tremendous hole. Batista made his debut for the Pirates and gave up a two-run homer to Phillies outfielder, Ruben Amarro. Bonds hit his third home run in as many games —and fourth of the young season—in the final game of the series, as the Pirates cruised to Smith's second win, 6-1.

The Pirates were 4-2 at that point and tied with the Expos for first place. Little did anyone realize that Smith's complete-game victory that Sunday afternoon would be the start of an incredible run that would put the Pirates 4-1/2 games in first place over the next 12 days. It started with Smith's win and kept going through a short five-game homestand with the Cubs and Phillies. The Pirates swept the Cubs in two games, 3-2 and 7-2, and Drabek raised his record to 2-1, as the Pirates rallied for a 7-4 win over the Phillies to make it four in a row. Smith raised his record to 3-0, as Pittsburgh used a five-run fifth to defeat the Phillies 9-2, in the second game of the series.

Cecil Espy had become a manager's dream coming off the bench in the early part of the season. His three-run, pinch-hit triple in the decisive fifth put the Pirates comfortably ahead and raised his early-season average to an incredible .800 (8-for-10). Gary Varsho closed the homestand with a two-run, inside-the-park home run in an 11-0 whitewash of Philadelphia. Andy Van Slyke had three hits and scored three runs, as he seemed to be settling in after developing serious back pain in spring training.

With six wins in a row under their belts, and a 3-1/2- game lead over Montreal and St. Louis, the Pirates embarked on a 12-game road trip that started with an early— but very important —four-game series with the Expos at Olympic Stadium.

Tomlin battled inning for inning with Montreal pitcher Ken Hill in the first game of the series, and the Pirates took a 2-1 lead into the top of the ninth. That's when they faced their former teammate, Landrum, and shelled him and another former Pirate farmhand, Bill Sampen, for nine runs to break the game wide open. Kirk Gibson highlighted the inning with a grand slam, his first home run as a Pirate, and Bonds added a three-run blast for his sixth homer of the season.

Neagle made his first start as a Pirate and lasted into the fifth inning  before Leyland relieved him with Palacios. Pittsburgh staked Neagle to a five-run first-inning lead behind Bonds' seventh home run, but had to fight  down to the wire, as Roger Mason earned his third save by holding off the  Expos in the bottom of the ninth, 8-7.

Pittsburgh improved its record to 12-2 in the third game of the series, as Drabek outdueled Martinez once again in a rematch of Opening Day. The Pirates scored one in the first and one in the ninth, as Drabek went the distance in  his second 2-0 shutout of the season over the Expos. Gibson hit his second  homer of the series to help the Pirates offensively.

The Pirates' nine-game winning streak came to a halt in the fourth and  final game of the series as Montreal capitalized on five Pirate errors,  including three in the first inning, and won, 6-3. It was the first loss of  the season for Zane Smith, who saw his record drop to 3-1.

"It was a big streak for us," Jim Leyland said. "It was a good way to get the season going, but we had to realize there was still a lot of baseball left. They weren't all going to come that easy, and I figured we'd need every  one of those nine straight wins at some point."

How true the manager's words were, as the Pirates went into May feeling good  about a 15-5 record in April and came out feeling lucky to be alive.

Right before one of the Pirates' darker periods of 1992, Leyland was faced  with the task of telling a former World Series hero his services were no  longer needed. Kirk Gibson was every bit the competitor the Pirates hoped he  would be, but his .176 batting average wasn't enough justification to keep  him on a team that was priding itself on youth. The fact was, Orlando Merced  needed a place to play, and the Pirates figured it would be better to release  the veteran Gibson outright, than to ask him to be a bench player, which was the best role they could have offered him.

The decision to release Gibson came on May 5, and it was just 10 days later that one of the more difficult slumps the Pirates had endured in a long time  began. The Pirates had just completed a series in Atlanta, where they took  two out of three from the Braves. They would play a short, three-game set  with San

Diego at Three Rivers Stadium before heading to the west coast for the first of their two annual trips to San Francisco, Los Angeles, and San Diego.

Pittsburgh was 23-10 and 3-1/2 games ahead of St. Louis when the bottom almost fell out of their season. Neagle failed to get out of the first inning as the Padres scored three times and won the first game of the series, 9-2. Benito Santiago had three doubles, and Tony Gwynn went 4 for 5, as the Padres racked up 18 hits off Pirate pitching.

Things got worse the following evening, as the Pirates blew a 6-0 lead after the second inning and lost, 10-9. Barry Bonds belted his 10th and 11th home runs—including the second grand slam of his career—and had a career-high six RBIs, but it wasn't enough as Gary Sheffield, who made a run at the triple crown in '92, and Fred McGriff hit towering home runs of their own. Sheffield's traveled 436 feet to centerfield and McGriff's was a 452-foot drive to right.

The Pirates dropped their third in a row on Sunday afternoon, as Tomlin's record fell to 4-3 in Pittsburgh's 6-5 setback. Van Slyke had three hits in the game, but could not deliver with the tying run aboard in the bottom of the ninth. It was the first time the Pirates were swept in a three-game series at home since August of 1990, and their old nemesis, Randy Myers, who helped shut down the Pirates in the 1990 NLCS, got the final out for San Diego to earn his 11th save.

The Pirates were swept in San Francisco as Drabek fell to 3-3, Smith to 5-2, and Walk to 1-3. Van Slyke had both of the Pirates' hits in the third game of the series to keep his strong pace going, and Walk was victimized by his own wild pitch that allowed Kevin Bass to score from third for the only run of the game.

They had found so many ways to win during a nine-game fiesta early in the season, but now the Pirates could do no right and seemed to be searching for the one event in a game that could give them a victory during this dreadful slump. Pittsburgh earned a slight reprieve in the first game against the Dodgers, as Tomlin won his fifth of the season, but even then the Pirates had to go down to the wire as Belinda gave up a three-run, pinch-hit homer to the Dodgers' Stan Javier in the bottom of the ninth before nailing down a 6-4 Pirates victory.

Belinda was not as fortunate in the second game of the series as Dodger rookie Eric Karros' three-run, pinch-hit homer in the ninth inning wiped out a 4-2 Pirate lead and sent the team to its seventh loss in the last eight games. Pittsburgh led 4-1 going into the ninth, but Mason gave up an RBI-single to Mike Scioscia before Karros' heroics. Los Angeles took the third game of the series, but not in as dramatic a fashion as Kevin Gross bested Drabek and won, 4-2. The loss left Drabek at 3-4 for the season and dropped the Pirates into second place at 24-18, a half-game behind the Cardinals.

"I said going into the season that this division [N.L. East] would probably be the toughest in baseball," Leyland said. "I thought we had a good team, and I was confident we could win it again, but all the teams were up around first place at some point in the season."

Bonds went 4-for-5 and hit his 12th homer, but the Pirates fell to San Diego, 7-6, in the first of a three-game series at Jack Murphy Stadium. St. Louis' win dropped the Pirates another game back, but the players all knew there was a lot of baseball left.

Improvement was bound to come sooner or later, but the Pirates were swept by the Padres for the second time in 10 days and closed their disastrous road trip by finishing 1-8. During their worst slump of the season, the Pirates lost 11 out of 12 and were outscored, 69-46. Their record fell to 24-21 and a 4-1/2 game lead in the standings turned into a 1-1/2 game deficit.

Fortunately, the Pirates wouldn't see the west coast again for a couple of months and they were heading back to Three Rivers Stadium for a 10-game homestand with the Giants, Dodgers, and Mets that they hoped would get them back on the right track.

It started off right as the Pirates scored eight runs in the seventh inning, and Palacios raised his record to 3-0 in a 13-3 shellacking of San Francisco. Van Slyke collected three hits against the Giants, while Jose Lind drove in three runs with a double and single. Neagle evened his record at 2-2 as the Pirates pulled out a 3-2, 10-inning decision over the Giants the next day. Jeff King scored the winning run on a sacrifice fly that outfielder Willie McGee caught along the rightfield foul line.

The Giants won the third game of the series, 5-3, as Bud Black bested Smith, whose record dropped to 5-4 after a 3-0 start.

The afternoon game was billed as, "Turn Back The Clock Day," as both teams wore 1939 uniforms, and the stadium took on the look of 1939 with billboards covering the outfield walls and stadium workers dressed in 1939 garb.

The Pirates took two out of three from the Dodgers before the Mets came in for the first meeting of the season between the two teams, despite the fact that the season was nearly one-third complete. The series featured Bobby Bonilla's return to Pittsburgh, but the Pirates were the ones who did most of the celebrating. Bonds greeted his friend in the first game with his 14th home run as the Pirates won 7-2, and Lloyd McClendon slapped an RBI-single in the 10th inning to give the Pirates a 5-4 win in the second game.

Bonilla went 4-for-4 with a home run and four RBIs as the Mets trounced the Pirates in the third game, 15-1. Neagle made his last start of the season as he allowed six runs in four innings and watched his record fall to 2-4. Tomlin raised his record to 7-3 for the season and 6-0 in his career against the Mets, as the Pirates blanked New York 3-0, to take three out of four.

The Pirates were in first place again at the All-Star break with a record of 49-39. They were 4-1/2 games ahead of St. Louis, but Montreal had started a surge of its own after a managerial change that saw Felipe Alou take over for Tom Runnels, who was fired about a month and a half into the season.

Alou was a lot like Jim Leyland in that he related well to his players and seemed to get the most out of them at every turn. The Pirates, despite their losses of Bonilla and Smiley, were picked by many to win the division again, while the Mets and up-and-coming Cardinals were expected to give them a battle. No one predicted the Expos to be the Pirates' main nemesis down the 1992 stretch after their fifth-place finish in '91.

Pittsburgh split a four-game series with the Cubs following the All-Star break and dropped two out of three in Houston before heading to Atlanta for a big three-game weekend series with the Braves. Right before the break, Ted Simmons made his first major trade during the season when he sent third baseman Steve Buechele to the Cubs for left-handed pitcher Danny Jackson.

The move was puzzling, because up to now Bonds was the Pirates' only source of home run power for the Pirates, and it was figured Buechele would be needed for his bat, as well as his defense. Buechele, however, had hit only eight home runs for the Pirates in '92, and news from the training room was not good when Zane Smith came down with some major discomfort in his throwing shoulder. Jackson was a proven veteran who won 23 games in 1988 for the Cincinnati Reds and had been a part of two World Series championship teams in Kansas City and Cincinnati.

Simmons also seemed to be using some psychology in his thinking for the trade, because up to July 4, Jeff King was batting just .187 with six home runs and 20 RBIs, playing mostly at second base in place of Lind once in a while. He was optioned to Class AAA Buffalo after Leyland admitted there was only so much time they could give King to come around. "If he's going to be a major leaguer, he's going to have to start producing," Leyland said of the Pirates' former No. 1-draft pick.

King hit .345 at Buffalo, with two home runs and five RBIs in seven games. The trade was announced on July 10, and four days later King was recalled to play third base for the Pirates for the rest of the season. It was almost as if the Pirates were telling King, "The position is yours. Go out and take it." Despite his anemic numbers, it was too early to give up on a young career such as King's, and when pitching help came along, Simmons figured Buechele was expendable. King responded by hitting .268, with eight home runs and 45 RBIs in 69 games after his recall. He started 61 of those games at third base.

The Pirates lost two of their three games in Atlanta, including a dramatic 1-0 decision in the second game. It was a Saturday night and there was a definite playoff atmosphere. Both teams were strong candidates to meet again for the National League pennant in October, but for now they were involved in tight races in their respective divisions.

Jackson was making his second start in a Pirate uniform, while the Braves countered with veteran left-hander Charlie Leibrandt. Atlanta scored the only run of the game in the bottom of the second when David Justice hit his ninth home run of the season to leftfield. Incredibly, that was the only hit the Braves would get the entire game.

In the top of the ninth, the Pirates had a runner on first base and one out with Van Slyke at the plate. Van Slyke was having his best year by far at the plate as he was hitting around .320. His change in his swing accounted for the better average, but his home-run production was down from years past. He had six homers to this point, but when he connected on Kent Mercker's 2-2 pitch, it looked for sure as though he had given the Pirates the lead with home run No. 7.

The ball floated into the Atlanta sky, and centerfielder Otis Nixon kept a watchful eye on it as he ran toward the outfield wall. In what was by far the catch of the year, Nixon leaped high toward the wall and robbed Van Slyke of the sure home run. His arm was above the wall up to his elbow and he needed every inch of that reach to grab the ball.

The Atlanta crowd let out a deafening cheer that lasted well beyond the third out of the inning. Nixon's teammates mobbed him as though the Braves had just won the World Series.

"It was an incredible catch," said Van Slyke, who has made quite a few spectacular catches in his career. "I thought I had a home run that put us ahead. When I saw him pull it down, my heart sunk. It took perfect timing, and he did everything right."

The Pirates won the third game of the series 5-4, but they continued to plod along as they dropped all three games of a series in Chicago. Pittsburgh was 53-48 following its miserable trip to the windy city and had dropped to a first-place tie with the Montreal Expos.

The Pirates were set to open a six-game homestand with the Cardinals and Mets that would mark not only the beginning of another important winning streak, but also would introduce the city to a young man whose best pitch traveled no faster than 60 miles per hour, but confused opposing batters in ways they had never seen.

⁂

Before their series with the Cubs, the Pirates found that Smith's shoulder injury was serious enough that he would have to be placed on the 15-day disabled list. Danny Jackson, whom the Pirates acquired to help in case Smith's troubles worsened, won his first game as a Pirate in the first game against St. Louis, 4-0. With a string of consecutive games coming up, Leyland and

Simmons agreed that the time was right to call up the rookie knuckle baller who had been working for most of the season with the Pirates' Buffalo farm club.

Tim Wakefield was the Pirates' eighth-round selection in the June 1988, free agent draft. He was originally signed as a first baseman, and he holds the school record for home runs in a career (40) at Florida Tech. Wakefield hit .344 with 22 home runs and 71 RBIs in 1987 at Florida Tech, and was named team MVP in '87 and '88.

He originally signed with the Pirates as a first baseman, but one day when he was with Class A Welland, he was spotted by one of the coaches toying with a knuckle ball as he was tossing a ball in the outfield. The coach asked him if he thought he could throw it in a game and Wakefield said yes. So he was given a try, and he has been a pitcher ever since. The pitch may have actually saved Wakefield's career, because he was never the same kind of hitter professionally that he was in college, but the Pirates' player development staff liked his potential as a pitcher and decided to hang onto him.

Wakefield went 15-8 at Class AA Carolina in 1991 and had a 2.80 earned run average. He started the '92 season at Buffalo and was 10-3 with a 3.06 ERA and a league-best six complete games before the Pirates bought his contract. It was July 31 and the Pirates were nearly two-thirds of the way through their season. Time was on the young man's side. Time to see if he could make a difference in the Pirates' quest for a third straight division championship.

The Pirates were playing the second game of their four-game series with the Cardinals, and Wakefield would make his major league debut in front of not only 20,299 Pirate fans that included his mother and father, but a national television audience that was tuned into ESPN.

"I really didn't mind it a bit," Wakefield said. "I was nervous when I first went out there, but that was because it was my first game with the Pirates and I was hoping to do as well as I could. My parents were at the game, and I just looked at being on TV as a chance for my friends from Florida to see me pitch."

His poise was incredible. To that, everyone affiliated with the Pirates will attest. Wakefield pitched against St. Louis like he had been a part of the Three Rivers Stadium mound all his life. He struck out 10 Cardinal batters in his debut and pitched out of a jam in the top of the ninth to go the distance in the Pirates' 3-2 win. Bonds hit his 20th home run of the season—a two-run shot in the first inning—and Bell added a solo homer in the third to supply all of the Pittsburgh offense.

"I didn't know whether Jim Leyland would come out and get me in the ninth or not," Wakefield said. "I kinda thought he would because it was such a big game and I was a rookie. But when they got somebody on base and I didn't see him come out of the dugout, I just told myself to dig down deeper and show him his faith was warranted in me."

When Wakefield got the last out, Leyland was the first one there to congratulate him, and Ray Miller told him what he tells every young pitcher making his first major league start.

"I just kinda talk to them in the runway and reassure them," Miller says. "I think it's better that a pitcher hear a lot of the confident things. When he wins his first game, I usually put my arm around him and tell him, 'I knew you could do it.' A lot of times he has tears in his eyes and it makes me feel the same way."

After his first game, Wakefield experienced the same media crush that most rookies do when they come from out of nowhere to win one for the home team. His was a curiosity that was doubly magnified because he was a knuckle ball pitcher with an interesting story. But that was another thing Miller prepared him for — and something Leyland wanted to keep a close watch over.

"We didn't want the media hounding him every step he took," Miller said. "I told him after that first game that he'd be getting a lot more attention. He asked me why, and I told him because there are very few knuckle ball pitchers and the media is going to want him all the time. I said, 'they'll want to compare you with others, and they'll keep reminding you that the only other knuckle ball pitchers in the league [Tom Candiotti of the Dodgers and Charlie Hough of the White Sox] wear the same number [49] as you do.'"

So Miller made a rule for his young pitcher, one that is practiced fairly regularly by all the pitchers in the Pirates' starting rotation. No talking to the media on the day you're scheduled to pitch, until after the game. The rule also applied to the day before a scheduled start.

"I figured that would give him two days to himself anyway," Miller reasoned. "I also reminded him about crediting his pitching coaches in the minors and his defense in the field. The point is to really play down your own success and spread the credit around to others. If you're good enough, people will notice you without you having to blow your own horn."

Wakefield had done his job in his first outing as a Pirate, and the team responded by winning the final two games against the Cardinals for a four-game sweep and a two-game lead over the Expos. Pittsburgh made it six in a row by sweeping a pair from the Mets, 3-2 and 6-2. Wakefield again pitched well in the second game, as he struck out nine in eight innings of work and raised his record to 2-0.

Having swept the Cardinals in four straight at home, the Pirates went to St. Louis and accomplished the feat again. Roger Mason won two of the games in relief, and Bob Walk continued his turnaround from a rough start as he raised his record to 6-4. Wakefield started the first of a two-game series in New York, but was long gone by the time Jeff King's RBI-single drove home the go-ahead run in the top of the 16th inning. Rookie pitcher Steve Cooke got his first major league hit, RBI, and win as the Pirates got past the Mets 4-2.

Pittsburgh had won 11 in a row and was 3-1/2 games ahead of the Expos as the Pirates raised their record to 64-48. Things mellowed a bit as the Braves came into Three Rivers and won three out of four from the Pirates. The only Pittsburgh victory in the series belonged to Wakefield, a 4-2 decision over John Smoltz that raised his record to 3-0.

The Pirates had some payback in store for the San Diego Padres, who left with a three-game sweep in their first trip to Pittsburgh in May. The Pirates got wins from Tomlin (12-7), Walk (7-4), and Jackson (6-11) to turn the tables on the Padres and pull off a three-game sweep of their own.

Wakefield suffered his first bad outing as a major league pitcher as the Pirates opened their second trip to the west coast in San Francisco. The Giants capitalized on a six-run fifth inning and a costly mistake by Wakefield that aided the big inning. The Pirates led the Giants 3-0, but Wakefield failed to cover first on a ground ball, and Robby Thompson made him pay with a three-run homer that broke a 3-3 tie. Wakefield tried to sneak a fastball by Thompson, but the veteran second baseman rode it over the fence in leftfield to send Wakefield to his first loss in four decisions.

Pittsburgh lost two of the three games in San Francisco, but won two out of three in both Los Angeles and San Diego. A highlight of the series against the Dodgers was the pitching matchup in the third game between Wakefield, whom Leyland hoped would maintain his strength and composure, and Tom Candiotti, the only other knuckle ball specialist in the National League. It was the first matchup of starting knuckleball pitchers in the same game in 10 years, and Wakefield was most impressive as he shut out the Dodgers 2-0. He even picked off two baserunners in the same inning.

It was a respectable 5-4 trip to the West coast this time, and nothing like the 1-8 disaster the Pirates experienced toward the end of May. They returned home 17 games over .500 and with a 3-1/2 game lead in the division. It appeared by now that Montreal would be the nearest roadblock to the Pirates' chances of winning the division once again.

The thing that favored the Pirates and hurt the Expos was that the two teams had only four games remaining against each other. That meant the Expos would need a lot of help from the other teams in the division if they were to have a chance at dethroning the Pirates.

Pittsburgh, meanwhile, took five out of six against the Giants and Dodgers at Three Rivers Stadium and then took two out of three against the Cubs. The Pirates continued their domination over the Cardinals in 1992 by sweeping a pair of games in St. Louis, and then came home for their final two games against Montreal in Pittsburgh. The Expos won the first one, 6-3, but the Pirates maintained their four-game lead by taking the second game, 3-2, and accepting a split in the series.

Pittsburgh then won four out of its next five games and forced a split in the last two games with the Expos at Montreal. By now the lead was seven games, and the Pirates were just days away from their third straight division title.

That day came in the 155th game of the season. The Pirates cut their magic number to one a day earlier by routing the Mets, 19-2 and 31,217 fans showed up at Three Rivers Stadium on a Sunday afternoon to see if they could do it against the hated Mets, who had by now turned into a mere shadow of the team that Pirate fans truly detested.

The Pirates led 4-2 into the top of the ninth, but the Mets started a rally. Lind made a terrific play on Daryl Boston's ground ball by diving to his right to get the second out, and Belinda blew a called third strike past Jeff McKnight to end the game.

"It was great to be out there in that situation," Belinda said afterwards. "It's something you dream about and practice as a kid. It was the most exciting time I've ever had in baseball."

By now the scene had become common to Pirate fans, but it was still something they would never get tired of. The entire dugout spilled out onto the field and hugged and congratulated each other on another successful season. They tipped their hats to the fans, and Jim Leyland got a ride on a couple of sets of shoulders—one of them belonging to Barry Bonds again, who pointed at Leyland and shouted over and over, "He's the best! He's the best!"

The celebration continued in the clubhouse, but it was nothing like the first one the Pirates had two years before and slightly more subdued than the one in '91. With each passing year and no National League pennant to speak of, the Pirates weren't quite content to spend themselves on a celebration they had been through twice before. The veterans took a few sips of champagne, or maybe smoked a cigar, but for the most part, they let the rookies enjoy the experience and soon everyone realized that a celebration wouldn't be complete until the Pirates got past the National League Championship Series.

ૐ

The Pirates drew 1,829,395 fans to Three Rivers Stadium in 1992, a figure that was down from the record attendance of 2,065,302 in 1991. Some attributed the lower number to the increased ticket prices for '92; others thought people were outraged at the escalating salaries made by some of the team's bigger name stars, as well as many of the mediocre names.

A major reason, however, may have been the newspaper strike that shut down both of Pittsburgh's daily publications. The *Pittsburgh Press* and *Pittsburgh Post Gazette* were the major source of daily news and sports for those who lived in the city and its immediate outskirts. While suburban areas had their own smaller newspapers, they were rarely seen by those who had grown up reading the city's only two publications since the turn of the century.

How could a newspaper strike affect a major league baseball team's attendance figures? If fans don't have their paper to read every morning, they don't see the scores, and they can't follow the progress of their favorite players on their favorite team that is so routinely reported by those newspapers. Consequently, the fans lose interest as time goes on.

Sure a fan can get scores off the local television news reports, but how much do they find out about a guy like Tim Wakefield, who came out of seemingly nowhere to help the Pirates in their title run? They hear his name on the news, but do they get the chance to absorb his background and what made him a knuckle ball pitcher?

Andy Van Slyke was in the race for National League batting champion, but the fans didn't get a day-by-day comparison of Van Slyke's and San Diego's Gary Sheffield's averages like they would have seen in the paper. These were some of the things fans missed because of the newspaper strike, which lasted through the entire season and was only resolved around the beginning of 1993.

Whatever the case, there was a lot to read and hear about as a result of the 1992 Pittsburgh Pirates' season. Besides their third straight division championship, the Pirates claimed a few award winners and made some new discoveries. Barry Bonds was named Associated Press Player of the Year in major league baseball, and he also won his second National League Most Valuable Player award in three years.

It was no big secret that Bonds was probably playing his last season in Pittsburgh. He was upset that Pirate management took him to arbitration before both the 1990 and '91 seasons and with the potential to become the highest-paid player in baseball, he was certainly going to shop himself around in the off-season.

Bonds insisted throughout the season that money wasn't his main objective. He said he liked it in Pittsburgh and couldn't play for a better manager in baseball than Jim Leyland. But he was also concerned about where the Pirates were headed, and he didn't want to stick around if they weren't going to be serious about keeping this current team as together as possible. Such an occurrence would have been impossible, because there was no way a small-market team like the Pirates could afford to keep Bonds and Doug Drabek, not to mention the team's other stars such as Van Slyke, whose contract would run out after 1994, Bell, Lind, Tomlin . . . With salaries approaching ridiculous propor- tions, that list could go on and on.

"I haven't closed the door to anything," Bonds said at the conclusion of the season. "I don't really want to get involved in the negotiations. My agent will let me know what's going on."

Being his probable last season in Pittsburgh, Bonds made it a memorable one. He hit .311 in 1992 with 34 home runs, 103 RBIs, and 39 stolen bases. It was the second time Bonds had reached the 30-30 club in home runs and stolen bases in his career, and his 109 runs scored and 127 walks were the most in the National League. Bonds also led the major leagues with 32 intentional walks, which broke the old club record of 27 set by Roberto Clemente in 1968.

Bonds, who missed 18 games in late June and early July because of a severe muscle strain in his right side, was the National League Player of the Week for the first week of Septem- ber as he hit .500 (7-for-14) with four home runs, seven RBIs, and 10 runs scored. He also walked 13 times during that period for a .741 on-base percentage. His seven home runs, 17 RBIs, and .317 average helped him earn Player of the Month honors for April.

Bonds appeared in his second career All-Star game in July and had his first starting assignment. He led the Pirates in home runs, RBIs, and stolen bases for the second consecutive season, and his consistency showed as he hit .303 (72-for-238) in 68 games before the All-Star break with 15 home runs and 49 RBIs, and .319 (75-for-235) with 19 homers and 54 RBIs in 72 games after. His home run total was a career best, and he became the first Pirate since Willie Stargell (1971-73) to post three straight 100 RBI seasons.

Tim Wakefield surprised the baseball world with his 1992 performance and finished second to Los Angeles Dodgers' rookie Eric Karros in the balloting for Rookie of the Year. He finished the season as the Pirates' most consistent pitcher with an 8-1 record in 13 starts and a masterful 2.15 earned run average. Despite his second-place finish to Karros in the major league baseball voting, Wakefield was named Rookie of the Year for 1992 by *The Sporting News*. His floating knuckle ball baffled opposing hitters and made believers out of everyone he came in contact with.

"Tim was a big pickup for us," Jim Leyland said. "We were struggling for pitching by the time August came around, and he stepped right in and did an unbelievable job."

Wakefield was expected to crack at some point in his short season with the Pirates. With each win came further requests from the media. Even on the road—and perhaps more so because he was a novelty— people from all parts of the journalistic world wanted a piece of him. He did interviews in San Francisco; he appeared on television with ESPN's Roy Firestone in Los Angeles, and he was asked to pose for baseball card pictures in San Diego.

"That was something we wanted to shield him from, but we knew we couldn't do it completely," Ray Miller said. "We just told Timmy to be humble and remember his defense whenever people asked about his success. I listened to him after he beat [Tom] Candiotti in Los Angeles, and he did a great job of passing the credit around."

When Wakefield pitched in the 1992 National League Championship Series against the Atlanta Braves, the media blitz got so overwhelming that the Pirates had to station the team's media relations director, Jim Trdinich, in front of Wakefield's locker after games so he could get dressed in peace.

Being a rookie, Wakefield found that following the advice given to him by Leyland and Miller was the best way to handle this new world he had stepped into. With microphones almost constantly in his face, he said what a thrill it was to be on the same pitching staff with men like Doug Drabek and Zane Smith and said he loved to just sit back and watch people like Van Slyke, Bonds, and Lind make the spectacular plays in the field look routine.

"The pressure will only get to you if you let it," Wakefield said upon returning from his first west coast trip as a major league baseball player. "I'm fortunate to have a father who brought me up well and taught me to be humble, and my coaches have been great at every level of the game."

Contrary to the pressures of professional baseball, Wakefield said his biggest thrill in Los Angeles was meeting actor Ed O'Neill, who plays Al Bundy on the hit TV series, "Married . . . With Children."

"He was great," Wakefield said. "He was a pretty quiet guy, nothing at all like Al Bundy. We talked for a few minutes about baseball, and he told me how he was originally  from Youngstown, Ohio, which is only about an hour or so from Pittsburgh."

"Tim has tremendous poise," Pirate catcher Don Slaught said more than just once during the second half of the season. "He came up when we lost  Zane, who was one of our best pitchers, and just stepped right in. He throws  the kind of pitch that can end up just about anywhere. But if he throws a  wild pitch, or if Spanky [LaValliere] or I let one get past us, he doesn't blink an eye. He'll throw the pitch ninety-five percent of the time and  nothing rattles him."

In a lot of ways, Wakefield was the answer to the Pirates' prayers, but  Pittsburgh had some other prayers answered in 1992. Probably the biggest blessing was having Andy Van Slyke in the outfield for the entire season.  Pittsburgh's problems with back pain were well documented, not only in baseball, but across town at the Civic Arena, where Penguins' star Mario  Lemieux missed half of the Penguins' first Stanley Cup championship season  in 1991 with severe back problems.

Pirate third baseman Jeff King initially injured his back in the 1990 NLCS against the Reds and missed most of '91 because of the tormenting pain.

"It was frustrating more than anything," King said of his experience. "It  hurt to bend over and tie my shoes, but no one could find anything wrong. I  traveled all around the country seeing six or seven different doctors, but no one had an answer."

King's problems were straightened out after he under-went surgery in late  November to repair a ruptured disc in his lower back. He started slowly in  '92, but came on strong in the second half of the season and played steadily  at third base.

When King's injury made it apparent that he would not be able to play again  in '91, the Pirates called up rookie third baseman John Wehner from their  Class AAA Buffalo affiliate. Wehner responded well to his promotion and hit .340 until a back injury ended his season prematurely. He  also had a  ruptured disc that was repaired surgically near the end of the season, but it took him  the whole off-season before he was able to play baseball again.

Through the entire winter before the 1992 season was set to begin, Van  Slyke began to experience the same kind of discomfort in his lower back that his teammates went through. He couldn't swing a golf club or play racquetball. Even running to stay in shape was a problem.

"I kept thinking about what Jeff and John went through and it concerned me," Van Slyke said. "I knew what I was feeling was pretty much what they said they had felt. It ran through my mind a lot about what could happen."

Van Slyke's nature through his entire career has been to dive for any ball that he feels is catchable. Outfield walls were not a major barrier to him. He would climb them, leap them, or run into them if it meant catching the baseball. But it seemed that his body was now trying to tell him that it could not be as resilient as it had been in the past.

Even now, it was tough to listen. He would undoubtedly spend another season sliding along artificial turf or hurling himself against the very walls that limit his talents.

"Andy never wants to come out of the lineup," Jim Leyland said. "You know something's seriously wrong when he asks for a day off."

The pain didn't end when spring training came around. He asked Leyland at one point in mid-March to remove him from the line-up before an exhibition game and immediately the dreadful thoughts of season-ending surgery came into his mind.

"It got to the point where something had to be done," he said. "I couldn't go on like that. I couldn't have been an effective player that way. I had to get the problem solved, so if it meant surgery, then that's what it had to be."

Van Slyke was immediately sent back to Pittsburgh to see team orthopedist, Dr. Jack Failla, who put him through a series of tests over the next couple of days. In a way, he did have the same problems that King and Wehner had, but the discs had not ruptured. Van Slyke was told he would not need surgery and could continue to play, but because of three degenerative discs and another bulging disc, he would have to be rested more throughout the season and would definitely have to cut down on the aggressive style of play that was so common to him.

"I guess it's like getting a speeding ticket," said Van Slyke, who almost always has a joke or anecdote to go along with his answer. "I got the ticket fixed, and I don't have to pay the fine. But I'm still getting points taken off my driver's license."

The injury helped Van Slyke in a way, because he no longer tries to generate power with his swing. Without that added stress on his back, Van Slyke's swing is cut down to a degree that he hits more line drives than fly balls, and that usually means more hits than outs.

He came into the 1992 season with a .269 lifetime average. His best season was in 1987 when he hit .297 in his first year with the Pirates. Through the month of June, Van Slyke was hitting .340 and leading the National League in batting average. He finished the season at .324, second behind the Padres' Gary Sheffield. Besides having his best season average-wise, Van Slyke also set career marks in doubles (45) and hits (199). As expected, his home run total was down (14), but he had 89 RBIs, which showed his ability to drive in baserunners from the third position in the order.

"I know I'm a better hitter when I don't try to hit home runs," said Van Slyke, who played in his second All-Star game in '92 and hit .415 during the month of May. "When I try to hit the ball out of the park, I end up trying to pull everything or striking out. Now, home runs aren't even on my mind when I go to the plate.

"I'm just going up there with the idea of putting the ball in play. I've had more opposite-field hits than ever, I'm making better contact, and I still feel I'm a productive hitter."

"Andy found out there is a left field he can hit to," Pirates' hitting instructor, Milt May mused.

Van Slyke, who batted a career-best .297 against left-handed pitchers in '92, enjoyed the individual race with Sheffield for the batting title and said he doesn't really mind the decreased production in home runs if it means he can help the team in other ways.

"I don't know if I'll ever hit many home runs again," he said. "Maybe if I get on the right workout program, where I can gain strength in the right areas of my body. I'll just have to wait and see. Maybe my back will feel better some day, and I'll be able to generate more power again with it."

The home runs Van Slyke can do without. But the lack of aggressiveness is what bothers him the most. He knows he can't afford to take the pounding that his dives usually involve, but it is frustrating to watch a ball fall in when he knows he probably could have caught it.

"There have been times when I've had to pull back a little bit," Van Slyke said. "That hasn't been easy. I'm used to playing the game hard all the time, and it's tough to have to stop and think before you do something.

"There have been a couple times where I know I've hurt the club because I haven't dived for balls. Maybe I would have made the catch and maybe I wouldn't have. I just have to be careful and that's the way it is. It's better that I not dive for a ball in one game than do it and wind up missing a lot of games."

Van Slyke said his main concern with each passing season is to stay healthy so he can be available to play every day. And Leyland couldn't agree more with that philosophy.

"Any time the back is involved, you can never be too sure," Leyland said. "If Andy says it's hurting or stiff, and he or the trainers feel he can't play, then he won't. With a chronic problem like that, you can't take any chances."

The daily heat treatments, ultrasound therapy, and pre-game stretching help him prepare for most of the games, but Van Slyke can't deny the anxiety that is created from the constant reminders about his condition.

"It's really more mentally draining than physically draining," he said. "You're always thinking about the back, and you hope that it doesn't hurt too badly. It's always in the back of your mind. I can't really ever avoid it. There's always some amount of pain in varying degrees."

One thing the back problems didn't take away from Van Slyke was an award that has almost become synonymous with his name. Although his outfield aggressiveness was slightly tempered, Van Slyke still made the outstanding catches and covered enough ground to win his fifth straight Gold Glove Award, which is something he will never get tired of.

"Yeah, that really means a lot," said Van Slyke, who was also named by the Pirates as the winner of the Roberto Clemente Award for 1992. "With the early pain in my back, I didn't think I'd get another chance at it. There's probably always going to be some kind of soreness in my back. I'll just have to learn to live with it the best I can."

The Pirates also received honors in the infield as Jose Lind, who had long lived in the shadows of the Cubs' Ryne Sandberg when it came to notoriety, finally won a Gold Glove for his tremendous plays at second base. Lind made only six errors all season, and it was the third straight year he had committed fewer than 10 errors in a season.

To cap off the Pirates awards for 1992, Jim Leyland won his second Manager of the Year award as voted on by the Baseball Writers of America. Leyland, who also won the award in 1990 and finished second to Atlanta's Bobby Cox in '91, received more votes than runner-up Felipe Alou, who guided the Expos to an incredible second-place finish in the N.L. East.

"I have a good staff around me and a great group of ballplayers," Leyland said unselfishly. "Our staff has been together for a while and the players relate well to them. I make the decisions, but it's a lot easier when you have guys like I do surrounding you."

๛

There was a lot of hoopla surrounding the Pirates as they prepared for Game 1 of the 1992 National League Championship Series against the Atlanta Braves. The biggest question coming from just about every reporter's lips was what would it take to shake the losses of the previous two seasons and get the Pirates to the World Series?

"We just have to play relaxed," Pirate leftfielder Barry Bonds said. "We can't come in and play nervous or feel like our backs are against the wall. If they beat us, they beat us, but I'm going to do everything I can not to let that happen."

Bonds' two previous playoff trips were simply miserable as he hit a combined .156 in 13 games over 1990 and '91. He had just seven post-season hits— and one extra-base hit— in 45 at bats, and struck out nine times. It was generally felt by everyone involved that if the Pirates were going to get past the favored Braves, they would need Bonds to have a big series.

Pittsburgh, which was 35-37 against the Western division during the regular season, won the East with a 96-66 record and finished nine games better than the second-place Montreal Expos. Atlanta had the best record in baseball in 1992 (98-64) and finished eight games ahead of the Cincinnati Reds in the West. The Pirates sent Doug Drabek, who was 15-11 with a 2.77 earned run average during the regular season, to the mound for Game

1 against the Braves' John Smoltz, who finished 15-12 and had a 2.85 ERA.

Smoltz, who was 2-0 in career post-season play, retired the Pirates in order in the first inning, and Drabek did the same to the Braves in the bottom of the first. The crowd immediately started to chant, "Ba-rry, Ba-rry," when Bonds led off the top of the second, and a sea of tomahawks chopped into the Atlanta night.

Three pitches later, Bonds endured another ominous beginning to post-season play as Smoltz snuck three fork balls past him without the bat ever leaving Bonds' shoulders. "I didn't expect three fork balls in a row, I'll tell you that," Bonds said afterwards. "He got me that time."

Atlanta struck first, as it had in five of the seven playoff games with the Pirates the season before. Sid Bream hit a one-out single to center and after Ron Gant struck out, catcher Damon Berryhill, who was replacing the injured Greg Olson, walked. Second baseman Mark Lemke then singled up the middle to drive in Bream with the first run of the game.

The Pirates got two runners on in the fourth inning, but Jeff King popped out to end the threat with Jay Bell standing at third. Bream stroked an RBI-double to left centerfield in the Braves' fourth and came around to score on Orlando Merced's throwing error to give Atlanta a 3-0 lead.

The Braves made it 4-0 in the bottom of the fifth on Jeff Blauser's solo home run to left, and they added another in the seventh when Otis Nixon singled, stole second, and scored on Terry Pendleton's single to left center field. The Pirates avoided a shutout—and a major league record for consecutive post-season scoreless innings (29) dating back to 1991—when Lind homered to lead off the top of the eighth, but Atlanta continued its playoff mastery over the Pirates and won the first game of the series, 5-1.

"It's disappointing because you want to get off on the right foot," said Drabek, whose 4-2/3 innings marked just the third time in 35 starts in '92 that he didn't last into the sixth inning. "You have to realize it's a seven-game series and even though you like to get that first game under your belt, a lot can happen to turn things around."

If anything, the Pirates remembered that they were the team that won the openers in their two previous playoff series, so losing this one may have been just what they needed.

"It's like the toss of the coin to start a football game," Bob Walk analyzed. "You want the ball first to see if you can go down the field and score, and then it's the other team's turn to see if they can score. They won the first game, now it's our turn to see if we can win one."

Losing the first game wasn't the end of the world in most of the players' eyes.

"Did we lose tonight?" Mike LaValliere asked when the subject of how important this loss was to the Pirates' approach to the rest of the series. "That's just my point. It's done and over with and there's nothing we can do about it. We made a few mistakes and they capitalized on them. It's just a matter of going out tomorrow and forgetting about this one."

So maybe the Pirates could forget about losing the first game, but losing the second one would put them in a most uncomfortable situation. Steve Avery, who won two games against the Pirates in 1991— both shutouts — and set an NLCS record with 17 scoreless innings, was on the mound against Pittsburgh left-hander Danny Jackson, who was 2-0 against the Pirates when he pitched for the Reds in the 1990 playoffs.

Jackson lasted just 1-2/3 innings as the Braves racked him for four runs and four hits in the bottom of the second and coasted to a 13-5 victory over the Pirates. Atlanta used three singles and a triple by Blauser to score its runs in the inning.

The Braves increased their lead to 8-0 in the bottom of the fifth on Gant's grand slam off Walk, who was the third Pirate pitcher of the game. The Pirates cut the lead in half in the top of the seventh when Bonds singled and scored on Lloyd McClendon's RBI-double to make it 8-1.

After Don Slaught walked, Lind tripled to right centerfield to drive in both McClendon and Slaught. Lind then scored on Avery's wild pitch and the Braves' lead was cut to 8-4. Relief pitching deserted the Pirates, however, as Denny Neagle gave up five runs in the bottom of the seventh to let the Braves put the game on ice.

"Being down 2-0 and having to fight back is not a good situation to be in," Bell said. "We can't make excuses. Those guys played good baseball and were prepared to play here. I don't think we played very good baseball at all. I think we were a poor example of the team that has been considered one of the best fundamental teams in baseball.

"The fact of the matter is, if we don't play better at home, we're going to get knocked off. It's as simple as that. But I don't think we'll play at home like we did here. Those guys are going to know they're in a series."

Like it or not; admit it or not, the Pirates were in a desperate situation. They were down two games to none to the Braves and had to win at least two out of three at home to send the series back to Atlanta. They needed a win, and they would have to rely on the rookie to get it for them.

Tim Wakefield was the talk of the National League over the last two months of the season. He had beaten the Mets twice and outdueled a fellow knuckle baller in Tom Candiotti of the Dodgers. He won eight games as a rookie and lost only one. He displayed the composure of a 10-year veteran and the modesty of a gentleman. Pirate supporters had known him for only a short time, but the 56,610 fans who packed Three Rivers Stadium for Game 3 believed he could pull their beloved team through.

Wakefield retired the Braves in order in the first inning and the Pirates seemed prepared to pounce on Atlanta starter, Tom Glavine, in the bottom of the first. Gary Redus, who was platooning with Orlando Merced at first base throughout the series, led off with a triple to right centerfield. But just like series' of recent past, the Pirates could not push the run across.

Bell grounded back to Glavine for the first out. Van Slyke hit one down the first base line that Sid Bream made a nice stop on—a play that Redus should probably have scored on as well — and Bonds also grounded out to Bream to let Glavine off the hook.

Bream gave Atlanta a 1-0 lead with his third career home run in post-season play in the top of the fourth, but Slaught tied it with a solo homer to left in the Pirates' fifth. It stayed that way until the bottom of the sixth when Van Slyke led off with a double and scored on Jeff King's one- out double.

Gant hit his second home run in the top of the seventh to make it a 2-2 game, but the Pirates scored the decisive run in the bottom of the seventh. Redus, who was 3 for 3 in the game, hit a one-out single to left center and moved to third on Bell's double. Van Slyke's fly ball to rightfield was deep enough to score Redus and the Pirates had a 3-2 lead.

The best the Braves could do after that was Nixon's two-out, eighth-inning double as Wakefield went the distance to record his ninth win of the season and first in post-season play. Wakefield struck out three, but allowed only five hits and one walk as the Pirates kept their heads above water in the series.

Game 4 was a rematch of Game 1, as Smoltz went up against Drabek for the second time in the series. As usual, the Braves struck first with a pair of runs in the top of the second. Smoltz helped himself with a two-out, RBI-single, and Nixon followed with another base hit to drive in the second Atlanta run.

The Pirates tied it in the bottom of the second when LaValliere and Lind singled with one out and Drabek walked to load the bases. Rightfielder Alex Cole, whom the Pirates acquired in a mid-season trade with the Cleveland Indians, singled through the box to drive home LaValliere, and when Braves shortstop Jeff Blauser couldn't get a handle on the ball, Lind hustled home with the tying run.

Merced's one-out double to right center scored King from first in the bottom of the third to give the Pirates a 3-2 lead, but the Braves regained the lead in the top of the fifth on David Justice's RBI single to right, and King's throwing error on a ball hit by Brian Hunter, who was pinch-hitting for Bream. Randy Tomlin's relief appearance for the Pirates after Justice's hit marked the second straight game that Drabek couldn't get past the fifth inning.

Atlanta added a pair of runs in the sixth as Smoltz singled with two outs off Tomlin, stole second, and scored on Nixon's double. Blauser added an RBI single off reliever Danny Cox, and the Braves were on their way to a 6-4 victory and a 3-1 lead in the series.

The Pirates were reminded all through the night and into the next day that no team had ever come back from a 3-1 deficit in NLCS play, but they still felt they had the makings to become the first. Bonds, who was 1-for-11 in the series and just 8 for 56 in post-season play, spent about two hours in manager Jim Leyland's office after the game. They talked about his slump and the many things that seemed to be going wrong for the Pirates.

"I think Barry Bonds is the best player in the game today," Leyland said earlier in the season. "A lot of players go through seven-game stretches or more when the hits aren't falling. It just seems that his come around playoff time, and it gets magnified a thousand times over with each out he makes. I don't worry about him, because I know he's the type of guy that can break out of it at any time, and if he does, look out."

Game 5 was scheduled for Sunday and when Bonds awoke in his suburban Pittsburgh home, there stood before him one of the greatest surprises he could possibly have received. Bonds' wife, Sun, flew Bonds' closest friend in baseball, Bobby Bonilla, in from New York in hopes that her husband would relax and not take the weight of the world on his shoulders every time he stepped to the plate that night.

Bonds and Bonilla spent the day together, and Bonilla was a guest of the Pirates in the press box as he hoped his former teammates could keep the series going.

Up to now, Steve Avery had been a wizard against the Pirates, who didn't score a run on him in the '91 playoffs and were beaten by him in Game 2 this year, 13-5. Danny Jackson was the starter for the Pirates in Game 2, but he never got out of the first inning as he dropped his sixth straight decision to the Braves. If the Pirates were to stay alive, they would have to count on their reliable veteran Bob Walk, whose last playoff win was Game 1 of the 1990 NLCS against Cincinnati.

Pittsburgh played inspired from the beginning, as it scored four first-inning runs and chased Avery after he faced just six batters. Redus continued his torrid series with a double to lead off the inning and scored the first Pirate run on Bell's single to center. Van Slyke's ground out to third moved Bell to second, and Bonds stepped in for his first at bat.

It wasn't as dramatic as the shot heard 'round the world, but one could see and feel the tension lifted from Bonds' shoulders as he drilled a double to the left centerfield wall. As he stood at second, his lips clearly mouthed the words, "Finally, it's over." Three long years of not delivering when his teammates relied on him. Three years of being known to the national audiences as a choker and a failure were lifted with that one at bat. The crowd roared around Barry Bonds, and he shook his head and smiled.

The Pirates weren't through as King and McClendon hit back-to-back RBI doubles to put the Pirates ahead 4-0. Bonds finished 2-for-5 with two runs scored; King was 3-for-4 with two runs; Redus was 2-for-4 and McClendon, who hit an astonishing 8-for-11 in the series, was 3-for-3. In all, Pittsburgh pounded out 13 hits, and Walk pitched the second complete game of the series for the Pirates as his three hitter shut down the Braves, 7-1.

"I just wanted to go as long as I could and give us a chance to win the game," Walk said. "Fortunately, we had a lot of guys come through, and now we're going back to Atlanta. We believe in ourselves, and we know anything's possible. That's why they play all the games until someone wins four."

The Pirates returned to Atlanta with renewed life and a confidence they had lacked through much of the first four games. "We had intensity and we were confident all along," Bell said. "But we just didn't play well in a couple of the games, and it cost us."

They were down three games to two, but the Pirates had their rookie phenom on the mound for Game 6. By now, no one with the Pirates felt this kid, Wakefield, knew the meaning of the word fear. "I told Timmy before he pitched his first playoff game to just go out and have fun," Ray Miller said. "When it was over, he said that's exactly what he did. I went up to him before Game 6 and said, 'Remember the fun you had your first time out?' He shook his head yes, and I said, 'Go out and have some more fun.'"

It was a game where all the Pirates had fun and carried over some of the momentum and enthusiasm that had carried them since the first inning of Game 5. After a scoreless first inning, the Pirates jumped all over Atlanta starter, Tom Glavine, in the second.

Bonds led off with his first career post-season home run, and the Pirates followed with three straight hits. King and McClendon had back-to-back singles and both scored on Slaught's two-run double. Lind reached safely as shortstop Jeff Blauser tried to make a play on Slaught at third, but threw the ball away, allowing Slaught to score the fourth Pirates run. Atlanta used poor fielding judgment again on Wakefield's sacrifice bunt when Glavine tried to make a play on Lind at third, but didn't get an out anywhere. Redus' double to right scored Lind, and Bell capped off the inning with a three-run homer to give the Pirates an 8-0 lead.

The Pirates added four runs in the top of the fifth as Redus and McClendon continued to swing the hot bats, and McClendon smacked a solo home run in the sixth to make it 13-1. Wakefield allowed a pair of home runs to Justice, but nailed down his second complete-game win of the series by getting Bream to ground out to Bell for the last out in the ninth.

"Tim had a nasty, nasty knuckle ball," Slaught said. "I couldn't catch it at first, but he kind of toned it down later and started getting it over for strikes. The big inning definitely gave us a lift. It takes a lot of pressure off the catcher to have an 8-0 lead when he's catching a knuckle baller. When we got the big lead, we tried to go back and forth with the fastball, curve, and knuckler, but Tim was losing his feel for the knuckle ball, so we decided it would be better to stay with that because that's what got him there."

When it became apparent the Pirates were going to force a seventh and deciding game, speculation immediately arose in the press box about the possibility of Leyland removing Wakefield early and saving him for some work —possibly even the start— in Game 7. The knuckle ball was not as strenuous on the arm as other pitches might be, so a lot of the writers thought such a scenario would be possible.

"That's why they're up in the press box and not down on the field," Ray Miller quipped.

"I knew I was going to be asked that question by somebody," Leyland said. "The answer is no. We were in an oxygen tent the last couple of days. We had to win that game [Game 6] so there was no way I was going to take Wakefield out as long as he could keep going. As hot as he is, I may use him to manage [in Game 7], but I won't use him to pitch."

"I've seen a lot of good young pitchers have impacts on a team," Miller said. "But I've never seen anyone like him [Wakefield]. He pitched two pressure-filled games and kept us in this thing."

If Tim Wakefield was to see any more action, it would be as the Pirates' Game 1 starter in the World Series. Their ace for the last five years would get the call for Game 7, and despite the fact that Doug Drabek did not make it through the fifth inning in either of his first two starts, everyone affiliated with the Pirates liked his chances in a third opportunity.

❧

While Leyland quickly ended all speculation about who his Game 7 starting pitcher would be, he could not seem to avoid the questions about his starting lineup.  For the entire season—and perhaps his entire managerial career— Leyland has believed in the theory of using a mostly right-handed lineup against a left-handed pitcher and vice-versa.

He did it throughout the Pirates' rough stages in 1986 and 1987 and continued to do so through the playoff years of '90, '91, and '92.  Through the first six games of these playoffs, Leyland's main three switches were at first base, rightfield, and behind the plate.  When Tom Glavine and Steve Avery pitched in four of the games, Leyland countered with right-handed hitters Gary Redus at first; Lloyd McClendon in right, and Don Slaught behind the plate.  Those three responded with a combined 19 hits, two home runs, 12 RBIs, and a .487 average through the first six games.  They were, in fact, the biggest reasons the Pirates made it to a deciding game because of their clutch hitting in Games 5 and 6— games in which the Pirates knocked Avery and Glavine out of the box very early.

Orlando Merced, Alex Cole, and Mike LaValliere were the left-handed side of Leyland's coin and they had done little to strike fear into the heart of John Smoltz, who was the Braves' only right-handed starter in their playoff rotation.  Through the first six games, Merced, Cole, and LaValliere had combined for just four hits, no homers, two RBIs, and a .190 average.

The questions surfaced immediately after Game 6.  "With Redus, McClendon and Slaught swinging the hot bats, would you consider starting them against Smoltz in Game 7?" the media begged to find out from Leyland.

Redus was 2-for-5 in Game 6 with two runs scored and two RBIs; Slaught was 1-for-4 with two runs scored and two RBIs; McClendon was 3-for-3 with a  home run off of Braves' relief pitcher, Marvin Freeman, who was right-handed.  For the series, Redus was 7 for 16 (.438) with four runs scored; Slaught was 4-for-12 (.333) with a home run and five RBIs; and McClendon was the most sizzling Pirate of all.  He had an astounding .727 average (8-for-11) with four runs scored, two doubles, one home run, and four RBIs.

The logic of making such changes seemed to have credence, but Leyland answered before the question was barely out of a reporter's mouth that he would stick with the system the Pirates had used all season.

"I don't think you change basically what you did all year," he said. "I don't think it would be fair to all of a sudden play somebody against a right-hander who hasn't played (in that situation) all year. I just don't think that's the right way to do it. You're putting pressure on a guy and all of a sudden asking him to do something he hasn't done all year. That's why I'm staying with the basic lineup."

And those that would be seated next to Leyland in the Pirates dugout in Game 7—Redus, McClendon and Slaught—had no problems with the decision, nor did they show any hints of displeasure following their successes in Game 6.

"All we've done so far is buy ourselves a Game 7," said McClendon, who was also 3-for-3 in the Pirates' Game 5 victory. We've been on a platoon system all year; that's the way we've played and it's worked. I don't see any reason for it to change now. We won 96 ballgames with the personnel we have. There's no reason to change."

"We're a team and you can't dictate what other guys are going to do," Redus said after Game 6. "I know Orlando is going to do the job at first base; I know A.C. (Cole) is going to do the job in rightfield, and I know Mike will do the job behind the plate. It has been the same all year. I know exactly when I'm going to play and it's going to be against left-handers. It's that simple."

❧

It was 6:15 p.m. on the evening of October 14. The starting time for the deciding game was still about two-and-a-half hours away, but Jim Leyland walked along the outskirts of the Pirate bullpen and practiced imaginary golf swings with his fungo bat. The man whom many feel smokes too many cigarettes and drinks too much coffee seemed as relaxed as ever for a game that would decide whether his team continued playing or not.

One by one, Pirate players sifted slowly out of the club-house and prepared to hear the shrill call of strength coach Warren Sipp's whistle that would signal the beginning of the team's pre-game stretch. Leyland continued to look relaxed as he exchanged pleasantries with several members of the media and honored a couple of interview requests.

At approximately 8:35 p.m., John Smoltz threw the first pitch to Pirate rightfielder Alex Cole and another 162-game season was down to just one last game for either Pittsburgh or Atlanta. Cole walked on four straight pitches, and after Bell was unsuccessful on a sacrifice bunt attempt, Van Slyke moved Cole to third with a double to right centerfield. The Braves intentionally walked Bonds, whom they feared was coming out of his three-year, post-season shell, but Orlando Merced gave the Pirates a 1-0 lead with a sacrifice fly to rightfield.

Drabek pitched well through the first five innings as he allowed only Damon Berryhill's lead-off double in the third. The Pirates added a run in the top of the sixth when Bell doubled to left and scored on Van Slyke's single to center.

Atlanta mounted a rally in the bottom of the sixth with three straight singles from Lemke, Jeff Treadway—who was batting for Smoltz— and Nixon, who reached on a bunt single. With the bases loaded and nobody out, Blauser hit a shot down the third base line that King stabbed out of the air and then stepped on third to double off Lemke for a quick unassisted double play. Pendleton then lined out to Bonds in left, and Drabek had pitched out of a major jam.

The Pirates had a chance to get a much-needed insurance run in the top of the eighth, but Merced was thrown out at the plate by Justice as he tried to score from first base on a double by King into the rightfield corner. "We said in the beginning that it would be tough to get runs off a lot of Atlanta's pitchers," Pirates third base coach Rich Donnelly said. "If there was anything even remotely close, we had agreed to keep the runners moving and try to manufacture runs."

The lost run turned out to be huge for the Pirates, and when they were set down with ease in the top of the ninth, it all came down to one unusual and unbelievable bottom of the ninth.

≈

. . . The fans would talk about it for the entire off-season and will continue to talk about it every off-season as long as there is baseball in Pittsburgh. "Remember the '92 series with the Braves?" they will ask. "Bases loaded, two outs. All we needed was one more out, and we were in the series. And it all fell apart because of some no-name."

Francisco Cabrera, the last hope for the Atlanta Braves took two balls from Stan Belinda, whom Leyland had decided to stick with the rest of the way. Belinda was throwing nothing but fastballs to Cabrera, and his 2-0 pitch was met first with a cheer, then a groan as the sharp line drive landed foul in the third base boxes.

Now Cabrera dug in, expecting another fastball from Belinda. "When I saw that foul ball pitch, I decided to move in a little bit," centerfielder Andy Van Slyke said. "I figured if he was going to beat me, he was going to have to hit it past me. I wasn't going to let him drop one in front of me."

When he came up with the idea of playing just a touch shorter in center field, Van Slyke motioned to Bonds to also move in. Bonds nodded at him and made a gesture as if to say he had the situation under control. Not a minute later, the ball was rocketed past Dell at shortstop on a line drive, and Bonds was running up and over to his left to try for a play at the plate.

Justice came home with the tying run, and Braves' third base coach Jimy Williams waved frantically for Bream to try to score. Bonds came up with the ball as Bream rounded third, and his throw made one hop in front of the mound and slightly to the right, which forced LaValliere's momentum away from the plate for just a split second. LaValliere caught the ball and hurriedly made a sweep tag of Bream as his left foot came sliding into home plate.

"I didn't know what happened," LaValliere said. "I tried to block the plate, and when I swept him with the tag, all I saw was dirt and chalk and Sid's steel cleats. Everything happened in such a blur."

"I thought of myself as a racehorse coming down the home stretch after I rounded third," Bream said. "All I kept thinking was, come on legs, don't fail me now."

If the saying was true about baseball being a game of inches, this was the type of play that gave the phrase its meaning. As Bream slid into home ahead of or behind LaValliere's quick tag, Randy Marsh stood over the play and wasted little time in throwing his arms out to signify the safe call.

LaValliere and the rest of the Pirates left the field in a slow daze. Bream was covered by a sea of Braves at home plate, and the new Atlanta hero, Francisco Cabrera, was first drawn into the mob of players, and then was hoisted high on someone's shoulders for the whole world to see.

Bonds remained on his knees in leftfield, frozen in the position that momentum caused from his last throw as a Pirate. Van Slyke sat in center field with his knees drawn close to his chest and stared in disbelief at the wild celebration going on around home plate. It was his team that should have been celebrating; his team that had the rug pulled out from under it in the bottom of the ninth inning.

Inside the locker rooms, a table full of opened champagne bottles were whisked out of the Pirates' clubhouse for the anticipated celebration and down the hall to their new party location in the Atlanta dressing room. The series Most Valuable Player trophy was also in the Pittsburgh clubhouse and it was going to be presented to Tim Wakefield once the game had ended. That too was transferred to the Braves' locker room, much like a child's favorite toy is taken away as punishment for an offense he should never have been held accountable for. It was presented to Smoltz, who wasn't even a factor in the game's final outcome.

Outside, Van Slyke remained stunned on the field. He was the last player from either team to exit as everything seemed like a horrible nightmare to him.

"All of my emotion, all of my adrenaline went out of me after that one play," Van Slyke said. "That's why I sat there for so long. I just couldn't believe something like that happened to us, and we were out of the playoffs again. I just didn't want to talk or say anything to anybody, and it was that way for me for about the next three days."

The two pitchers involved in the ninth inning for the Pirates could have easily hidden in the training room after the game, but both braved the questions of what went wrong.

"It was a do-or-die situation, and every pitcher has got to like being in that spot," Drabek said of going out to start the ninth. "Fortunately, I was in that situation and I still felt good. But it was just something that didn't work out."

"I don't think there's a person among you [the media] who wouldn't like to be in that situation at some moment in your life," Belinda said. "I wanted to and I was, but I just didn't get it done. The guy just hit a good pitch, there's not much else to say. Tonight he got me."

Most of all, the players and even the national media felt for Jim Leyland. His genius had carried the Pirates to three straight division championships, but just when it looked like he was finally going to manage in his first World Series, the opportunity was cruelly snatched away from him.

Leyland graciously commended Bobby Cox and the Braves on a great series in an interview with CBS and then talked about the bottom of the ninth.

"It's definitely a heartbreaker," he told CBS analyst Tim McCarver. "It goes back to that old Yogi-ism, 'It ain't over 'til it's over.' You have to be a competitor. You go to work and do your job and this is the ultimate, to get in a situation like this. I manage all games to the best of my abilities, and I'm confident I'll get back here again some day."

Later, Leyland met with the press and gave his assessments all over again.

"It's a little tough to have to tell you for the third year in a row how much we appreciate the job you did and the patience you showed to our players," Leyland said as his voice cracked, and he was heard to choke back a few tears. "I'm very proud of what this team did, and I never doubted we could win the series. Even when we were down three games to one.

"This is, without question, the toughest loss I've ever been through. I'm still in shock somewhat, and I don't know if I'm answering questions very well right now. It's a heartbreaker, but the Pittsburgh Pirates still walk tall tonight and will continue to do their best to make it back again. We'll look back on it later and say this was a very good year for the Pirates. I'm very proud of this club because they never quit. We've come up short by one game for two years in a row, but there are a lot of other teams that would like to have been where we are."

The post-game media crush was gone, and most of the players had their gear packed and were situated on the buses that sat just outside the clubhouse doors. Jim Leyland was dressed in a shirt and tie as he walked around to some of the players who remained in the gloomy aftermath.

He thanked them for a terrific season and accepted their condolences with a smile and a hearty slap on the back that said his appreciation to them far outweighed the disappointment he felt for this one evening.

The Pittsburgh Pirates may have felt the sting of playoff failure for another year, but led by the shining example of their manager, 1992 was a year that showed failure is only a word to describe quitters. The Pirates were by no means quitters, and they were definitely not failures.

# A Look at the Future

A little less than a month after that fateful October night when gloom and torment had descended upon the Pittsburgh Pirates for a third straight post-season, Jim Leyland was no longer the victim of the harsh and brutal crime that seemed to have been played out in Atlanta-Fulton County Stadium. It wasn't since 1951, when the Giants' Bobby Thompson hit his famous "Shot Heard 'Round The World" that any team had lost the pennant to the team that was behind at the time of the final pitch.

Leyland, as is his custom, had looked at the positives and forgotten the incident. Instead, he remained upbeat and talked of warm, glowing Florida sunshine in February — the coming of another spring training, and the chance to live the dream all over again. But even now, weeks after the Pirates' heartbreaking loss, he still receives the condolences of what might have been.

"I don't want people to feel sorry for me," Leyland says adamantly, "My God, we've been in the playoffs three straight years. We played in a seventh game twice. We played 20 of a possible 21 playoff games. I'm paid well. I have an excellent contract, I have an excellent family. We're healthy. I don't want sympathy. That's not what it's all about."

He went on to explain — for what he hoped would be the last time — what feelings he experienced when his team went down in defeat.

"We needed to get 27 outs," Leyland continued. "We only got 26. I can appreciate loyalty and concern from people, but it's been kind of odd. A lot of people seem to be saying, 'Hey, don't let it get you down.' To me, this thing is long gone. It's a memory. I'm not sure whether it's a good or bad memory, but it's life. We were down three games to one, the kids played their hearts out. It's part of life. Kids crying in the locker room, that's part of life. I enjoy life.

"I totally appreciate all the very good friends who called me to tell me how bad they felt, but they seem to be implying that there was something unfair about it, that it doesn't seem fair. I don't understand that. We played nine innings, they got one more run than we did. I have no hangups about that whatsoever. Things were fair. We played 162 plus seven, but we didn't get done what we had to. That's the game."

Mike LaValliere, a part of the Pirates' two-catcher system and the one who made the gallant sweeping tag of Sid Bream to try to save the Pirates' season in the bottom of the ninth, remembered the loss of Leyland's first child and felt there was little comparison in losing a playoff game in the last inning.

"People show their emotions in different ways," LaValliere said. "Everybody knows Jim's really into the game and he shows it, but a lot of guys who are really quiet are just as much into it as everybody else. Jim's just as fragile as the rest of us, but I don't worry about him. He's gone through worse losses in his life, and they don't all involve baseball. If losing the playoffs three years in a row is the worst thing that happens to him, then he's had a helluva life."

But when a young and obscure, last-minute replacement named Francisco Cabrera altered the course of Pirate baseball history, everyone around Jim Leyland treated the situation as though it would end his world forever. And that just was not the way Leyland wanted it to be.

"I felt pretty bad in the days after the game," he said. "I just wanted to be with my wife, and we stayed in the house because the minute we went outside, everybody was telling me how bad they felt. I felt bad for them, too. It was the same way when I got on the plane to come home that night. Seeing the faces on the people, on my wife, seeing that they were wondering what I was going to do. I thought, 'This is nuts.'

"After a few days of discussing it with Katie, I knew I couldn't let that kind of stuff go on any longer. I watched the World Series and I rooted for the Braves. They were the National League champs and Bobby Cox is the best. I decided to have a nice winter, enjoy a great off-season, and then continue to work my tail off to contribute the best I can to the Pittsburgh Pirates' organization.

"Is the loss heartbreaking? No question. But if somebody's waiting for it to dampen my spirit or dull my enthusiasm, forget it."

❧

As time goes on, the players involved can wash away the hurt and anguish that swept past them in that dreadful ninth inning. But the memory will last forever.

"It took three days; three solid days," Andy Van Slyke said. "It was all I thought of, and I did nothing but mope around the house and relive that last inning the whole time. But then I got over it. It was over and there was nothing any of us could do to change the outcome. Life would have to go on, and we would have to look forward to 1993."

The Pirates would have to look at the very real possibilities of facing 1993 without a couple of the faces that had been so vital to their successes over the past three seasons.

Doug Drabek had played out his option in 1992 and could shop his services around the league to the highest bidders. He played true to his word in '92 when he said if no deal was worked out before spring training ended, he would close the subject until the end of the season. He was not a difficult case by any means in terms of negotiations, but Drabek was, and always has been, the consummate professional who believed in giving 100 percent effort to his job. His job was to pitch for the Pittsburgh Pirates and he wanted no outside distractions that could possibly hinder his and the Pirates' chances for success.

There was a certain feeling throughout the season that the Pirates would work out some kind of deal with Drabek to keep him in a Pittsburgh uniform. Somehow it never seemed right to consider he would pitch for anyone else, considering what his presence both on and off the field had meant to the Pirate organization.

Drabek had always been a leader for the Pirates. He displayed Roberto Clemente-like qualities in terms of dignity and never turned down a request for an autograph from a fan or an interview from the media. Win or lose, good outing or bad, Drabek was forever the gentleman. He was one of the most popular Pirate figures when it came to charitable requests and appearances. He, like Van Slyke, has also worked his magic for young people whose wish it was to meet their favorite Pirate.

To Pirate fans, the possibility of losing Drabek was one of those situations that you would think about for a second, maybe run your fingers along your chin, and then say, "Nah, it'll never happen."

It happened.

On December 1, 1992, nearly two months after the National League pennant was snatched from the Pirates' fingertips, Doug Drabek was no longer a Pittsburgh Pirate. Instead, he became a member of the Houston Astros as the result of a four-year contract that netted him $19.5 million.

For Drabek, it was a chance to go home. He is from The Woodlands, a suburb of Houston, and when he thought of the possibility that he, his wife, Kristy, and their three children could live in one place year-round, he knew it was an opportunity he couldn't pass up.

"I said all along that I would do what was best for my family and myself," said Drabek, who has a 99-70 career record and a 3.11 earned run average. "My family is very important to me, and my kids [Justin, age 6; Kyle, 5; and Kelsey, 1] are school age, which is another important factor.

"This contract is the most important one of my career. At my age, I'll probably not get the opportunity to sign another one for this length. The idea of keeping my kids in a stable environment and not having to move twice a year was very appealing. All things considered, this is the best thing that could have happened."

Drabek received a $1 million signing bonus and will receive salaries of $4 million in 1993 and 1994 and $4.75 million in 1995 and 1996. The Astros hold the option on the 1997 season when Drabek can possibly earn $5 million or be bought out at $1 million. He made $4.5 million in his last season with the Pirates.

Pirates general manager Ted Simmons made the same offer to Drabek in April and even proposed the same money to be dished out in the same time frame. But when the Astros' offer was put on the table in December, Simmons wouldn't budge. At that time, he was only willing to offer Drabek a three-year contract.

"In April, we made a four-year offer that would have rewritten his contract for 1991 and carried him through 1992, 1993, and 1994," Simmons said. "In essence, we offered him the same kind of deal that would go through 1994. I don't want to go beyond that for a pitcher. The chances of them breaking down are too great.

"He's 30 now. He was 29 when we made the offer. The older a pitcher gets, the more of a risk he is. We made the same offer in April that Houston made now. At the time, our offer was unacceptable. I was disappointed to lose a pitcher of Drabek's caliber. But I wasn't surprised."

In late November of 1992, Drabek's agents, Alan and Randy Hendricks, told Simmons he could sign Drabek to a three-year contract, but it would cost the Pirates $17 million. "I couldn't go that high. No way," Simmons said.

Although Doug Drabek had sworn himself to silence during the season regarding his contract, he too had thoughts of returning to Pittsburgh for 1993 and beyond.

"I thought we had it done in spring training," Drabek said. "We were willing to give some stuff up and I was ready to sign. I really thought I was going to stay in Pittsburgh."

When Drabek apparently signed the same type of contract in Houston that the Pirates offered him in spring training, he left many Pirate fans with the impression that he didn't want to stay in Pittsburgh. But Drabek says that wasn't the case at all.

"I always said my first preference was to sign with the Pirates and it was," Drabek told *Beaver County Times* sportswriter John Perrotto. "But the contract I signed with the Astros is not the same contract I talked about with the Pirates. The Pirates wanted to renegotiate my 1992 contract and extend my contract through 1995. The contract I signed with the Astros takes me through 1996 and also has an option for 1997. It's like getting two extra years."

Drabek said he was willing to sign a three-year deal back in March, but when the four-year contracts were being offered by at least eight other teams after the 1992 season, he and his agents decided they weren't ready to settle for three years.

"We came down on our end [in March]," Drabek told Perrotto. "We offered to sign for three years, which would have reduced their risk. I'm not going to take the blame for not signing with Pittsburgh. We were willing to compromise. I think we were fair."

Drabek also had to wonder if the Pirates may have been overlooking his situation just a bit because they had another big free agent to think about in Barry Bonds.

"Much of the focus did seem to be on Barry and rightfully so," he said. "He's the best player in the game. I think some people forgot, however, that I was going to be a free agent. I had the feeling some people were assuming I was going to stay in Pittsburgh under any circumstances."

The main decision came down to location for Doug Drabek. When your hometown team comes calling, it can be a tough proposition to pass up.

"I know some people are going to look at it and think I just wanted out of Pittsburgh," Drabek told Perrotto. "That is not the case at all. I was very happy there and the people treated me and my family great. I wasn't purposely looking to leave."

ঌ

Through the 1991 and '92 seasons, Barry Bonds made it no secret that he was probably going to leave Pittsburgh. He and former teammate Bobby Bonilla suffered bruised egos when both lost salary arbitration cases after spectacular seasons in 1989 and 1990. Both said after their second arbitration setbacks they would remember the Pirates' stance on long-term contract negotiations when their time for free agency came up.

Bonilla celebrated his freedom following the 1991 season by signing a five-year, $29 million contract with the New York Mets. Bonilla, who is a Brooklyn native, said at the time that he would miss playing for Jim Leyland, but signing with the Mets was his opportunity to go home.

Bonds is another player who had thoughts of going home. He was born and raised in Southern California and as his days apparently became numbered with the Pirates, he often spoke of playing full-time on the west coast. During most of the 1992 season and the latter part of '91, Bonds frequently talked about playing for the San Diego Padres.

The Padres already had perennial National League batting champion, Tony Gwynn and power-hitting first baseman, Fred McGriff, and they added third baseman, Gary Sheffield, who challenged for baseball's Triple Crown (average, home run, and RBI champion) in 1992 and won the batting championship over Andy Van Slyke. "Imagine the lineup we could have," Bonds said on more than one occasion to reporters in 1992. "We'd be strong through the first six or seven batters."

Bonds did a one-on-one interview in the March, 1992, issue of *SPORT* magazine and said that he wouldn't mind playing for the San Diego Padres or any of the other California teams. "Except San Francisco," Bonds said. "It gets too cold there."

Bonds was probably thinking of the familiar phrase, "The coldest winter I ever spent was a summer in San Francisco" when he uttered those words. The city by the Bay is well known for its calm and beautiful summer afternoons, but blustery and often chilly summer evenings. It is not uncommon to see Giants' fans wrapped in blankets or wearing winter coats during night games at Candlestick Park in the middle of June. Players who usually bask in the short-sleeve weather of their profession layer themselves with T-shirts and turtleneck sweaters on a baseball night in San Francisco, and cover themselves with parkas that are usually reserved for the final days of the season in early-Autumn.

The Pirates went into the 1992 season with little hopes of signing Bonds to a long-term contract. Their final offer came in in February — $25 million over five years —but Bonds declined. The best the Pirates could do from there was hope to ride the All-Star outfielder's coat tails to another N.L. East title and whatever else could be accomplished from there.

Bonds did his share to help the Pirates win during the regular season by earning his second National League MVP award in three seasons. And although he had a third consecutive sub-par playoff performance, his talents were figured to be courted by many interested — and wealthy — suitors.

San Diego came up again in the first "Where will Barry Bonds end up?" conversations following the Pirates' playoff loss to Atlanta. The Braves were another team apparently courting Bonds, who was reportedly seen house hunting in Atlanta during one of the Pirates' visits there in the post-season. Rumor also had the Dodgers, Angels, Yankees, Mets, Cubs, and White Sox seeking his services.

Pirates General Manager Ted Simmons had his hands full in his first season of dealing with negotiating player's salaries *and* potentially losing two of his stars to free agency. He truly thought the Pirates had a chance of hanging onto Doug Drabek, but he knew the writing was on the wall as far as Bonds' departure.

Many times during the season, Bonds said he was happy in Pittsburgh and would continue to listen to offers from the Pirates. Bonds told a group of four or five reporters after one game more than halfway through the season that he only wanted to make sure the Pirates remained committed to winning, and if that was the case, he said he might even consider staying for less money than other potential bidders might offer. Simmons, however, felt that was a game the Pirates could not play.

"We're a small-market team," Simmons said during the National League playoffs in Atlanta. "We want to do everything we can to keep Bonds in Pittsburgh, but we can't get into a bidding war. Basically he's saying, 'If another team offers me $30, 40, or 50 million, I'll talk to you about staying in Pittsburgh for less.' Does that mean if another team offers him $50 million, he'll stay with us for $47 million? If it does, then I can't play. It's just not realistic to think he'll stay in Pittsburgh."

At the time, Simmons' hypothetical figures seemed somewhat farfetched, even for the current salaries that seemed to be skyrocketing by the minute. But as it turned out, his numbers weren't so very far off.

Bonds was apparently ever-so-close to signing an agreement with the Yankees. New York was reportedly offering him a whopping $36 million for five years, but Bonds' agent, Dennis Gilbert, who handled Bobby Bonilla's bonanza contract with the Mets just a year before, told Yankees' general manager Gene Michaels that his client was interested in a six-year deal. Michaels hedged on the extra year, saying that even though Bonds was the best player in baseball, teams had to draw the line somewhere.

Teams like the Padres, Dodgers, Angels, and Mets drew the line much earlier. With figures reaching levels that were previously unheard of in baseball, those teams all decided they would have to find a way to win without the best player in the game.

While Pittsburgh fans secretly hoped that Bonds would somehow be left out in the cold and maybe even become the example to every owner's decision to put an end to the levels of spending insanity that baseball had reached, Gilbert continued to shop his prize around.

Remember the place with the settled afternoons and unsettled evenings? The place where winter makes its appearance in the summer? Remember the place that was last on Barry Bonds' list of California baseball cities?

The 1992 season ended with much uncertainty for the San Francisco Giants. They were a team that finished just a few notches above the Los Angeles Dodgers at the bottom of the National League Western division standings. Their owner, Bob Lurie, had put the team up for sale during the season, and there were very strong indications that the Giants were about to be sold to a group of Tampa Bay investors, which meant Florida would suddenly have two major league franchises after having none in all the seasons before.

Talks persisted. Votes were cast. And when it all was over, baseball's owners voted in a majority to reject the sale to the Tampa group, which obviously blocked the Giants' relocation. While Tampa's elected officials fumed at baseball's utter disregard for their many efforts to bring major league baseball to their city, Lurie knew he had to look for buyers elsewhere.

With the Tampa deal all but forgotten, Lurie's attention turned to a group headed by Peter Magowan, who is chairman of Safeway Inc., a major supermarket chain on the west coast. There was no word on whether the deal would go through in early December, but as the Yankees continued to drag their tails in their negotiations with Bonds, someone in the Giants' organization acted smoothly and quickly.

On Saturday December 5, 1992, it was reported from baseball's winter meetings in Louisville that Bonds and the San Francisco Giants had agreed to a six-year, $43.75 million contract. The next day Bonds showed up at a press conference in a brand new suit with his wife, Sun, and father, Bobby, supposedly for a press conference to announce the signing. The only problem was that no one from the Giants' organization decided to attend.

As it turned out, Bonds had made the initial agreement with the Safeway group even though a deal had never been formally struck between Magowan and Lurie, and even without an OK from the other owners around the league. It was Lurie who put the deal on hold because he said he would not be responsible for paying Bonds if the sale of the Giants was not approved.

Just when it appeared that Bonds might be finding himself in a Pittsburgh Pirate uniform in 1993 after all, the three sides worked out a deal two days later that confirmed Bonds' agreement in San Francisco and his departure from Pittsburgh.

The deal was by far the richest in baseball history as it surpassed the old record of $32.5 million over five years that Cal Ripken, Jr., received when he re-signed with Baltimore. Bonds received a $2.5 million signing bonus on top of annual salaries which began at $4 million in 1993; $4.75 million in 1994; $7.75 million in 1995; $8 million in 1996; $8.25 million in 1997, and $8.5 million in 1998. His $7,291,166 average annual salary surpassed the record $7.1 million annual salary Ryne Sandberg has in his contract with the Chicago Cubs.

"This is the greatest day of my life," Bonds said when the official press conference to announce his signing finally took place. "It's really so unbelievable."

Bonds said he would look forward to hitting in the Giants' lineup between All-Star first baseman Will Clark and slugging third baseman Matt Williams. He also took one more opportunity to reflect on his days with the Pirates, finding it hard to believe that his time was already behind him.

"I never really wanted to leave Pittsburgh," Bonds said. "They had plenty of chances to try to work out a contract in seven years. I was right there the whole time. I don't understand why they never ever really tried to sign me to a long-term contract. Really, though, I never *did* understand the Pirates management."

While his words toward Pirate management were more stinging than anything, Bonds had nothing but praise for Jim Leyland, who was now all of a sudden his former manager.

"Jim Leyland is the best coach I have ever played for," Bonds said. "I would've played for him for nothing. I will especially miss him now that I'm no longer with the Pittsburgh Pirates."

An interesting sidelight to Bonds' signing was the fact that the Giants were the same team his father played for from 1968 to 1974. When Bonds gave more thought to the Giants' offer, he looked back on his days as a young man shagging fly balls in the Candlestick Park outfield with his father on one side of him and his godfather on the other side.

Willie Mays wore No. 24 during his illustrious playing career, and when Barry Bonds signed his lucrative deal with San Francisco, he asked if it would be all right to wear his godfather's number, because that was the number he had worn as a Pirate. Mays' number had been retired and commemorated on a sign on the outfield fence at Candlestick, but when Barry asked permission to display the number once again, Mays granted it.

The issue brought outrage to fans and media alike in San Francisco. Most felt this business of coddling players had gone just a bit too far. Willie Mays was a legend in every Giant fan's eyes and godson or no godson, almost everyone felt Bonds should leave the number in its proper place.

And when Bonds thought more about it, he agreed that history should be left alone. When he showed up at a press gathering in San Francisco two days after his official signing, Bonds held a Giants' jersey in front of him with the No. 25 on the back.

"I'm going to wear the No. 25 in honor of my own father, whom I love very, very much," the younger Bonds told the media. "I think it's best to let a great, great athlete who deserves everything keep his number retired. The only place the number 24 belongs is on that fence."

Both Bonds' confirmed that Mays had given permission to allow Barry to wear his number, but he decided he could still gain inspiration from Mays without wearing the same number.

"It'll be a great honor for me to play leftfield and still see the sign up there," he said. "Because I can still be a little boy pretending I'm in the outfield with my father and godfather.

"When you have someone you admire, and he's your godfather and he loves you very, very much, he wants to do something very special for you. I think that's what Willie wanted to do for me."

It was a chilly, rainy, and foggy day in San Francisco when Barry Bonds met the press for the first time. What other kind of day should it have been for the man who thought that city was too cold to play in? Eventually the question of Bonds' past dislike for San Francisco's seemingly antiquated stadium came up, but he was ready with an answer.

"I didn't like the visitors' accommodations," Bonds said. "The dugout was bad because we didn't have any heaters and there were no bathrooms nearby, so it made things a little tough for the visitors. That's all it was."

                                        ❧

The changing of the guard began for the Pittsburgh Pirates even before the departures of Doug Drabek and Barry Bonds and it continued afterwards. Some of the changes were expected and when faced with losing two of your top performers, a different look or makeup is bound to develop. But no one expected the swift and abrupt change in the chemistry of the three-time National League East champions.

The alterations began with the expansion draft, which was held in mid-November, 1992. The new teams for 1993 — Florida and Colorado — opted mostly for minor league talent, but the Pirates felt their share of losses on the major league level. The first undressing began when outfielder Alex Cole, who became a starter in rightfield through the second half of the season after a trade from Cleveland, was taken by the Colorado Rockies. Pittsburgh also lost starting pitcher Danny Jackson, who was acquired in a mid-season trade from the Cubs and figured in Leyland's plans as a possible left-handed closer in 1993.

Knowing they were about to lose Bonds to the highest bidder, the Pirates were suddenly down to just one regular outfielder in Andy Van Slyke. They were also aware of Drabek's possible departure and with Zane Smith's season-ending shoulder problems, the Pirates were also becoming thin on the mound.

"We're going to have to do some patching," general manager Ted Simmons told John Perrotto of the *Beaver County Times*. "We feel we have outstanding pitching depth in our organization, and we've taken great pains to ensure we don't lose any of our young pitching. That's where we're trying to build a good reserve."

After losing Cole in the expansion draft, Simmons said there was no need to panic and cited the possibilities of signing a free agent, which was something the Pirates hadn't done since 1989. "There are some mid-level guys out there who might help us," Simmons said.

The real house cleaning began on the afternoon of November 19 when second baseman Jose Lind was traded to the Kansas

Foley, like most players around the league, was curious about the prospects of playing for Jim Leyland, so he jumped at the opportunity.

"I have a lot of respect and admiration for Jim Leyland after playing against him for so many years," Foley said. "I know he gives everybody on the bench a chance to play, and that's why the Pirates were an attractive option to me."

Simmons felt that left-handed pitcher, Dave Otto, was an attractive option at the Rule-5 Draft, so he selected the 28-year-old veteran from the Cleveland Indians in the minor league phase of the draft. But he did so without realizing that Otto had a guaranteed contract with the Indians.

Otto had signed a two-year deal in '92 with an option year. He went into the 1993 season with a $525,000 guaranteed salary and a club option for $1.2 million in 1994. Because it was a multi-year deal, his 1993 salary was guaranteed even if the Pirates decided to release him. Simmons' uncertainty immediately brought to mind Larry Doughty's waiver-wire snafu in 1990 that cost the Pirates two of their top minor league prospects.

"Frankly, I didn't know he had a guaranteed contract," Simmons told Perrotto. "I wanted the guy, though. That's why I drafted him. He's a left-hander and we're short on lefties. He can start, he can pitch short relief, long relief. He can throw the heck out of the ball, and I think he can help us. He may even be a bargain."

In the 1970s, John Candelaria pitched a no-hitter for the Pirates and also helped the team capture its fifth World Series championship. In the mid-1980s, he wanted out of Pittsburgh and didn't care who knew it.

Candelaria oozed with contempt as he once referred to then-general manager, Harding Peterson, as a "bozo" and joined the likes of George Hendrick, Dave Parker, and several others in directing the mutiny that almost steered the Pirates out of Pittsburgh.

He finally got his wish near the end of the 1985 season when he was traded to the California Angels. Since then, Candelaria has played for seven other teams and has been an adequate middle reliever in his later years. As difficult as it may seem to believe, the 39-year-old left-hander returned to the days of his turbulent youth as he signed a one-year contract to pitch for the Pirates in 1993.

"He'll be a big help to us out of the bullpen," Simmons explained. "John Candelaria is a proven veteran who can provide us with some middle inning relief."

Pirates fans would beg to differ with Simmons in that regard. While it was true that Candelaria had pitched long and middle relief over the last few years with teams such as the Dodgers, Yankees, and Mets, he pitched a total of just 25 innings in 1992, and was not one of manager Tommy Lasorda's first choices out of the Dodgers' bullpen.

The biggest question the fans and media pondered was why Simmons would sign a known malcontent to a $740,000 contract when he had just released a proven left-hander in Bob Patterson, who had a $785,000 salary, enjoyed playing in Pittsburgh, and was six years younger.

For whatever direction the Pirates were heading, the senior citizen brigade continued. Not long after Candelaria was stirred into the mix, the Pirates signed a pair of Atlanta castoffs in relief pitcher Alejandro Pena and outfielder Lonnie Smith. Pena was 33 at the time of his signing and his season was cut short in '92 with elbow problems. Although Pena said he would be ready to go in 1993, Simmons did not sign him until he got a clean bill of health from several doctors. Smith played in 84 games with the Braves in 1992 and hit .247 with six home runs, 33 RBIs and four stolen bases.

Those numbers were nowhere near the statistics Smith had put up in the past, but Smith insisted that age was not hampering his athletic ability. Smith, who played for three different World Series champions (Philadelphia, St. Louis, and Kansas City) during his career, is a career .289 hitter with 90 home runs, 504 RBIs, and 360 stolen bases. His best season was in 1989, his first full season with the Braves, when he hit .315 and had 21 home runs, 79 RBIs, and 25 stolen bases.

Smith said it wasn't his production that kept him on the bench, but the Braves' multitude of younger outfielders. He said the Braves made it clear to him in spring training that he would be Atlanta's fifth outfielder behind David Justice, Ron Gant, Otis Nixon, and Deion Sanders, and that he would be primarily used as a pinch hitter.

"It was a tough year because I was very disappointed from the beginning," Smith said. "I thought I was still a productive player, but the Braves didn't seem to think so. It was tough sitting on the bench so much. They said they tried to trade me, but nobody wanted me. I found that a little hard to believe. I think I can help the Pirates. All I need is the opportunity, and I believe I'll get that in Pittsburgh."

The Pirates considered several other veterans as they tried to fill the holes left by the 1992-93 off-season. San Francisco outfielder Willie McGee's name came up in trade talks at one point, and 37-year-old free agent Willie Wilson was also courted for a time. Another name considered was 38-year-old catcher, Jamie Quirk, who played out his option in 1992 with Oakland and was looking for a new team. Eventually the Bucs re-signed another of their former outfielders in Glenn Wilson, who played with the Pirates in 1988 and '89 and was a solid power hitter from the right side of the plate. He signed a minor league contract with Class AAA Buffalo and will try to work his way back to the Pirates' roster.

Where will these drastic changes take the Pirates? No one really knows. Many think their first direction will be downward to the bottom of the National League Eastern division standings. After all, this plan of signing over-priced veterans looking for a team was tried once before and failed miserably. At that time, it seemed to be a drastic, last-ditch effort to keep the glory days alive, but it nearly accomplished the demise of baseball in Pittsburgh.

Ted Simmons, however, doesn't see that happening this time around, and he is of the feeling that the Pirates will remain contenders for years to come. Not because he believes the veterans the team signed will carry on into the 21st century, but because their leadership and experience will provide the Pirates' younger talent with just the right amount of guidance to handle the everyday rigors of life in the big leagues.

Youth is something the Pirates do indeed possess. When the team struggled through the first couple years of manager Jim Leyland's tenure, it was teething with names such as Bonds and Bonilla; Van Slyke and LaValliere; Drabek and Smiley; Lind and King. They were young and nurturing, but they were determined to take this team to the heights of success that Pittsburgh baseball had been so accustomed to in the 1970s.

While some of those names remain on the Pirates' roster, the new youth movement involves kids such as Albert Martin,

Carlos Garcia, Kevin Young, William Pennyfeather, Steve Cooke, Paul Wagner, Tim Wakefield, and Denny Neagle. Wakefield, Neagle, and Cooke contributed greatly to the Pirates' run in '92, while the rest all made appearances on the major-league level at one time or another.

"The only way a small-market team has a chance of surviving is developing its own players," Simmons said. "If you're losing them at the top end and not bringing them back at the bottom end, where do the players come from?"

While most view Simmons' off-season signings of Candelaria, Foley, Smith and Pena — who had a combined 55 seasons of major-league experience between them going into 1993 — as border-line insanity, Simmons contends there is solid reasoning behind the moves.

"We're very high on our young people and our prospects are the future of this franchise," he said. "At the same time, I'm not going to throw a bunch of kids into the major leagues naked. I believe in giving kids a chance, but I don't believe in just throwing them to the wolves. You need to have some veteran players around to provide insurance."

Simmons' hopes are that each of the four veterans will match up with one of the younger players in some way to help carry the load through the tough times and offer advice when it is needed. For instance, Al Martin is a left-handed hitter, who has been tabbed as Bonds' replacement in leftfield. Anyone who thinks there won't be pressure in that position hasn't been following baseball these past few years.

Leyland plans to platoon Martin with the right-handed hitting Smith because he feels it is important not to rush him or let him go through his entire career with "Barry Bonds' replacement" constantly burdening him.

"That wouldn't be fair to Albert Martin," Leyland said. "Barry Bonds is the best leftfielder I've ever seen. That doesn't mean Al Martin isn't going to be a good leftfielder, but it takes time."

Martin, who hit .305 with 20 home runs, 16 doubles, 15 triples, 85 runs scored, 59 RBIs, and 20 steals at Class AAA Buffalo in 1992, can also do without the inevitable comparisons.

"It's not like the Pirates got rid of Barry Bonds because of me," he said. "He left on his own free will. But I can't think of a better person to play leftfield than me. I'm not Barry Bonds. I'm just going to be Al Martin. I think it's my time to show what I can do, and whatever happens happens.

"I'm not really looking to fill Barry Bonds' shoes. I look at it as a job that opened, and it just so happens Barry Bonds is the one who vacated it. Hopefully, I can make a name for myself."

One of the things Ted Simmons liked about Tom Foley was his versatility in the infield. He is capable of playing all four positions and with two newcomers at key positions, that versatility is expected to come in handy through the course of 1993 for the Pirates.

Carlos Garcia has spent parts of the 1990, '91, and '92 seasons with the Pirates and was originally tabbed as the next shortstop of the future. But assuming there are no trades involving Jay Bell (which was another hot off-season rumor), that position is solidified for years to come. In 1992, Jose Lind missed several games in late-August and early-September with a sore back. During much of that time, Garcia stepped in and did an admirable job. He is much like Lind as far as range and depth go, but his .303 batting average, 13 home runs, 70 RBIs, and 21 stolen bases at Buffalo in '92 proved he can also swing the bat. The Pirates felt Garcia was ready for a full-time position in the big leagues — despite just 67 career major-league at bats — and that was why Jose Lind and his soon-to-be $3 million contract suddenly became expendable.

Kevin Young was the Pirates' seventh-round selection in the 1990 amateur draft and was already seeing major league action in 1992. He has just seven big-league at bats, but he is considered the Pirates' third baseman of the future. Together, Young and Garcia ranked 1-2 as the best prospects in the American Association while playing at Buffalo in 1992.

It is Simmons' hope that Foley can provide instruction to these young infielders when needed and also fill in when any of the Pirate infielders need a day off or happen to fall into one of the normal mid-season slumps that players often experience.

Alejandro Pena took the city of Atlanta by storm at the end of the 1991 season when he literally nailed down the Western division championship for the Braves with two wins and 11 saves after being traded from the Mets in the last days of the '91 trading deadline. He also had three saves in the Braves' National League Championship Series win over the Pirates.

Pena's production slacked off considerably in '92 as he finished 1-6 in 41 appearances with 15 saves in 18 opportunities and a 4.07 ERA. He finished the season on the disabled list with elbow problems and goes into 1993 with something to prove to Pirates fans. Simmons, however, is convinced that Pena will be a welcome addition to the Pirates pitching staff.

"He's a veteran who can help with a young guy like [Stan] Belinda out of the bullpen," Simmons told John Perrotto. "People have to remember that Belinda is only 26 years old with just three years of major league service time. He's just a kid. It's asking an awful lot of someone that age to be the closer all by himself. Young kids are going to have tough stretches just like veteran players. The difference is they have a tougher time handling it if they go 2-for-50."

In 1992, the Pirates very seldom needed middle-inning relief work because of the impressive innings their starters put in night after night, day after day. But when the outings were less than spectacular for the Pirates' starting pitcher on those rare occasions, Jim Leyland could usually turn to someone like veterans Bob Patterson, Bob Walk (if he wasn't in the starting rotation), or Dennis Lamp, who gave the Pirates some much-needed veteran innings out of the bullpen until his June 10 release.

Denny Neagle was the rookie in the bullpen. He was the one under the spotlight as far as the fans were concerned because it was he who was traded to the Pirates for their 20-game winner, John Smiley. Neagle admittedly tried too hard when he pitched in Three Rivers Stadium, despite the advice of Leyland and pitching coach Ray Miller, who told him to just be himself and not try to be John Smiley.

"That was hard at first because I didn't want the fans to think they were getting some nobody," Neagle said. "I think I was just trying to impress too many people when I started some games, and that kind of got me off track."

Leyland and Miller put Neagle back on track by placing him in the bullpen after he was bombed for six runs in less than three innings' work by the Mets in a 15-1 home loss. That was the last game Neagle started in 1992, but he seemed a lot more relaxed coming out of the bullpen and his numbers improved with the change of scenery. He finished the season at 4-6 with two saves and a 4.48 ERA.

Neagle is just one of the youngsters the Pirates are grooming in the stable of pitchers. Left-hander Steve Cooke also displayed impressive numbers after being called up from Buffalo during the second half of the season. The moment he will always remember is his first big-league win, which came against the Mets in New York. Jeff King broke a 1-1 tie for the Pirates in the top of the 16th inning with a run-scoring single, and Cooke added to the lead with his first major league hit and RBI. He also worked the last two innings in relief to pick up his first major league win.

Cooke also impressed Pirate brass near the end of the season when Leyland called for him unexpectedly after starter Bob Walk suffered a slight groin strain while covering first base in the second inning of a game against St. Louis. The Pirates had a 1-0 lead at the time, and Cooke limited the Cardinals to just three hits over the final seven innings to register his second major league win.

He is one of several that could be the Pirates' next most talked-about pitcher. In '92 it was Tim Wakefield, with his dazzling knuckle ball and remarkable poise, who came out of nowhere to post an 8-1 record in the second half of the season and two pressure-filled victories in the Pirates' post-season series against the Braves. Two years before that Randy Tomlin used his left-handed, shoot-from-the-side delivery to help the Pirates win their first of three straight National League East titles as he finished 4-4 with a 2.55 ERA after his call-up in early August.

Cooke, Neagle, and a couple of other young pitchers, including Paul Wagner and Paul Miller, should get their opportunities with the Pirates at one time or another in the near future, as well as Dennis Moeller and Joel Johnston, the two players the Pirates received from Kansas City in the Jose Lind trade. Most will come out of the bullpen because the Pirates figure to have a starting rotation that includes Wakefield, Tomlin, Walk, and, hopefully, a healthy Zane Smith, who had minor shoulder surgery in the off-season. But with Leyland's frequent usage of a five-man rotation, Cooke appeared headed for the fifth starting position heading into spring training, 1993.

No matter who comes out of the bullpen for the Pirates in those games where long and middle relief are a must, Ted Simmons hopes Candelaria will be a positive influence to them and everyone else in the Pirates clubhouse and not revert back to the days when he was known as a "cancer" to the organization.

"As I said, we're very high on our younger players," Simmons reiterated. "But we can't just throw them out there and say, 'go at it.' You need some veteran players for those times that come along when the younger players will struggle."

With all the off-season moves — some manufactured from necessity, some laden with confusion — the Pirates will most likely not be one of the pre-season favorites to return to the National League playoffs. Fans, however, remember that they weren't really the strong favorites to return in 1991 or '92, either. That they did win three straight division titles was a testament to the awesome talent the Pirates put on the field as well as an infinite amount of wisdom and confidence displayed by a youthful and energetic coaching staff. Jim Leyland's two Manager-of-the-Year Awards coincided with the Pirates' success on the field.

Many people believe that no matter what kind of team is put on the field in 1993, Leyland will somehow wave his magic wand, and the Pirates will be right there come October. But Leyland knows it takes a lot more than that. Montreal and St. Louis appear to be the early favorites as they are in the same positions as far as youth and talent that Pittsburgh was in around 1990.

"To tell you the truth," Leyland said. "I think we're gonna be right there again in 1993. I don't see why not. I know the other teams in the division will be tough once again, but I don't even worry about them. My job is to worry about the Pittsburgh Pirates, and I'm going to do everything I can to have us ready for 1993 and beyond."

Fan interest dwindled just a bit in 1992 despite the Pirates' third consecutive playoff finish as attendance fell to 1,829,395 — a dropoff from consecutive record-breaking years of 2,049,908 in 1990 and 2,065,302 in 1991. With the wholesale changes that took place in the previous off-season, Pirates management had to be concerned that fan interest had the potential to drop even further.

As of mid-January, 1993, however, advanced season ticket sales were up over 10 percent from the season before according to Steve Greenberg, the Pirates' Vice President of Marketing and Operations. He said only 29 full-season ticket plans had been canceled since the '92 season ended while 625 were added. This at least gave evidence to management that the fans were willing to give the team a chance in the coming seasons before they applied for disaster relief.

"We're very pleased," Greenberg told John Perrotto of the *Beaver County Times*. "We've reached our goals over last season and then some. For us to draw over two million fans twice and nearly do it a third time is remarkable when you take into account our number of season tickets. This gives us reason to be optimistic about the interest in single-game ticket sales, which will come later."

&

Had the Pittsburgh Pirates come full circle when Sid Bream lumbered home from second base for the Atlanta Braves in the last inning of the last game of the 1991 National League Championship Series? They did not reach every team's ultimate goal — The World Series — in three straight tries, but would they have to settle for just coming close? Was the cyclical nature of baseball about to send the Pirates into their next downward spiral?

The radical changes in the chemistry and makeup of this once finely tuned championship team made this a definite possibility. The Pirates headed into spring training, 1993, with 11 of the 25 players from their '92 playoff roster missing due to free agency, expansion, trade, or outright release. When some of those players' names are Bonds, Drabek, and Lind, it makes the prospects of a down year all the more realistic.

But Ted Simmons and Jim Leyland aren't about to give up the Pirates' ship as it sails toward the future. Simmons is oh-so-quick to rattle off the names of the Pirates' future as well as those from the present. "Our four young pitchers [Wakefield, Neagle, Cooke, and Wagner], I wouldn't trade for anybody," he said. "Name me a team right now with first-year players who can match that. We have Martin, Young, Garcia, and Pennyfeather, and I wouldn't switch those young kids for any others. We have [Jeff] King, [Orlando] Merced, Van Slyke, Tomlin, Zane Smith, [Stan] Belinda, [Don] Slaught, [Jay] Bell, [Mike] LaValliere ... All I'm saying is I kinda like the way it looks."

Leyland likes the mixture as well, and he realized after 1992 that some major changes were probably going to take place. "I knew Bonds was gone," he said. "Hey, he's the best player in the game. We couldn't afford to pay him what the market said he was worth, so you wish him all the best and send him on his way. I

knew some of the other moves were done for cost-cutting measures, but the only thing I was a little disappointed about was that
we didn't use some of the money we saved to re-sign Drabek. But
I'll take the team I have, and I think we'll be right there."

One may wonder where the relationship between baseball
and hockey lies, but when the Pittsburgh Penguins were in the
process of defending their Stanley Cup championship in 1992,
Mario Lemieux, the team's captain, star, and probably the greatest hockey player in the world, did something away from the ice
that may have lent as much to the team's successful defense as
anything he may have done on the ice.

The Penguins were struggling in March and were facing
the possibility of not even making the National Hockey League
playoffs when their general manager, Craig Patrick, shipped two
of the team's more popular players, defenseman Paul Coffey,
and winger Mark Recchi, to Los Angeles and Philadelphia,
respectively. The Penguins needed a shakeup in a big way, and
they received a great abundance of talent in return, including All-
Star winger Rick Tocchet from Philadelphia.

While several of the Penguins showed a quiet displeasure
in losing two of their friends, Mario Lemieux stepped forward
and said it was probably time for a change. It wasn't that Lemieux
disliked Coffey or Recchi — they were two of his closest friends
— but he said what he felt and the Penguins did need a change.

If Mario Lemieux didn't back the team's decision, think
what that might have done to the fan's way of thinking. Lemieux
has become the newest of sports heroes in Pittsburgh and when
he speaks, every hockey fan in the city listens. So do his teammates, and if he would have criticized Patrick for trading two of
the team's higher-profile players, the Penguins may never have
recovered enough to experience the incredible playoff run they
had that ultimately led the team to a second straight Stanley Cup.

In a way, the Pirates needed a Mario Lemieux to step
forward in the off-season. Someone to get the fans off of Ted
Simmons' back and say "Don't sell us short just yet" Andy Van
Slyke took that role a little bit when he answered many people's
remarks that the Pirates had turned themselves into a minor
league team.

"People are entitled to their opinions," Van Slyke said. "But
there's no way of judging this team until we get to spring

training. We'll be working together and learning together. We started from square one before and got where no one thought we could. There's no reason to think we can't do it again, and I think we have some pretty good talent stepping into the holes that were left open. I can't say whether we'll win or not right away. Usually I have a good feel for that. All I can say is that people shouldn't write us off so quickly."

The Pirates got another blessing from their captain in the infield when Jay Bell told Paul Meyer of the *Pittsburgh Post Gazette* that he was happy with the way the Pirates handled the changes and was looking forward to the '93 season.

"Every one of the guys we lost had their own special qualities, and they were very instrumental in helping us win the last few years," Bell said. "But we signed some guys who can help us win. Every year, you're going to lose some guys and gain some guys. It was more of a lose-gain situation after '92 for us. We lost a lot more than usual. We gained more than usual. It should be a really fun spring training because we have a lot to work on."

❧

Fun. That's what it's all about to the many professional athletes in major league baseball. They hit a ball. They throw it, they catch it. They circle the bases at all different speeds and make the spectacular plays in the field more so than the bloopers that are highlighted on sports reels throughout the country.

They love the game. It is what they grew up learning, whether it was from their coaches or their fathers. Take away the television and glamour; the massive stadiums and sellout crowds. Throw out the megabuck contracts and sometimes ridiculous incentive clauses. They would still play the game. For over a century, men have played baseball, and not always because it was their profession.

The game grew on those men, and it grows on youngsters today, even though it is now a business, and every man seems to be out for himself. People scoffed at Barry Bonds when he said after signing his lucrative contract with the San Francisco Giants that he would play for Jim Leyland for nothing. But you know something, he probably would have. Not only did Bonds have the best manager in the game when he played for the Pirates, he had an honest and trustworthy friend.

Money didn't take Barry Bonds away from the Pittsburgh Pirates. Status did. Even Leyland said at one point during the 1992 season that Bonds should not be ridiculed for seeking a contract for what he is worth, even if that meant joining another team. "He's the best player in the game, why shouldn't he be paid like the best?" Leyland said.

Through the 1990, '91, and '92 regular seasons, Bonds played like the best in the game, but his status reached proportions that a small-market team like the Pirates could not fulfill. But if there was no money — if each player was payed on the exact same scale — Barry Bonds would still play the game, and maybe still be playing for the manager he has always respected the most. All the players would still play. Because they love it.

In the mid-1980s, baseball was almost lost to the city of Pittsburgh, but through the efforts of Malcolm Prine, the late Carl Barger, the late Mayor Richard Caliguiri, and a host of others, it stayed. Did they do it for the money? At that time, all that could be said was, "what money?" Their efforts were sown because of their love for the game. They weren't players, but they put themselves into the game anyway. Without these men, there would have been no Jim Leyland, or Barry Bonds, or Andy Van Slyke, or Doug Drabek, or Jay Bell, or Sid Bream, or Jose Lind, or Tim Wakefield to admire. None of them would have been members of the Pittsburgh Pirates and fans would never have known their true greatness unless they saw their names on the backs of other uniforms.

Current speculation has the Pirates being run out of town once again. Many believe it is because of the off-season maneuvers that saw general manager Ted Simmons sign a handful of over-aged veterans to mix with the youth that is the future of the Pirates.

People say the team is headed back to the basement. But what if they are? Isn't that the cyclical nature of the game? Sometimes you have to suffer the down side to make it back to the top. The Pirates had some of the best players in the game through the early-90s and didn't win a World Series championship. They have won more games in the 90s than any other major league franchise, but don't have a title to speak of.

What is so wrong with change? The Pirates still have some of the best players in the game, and they definitely still have the best manager. There will be some young, but determined faces who will look unfamiliar at first, but eventually leave fans thinking, "Wow! He made that play just like Bonds used to." Whether it is Bonds in leftfield or Albert Martin, or whether Jose Lind is at second base or Carlos Garcia, the fans will be there.

Some April afternoon or evening every year, fans will hear that old familiar train whistle inside Three Rivers Stadium that signals the start of another baseball season in Pittsburgh. The animated train with its lone engineer will pick up steam as it lumbers slowly at first across the massive stadium scoreboard. The chugging will sound faster and faster and the fans will clap and stomp their feet in unison. Finally, the train will rumble at full speed down its single track and a stream of smoke will trail from the engine's mighty stack to spell out the words, "LET'S GO BUCS!"

These are the Pittsburgh Pirates and, hopefully, they will be around for baseball generations to come.

# DAWN OF A NEW STEEL AGE:
## Bill Cowher's Steelers Power Up for the 90s

THE STEELERS were corroding in Pittsburgh. Chuck Knoll had retired and the franchise was searching for a man who could lead them into a new era. From their search, the Steelers found young, granite-jawed Bill Cowher, who not only led them out of the darkness, but took them farther than anyone could have dreamed.

STEELER FANS called it Cowher Power, and the new coach energized not only a franchise, but an entire city. He led the Steelers to the best record in the AFC, their best record since the team's last Super Bowl victory, and he had everyone in Pittsburgh believing that the time was at hand for the Steelers' fifth Super Bowl Championship.

BUT THIS BOOK is more than a story about Bill Cowher's stunning success in his first season. It is the story of the Steelers' entry into a whole new era, with new bosses on the field and in the front office. It shows how the Pittsburgh Steelers have changed over the past several years, and looks to the future at some dramatic moves yet to come—including a possible change in ownership. It gives an inside look into the Rooney family, including the painful falling out between the two brothers who helped build the team into four-time Super Bowl champs.

DAWN OF A NEW STEEL AGE opens with a revealing look at what prompted Chuck Noll to retire, a move he did not want to make, but one in which he had little choice. It shows how the Steelers were rocked by several suspensions for drug use and a suicide attempt by one of their players. The book shows what the current players think of those who won the four Super Bowls—and what the players from the 1970s think of the modern Steelers. It tells of the struggles and triumphs of stars such as Rod Woodson, Greg Lloyd, Neil O'Donnell, and Barry Foster. It also reveals how one of them severely tested the new coach early in his tenure and how it affected both of them.

THE BOOK ALSO FOCUSES on the Steelers' longtime owners, the Rooney family. Through all the years, the Rooney name remains one of the most revered in all of sports. The book reflects on the family warmth and the cold realities of running a pro football team, and how one Rooney turned down an appointment to become a United States Senator—perhaps to take over as the next president…of the Pittsburgh Steelers.

**Look for this exciting new title in your local bookstore in October.**

***Marge Schott...Unleashed!:*** Explores the controversial tenure of Marge Schott as owner of the Cincinnati Reds, and what really led to her suspension. Available June 1993.

***Glory Jays: Canada's World Series Champions:*** The Blue Jays are the first team to take the World Series trophy north of the border. *Glory Jays* details the highlights of their exciting season, and gives a preview of this year's team. Available April 1993.

***Lady in the Locker Room: Uncovering the Oakland Athletics:*** Follow the career of Susan Fornoff, one of the few female reporters to cover a major league baseball team on a daily basis. Find out what a female reporter "sees" in the locker room. Available April 1993.

***Lou Boudreau: Covering All the Bases:*** Boudreau tells the story of his exciting career in this autobiography. His years as a player manager with the Cleveland Indians, and his nearly three decades of announcing for the Chicago Cubs. Available June 1993.

***Phil Rizzuto: A Yankee Tradition:*** Tells the story of Rizzuto's rise to baseball stardom, including his years in the minors, four All-Star appearances, and 1950 MVP performance. Available June 1993.

***Down for the Count: Investigating the Mike Tyson Rape Trial:*** This controversial new title gives an in-depth description of the trial of the year; including the numerous miscalculations by Tyson's defense team, the testimony of Desiree Washington and of Mike Tyson himself. Available May 1993.

**Please call Sagamore at 1-800-327-5557 to order any of our spring sports titles or to receive a free catalog of the best fall sports titles.**

---

*Against the World: A Behind-the-Scenes Look at the Portland Trail Blazers' Chase for the NBA Championship* ISBN 0-915611-67-8 $19.95

*Best in the Game: The Turbulent Story of the Pittsburgh Penguins' Rise to Stanley Cup Champions* ISBN 0-915611-66-x $19.95

*Blue Fire: A Season Inside the St. Louis Blues* ISBN 0-915611-55-4 $22.95

*The Fighting Irish Football Encyclopedia* ISBN 0-915611-54-6 $44.95

*Hail to the Orange and Blue* ISBN 0-915611-31-7 $29.95

*Lady Magic: The Autobiography of Nancy Lieberman-Cline* ISBN 0-915611-43-0 $19.95

*Lou: Winning at Illinois* ISBN 0-915611-24-4 $18.95

*Metivier On: Saratoga, Glens Falls, Lake George, and the Adirondacks* ISBN 0-915611-60-0 $19.95

*Stormin' Back: Missouri Coach Norm Stewart's Battles On and Off the Court* ISBN 0-915611-47-3 $19.95

*Take Charge! A How-to Approach for Solving Everyday Problems* ISBN 0-915611-46-5 $9.95

*Undue Process: The NCAA's Injustice for All* ISBN 0-915611-34-1 $19.95

*William Warfield: My Music & My Life* ISBN 0-915611-40-6 $19.95

*Winning Styles for Winning Coaches: Creating the Environment for Victory* ISBN 0-915611-49-x $12.95

*Woody Hayes: A Reflection* ISBN 0-915611-42-2 $19.95